FACTS OF LIFE

TEN ISSUES OF CONTENTMENT

MICHAEL C. GRAHAM
WITH LYNDA PRIDDY AND SANDY GRAHAM

outskirtspress
DENVER, COLORADO

The opinions expressed in this manuscript are solely the opinions of the author and do not represent the opinions or thoughts of the publisher. The author has represented and warranted full ownership and/or legal right to publish all the materials in this book.

Facts of Life
Ten Issues of Contentment
All Rights Reserved.
Copyright © 2014 Michael C. Graham
v3.0

Cover Photo © 2014 Michael C. Graham . All rights reserved - used with permission.

This book may not be reproduced, transmitted, or stored in whole or in part by any means, including graphic, electronic, or mechanical without the express written consent of the publisher except in the case of brief quotations embodied in critical articles and reviews.

Outskirts Press, Inc.
http://www.outskirtspress.com

ISBN: 978-1-4787-2259-5

Outskirts Press and the "OP" logo are trademarks belonging to Outskirts Press, Inc.

PRINTED IN THE UNITED STATES OF AMERICA

In memory of
David Thomas Lesselyong.
He lives in these pages.

Contents

ACKNOWLEDGMENTS I
INTRODUCTION III
IT'S AS EASY AS 1, 2, 3: THREE BASIC IDEAS 1
IT'S AS EASY AS A, B, C: HOW WE WORK 15
   A = ACTIVATING EVENT 16
   B = BELIEF SYSTEM 19
      Core Beliefs *20*
      Memories *23*
      Values *25*
      Automatic Thoughts *27*
   C - CONSEQUENCE 31
   ACT TO CHANGE COGNITIVE DISTORTIONS 41
      Awareness *41*
      Critical Thinking *54*
      Train *57*
EMOTIONS 60
HOW WE DON'T WORK: A MODEL OF
DYSFUNCTIONAL DEVELOPMENT 83
   SAFETY 93
   VALUE 98
   SPIRITUALITY 108
PRACTICAL COMMUNICATIONS AND
CONNECTION SKILLS 113
   USE ACTIVE LISTENING 126
      Nonverbal management *127*
      Minimal Verbal Responses *132*
      Paraphrasing *132*
      Reflecting *133*

    Clarifying *134*
    Summarizing *135*
  Speak For Myself 136
  Pay Attention to Underlying Messages......................140
RELATIONSHIPS AND ROLES **155**
  Personal Boundaries 156
  Codependence 165
  Enabling/Caretaking 169
  Rules & Roles in the Family of Origin 184
TEN FACTS OF LIFE SUMMARY **191**
MOOD DISORDERS AND GRIEF **192**
  Anxiety 194
  Panic Attacks 203
  Phobias 206
  Depression 208
  Grief 224
ADDICTIONS **233**
  Behavioral Habits 234
  Psychological Dependence 241
  Triggers 252
  Relapse Prevention...254
THINGS THAT HELP **259**
  Therapy 259
  Forgiveness 266
  Sleep 269
  Exercise 271
  Meditation 278
  Humor...283
BIBLIOGRAPHY **286**
INDEX..**294**

Acknowledgments

There is no way to chronicle all of the influences that led to this work. I suppose everyone I've ever met would have to be listed. After all, this book is a reflection of all that I am; and all that I am includes echoes of everyone I have ever known. However, there are a few who have been most influential and helpful with this project.

First I have to especially acknowledge my co-author and friend Lynda Priddy. Your influence on me professionally and personally is far more than I could ever have expected when we met. Your persistence and love kept me on task and kept me thinking more times than I can remember. This book would not exist if it were not for you and your belief and determination.

Also, my other co-author, Sandy Graham, deserves special thanks. There truly are no words adequate to express my appreciation and respect for the thoughtfulness and wisdom you have provided. You have brought clarity to many of the concepts and, in addition, brought them to life.

A number of friends and a couple of relatives have also provided insight and valuable suggestions: George Gridley for thirty years of conversations on the back porch; Bill Kelty for all of the breakfast encounters; John Graham as good a brother as can be and the true "Don."

There are also a number of folks who directly helped with readings, suggestions, and insight. I know I will not remember them all, but they include Arnold Lopez, Nick Hannan, Rick Peterson, Anne Brown, Brian Jackson, Bobby Pepper, Meagan Foxx, Sonya Chambliss-Alexander, Windy Elliott, Vanessa Richards, Doug Dodge, and Angela Hairapetian.

I want to especially thank my brother, James T. Graham and my daughter, Natalie Graham who unknowingly provided by example the final motivation to complete this project.

I will never forget Gail Loose for her contribution to my personal and professional development. She was as good a friend as there can be. Her love of children and dedication to their welfare will always be a source of inspiration.

There are hundreds of clients over the years who have helped deepen my understanding of my self and of the processes that affect us all. That is the point, and you are the reason.

Introduction

This book is for anyone who wants to feel better, anyone seeking happiness. Its purpose is simply to acquaint everyone who does not already know with the concept that in all circumstances and situations, and for every human being, happiness is always possible. There are literally millions of people who are at this moment unhappy and suffering psychological pain. This is all unnecessary suffering. It does not matter what is happening to us or around us; there is one thing we can always do. We can always decide to be happy anyway.

There is one thing we can always do. We can always decide to be happy anyway.

There is no new information in here. Everything in this book has been written about and talked about for hundreds, in some cases thousands of years. This book does not hold any secrets. Everything here is known by millions of people and is public information all over the world. I do not want you to approach this little book with any expectation that I have discovered something new, or that I am going to reveal some closely held secret of happiness, or even a secret that makes it easier.

What you will find herein is a discussion of a number of facts. These are not *the* facts of life. They are also not all of the facts of life. They may not even be facts. They are the beliefs, values, and perceptions that I have observed operating in people who are happy. They are the concepts that helped me learn to be happy. They are the characteristics of the mentally tough individuals I have met who seem to handle life better than most. The beliefs, attitudes, assumptions, and expectations with which we face the world determine the extent to which we will be able to cope with, endure, and enjoy life. This book presents a discussion of these personal issues all of us face.

I refer to these issues as "facts of life" because I believe certain dogmatism is required for emphasis. The important facts are shown in boxes as they appear in the text, and they are listed at the end of each of the first five chapters. In addition, some associated facts about the facts are provided in an expanded list listed following Chapter 6. These are the points that I really wish to make despite my digressions and ramblings. If you do nothing more than read and consider the "facts of life" as they are listed, my aims will have been accomplished.

For almost forty years I have worked in the behavioral health field. Almost always my jobs involved some form of public presentation: training sessions, lectures, workshops, and retreats. Most recently these talks have occurred in the form of the introductory workshop at Consiliom. Often I would be asked if there was a book I could recommend that covered the material I was presenting. These requests were problematic for two reasons. First, it seemed to me that the material I presented most often was pretty basic stuff. I was mildly surprised that people found it especially useful, as it seemed to me that it was simply common knowledge. I finally have come to see that what may be common knowledge in psychological and philosophical literature, and in my work, may not be so common in everyday life.

Secondly, I never found a book that covered the basic material in a succinct manner, without unnecessary theoretical ramblings or superfluous political and social comment (though I have found myself unable to totally avoid that activity herein). There are many texts that describe the ideas presented here. I have often recommended them, only to have people tell me later that "it wasn't the same" as my lecture. In addition, some of the best books are not always in print or easily available. Eventually I became persuaded that I should at least write up my lecture notes in a format I could hand out. That was the beginning of what became this book. Publication of this book, however, involves considerable trepidation, which I relieve somewhat by including the following cautions.

First, this is not an academic work. It does not stand up to any standard for adequate citations or documentation of sources. It is difficult to tell whether these ideas came from someone else or are just stuff I made up. I have included a reference list, and I have made a number of citations. However, the annotations are incomplete at best. This book consists of things I have read, experienced, or learned that seem to be true based on my years of clinical practice and my life in general. It is impossible to completely credit everyone who contributed to the ideas in this book, so just assume it is everyone except me. I will not quibble or deny any charges of not being the first to think of or write about anything you read here.

Also this book is not exhaustive. It is intended as a brief orientation to the concepts we all must grapple with when we are struggling. My goal has been to apply the basic facts to a number of the critical topics in mental health, and many of the predominant problems in our society and, at the same time, to keep it simple. This was originally envisioned as a quick guide, a follow-up to our workshops at Consiliom. I have attempted to keep it short and simple, as I believe that is what folks have been asking for. This is especially true of the discussion of various problem areas beginning in Chapter 7. I have attempted to show how the facts we describe operate in each of the problem areas. These are not intended as complete discussions of the various problems or diagnoses. There are many books devoted exclusively to discussion of anxiety, depression, enabling, addictions, et cetera. Here I have only provided some examples of how to think about these problems using the facts of life. For more complete discussion of any of the topics covered, a bibliography is provided. If it is pathology you are interested in, each topic I have addressed is covered much more thoroughly by one or more of the authors listed.

A third caveat relates to the stories and examples I have used. I have made every effort to hide identities and distort details enough to insure confidentiality. In the distortion of details, I have, in some cases, drastically altered the story. It is my hope that everyone will recognize himself or herself in some story. It is also my hope that the real people involved will not recognize themselves at all. Thus, as with citations, I will have no problem accepting a claim that something did not happen as I described, or did not happen at all. My veracity is not the point; it is my point that matters.

Finally this book is not for the public—it is for you. In other words, this is not a book to be used to explain to someone else what they are doing wrong or why they are not happy. The sole purpose of this book is to help *you* find a path to your own bit of tranquility. I intended it as a description of the findings of my own life journey, not a remedy for others. Those findings are the facts of life, the terms of our existence, which I believe all of us must acknowledge and resolve. They are for self-application only and not to be administered to anyone else. I suppose if all are consenting adults, the contents might be discussed in small groups, but only if it is understood that everyone present is totally responsible for whatever happens to them as a result and that I am responsible for nothing.

Also this book is not intended as, nor will it function as, an insight that, once read, will change your life. In fact this book will not change your life. Change only occurs when you confront the ten facts in your life. The ten facts of life are the issues of the human condition. This book is designed to provide a bare-bones description of the tried-and-true methods of facing the issues of our lives. Apparently some people do experience a flash of insight while reading a book or doing the laundry or whatever, and their lives are changed forever. That has never happened to me. I suspect that does not happen for most of us. For most of us happiness comes only by slogging our way through life day to day. So, this book is not supposed to provide a quick fix; it is for the rest of us who have to plod through, figuring things out as we go. This book will help you do some of the figuring.

I have been extremely lucky in my life. I was blessed with an outstanding family in which to grow up; I have always been surrounded by people who love me and can honestly say I have always done pretty much what I wanted to do. I clearly have not always made the smartest decisions or gotten the outcomes I expected, but it has been a thoroughly enjoyable slice. And though I often try, I cannot find any real regret. One of the most fortunate aspects of my life has been the astounding privilege of being with hundreds of people during their own, very private struggles for happiness. In many cases the experience was so intimate and personal that it seemed as if the struggle was my own. In the spirit with which all of you have shared with me, I offer these "lecture notes" to whoever might find them useful. Thank you.

Here is a preview of all ten facts in case you don't wish to actually read the whole book.

People are people.

Happiness is not something that happens to us. It is something we do.

We all have everything we need to be happy.
Everyone's reality is different, and everyone's reality is valid.
My feelings come from my thoughts.
Things always happen the way they happen.
The belief system consists of ideas, not facts.
Ideas can be changed.
Everyone's behavior is mostly about them, not me.
Meaning depends on context.

CHAPTER 1

It's As Easy as 1, 2, 3: Three Basic Ideas

All people—male, female, white, black, brown, red, or yellow— all human beings share a common ancestry and basic biological and mental processes. While popular wisdom maintains that it is our differences that are significant, I believe it is what we have in common that is most important. To be sure, there are exceptions to everything, and there are probably a few people out there who do not share the same DNA as the rest of us. Most of us, however, are pretty much the same. Genetic studies have determined that all of the differences we pay so much attention to involve less than 1 percent of our genome.[1] This means most claims to uniqueness are somewhat exaggerated. Nevertheless, claims of difference, and the pain of difference, abound.

At every party, there is a wallflower. In every large crowd, there is someone apart. In many of these situations the one alone concludes, "I am different" or, "There is something wrong with me." These are erroneous conclusions but, along with many other mistaken beliefs, they produce most of the suffering of humankind. This book is about the thoughts that create our emotional anguish, the beliefs that lead us to despair. In general many of these beliefs are founded on the notion that somehow "I am different." Not just different in perspective, upbringing, culture, or temperament, but unlike others in a fundamental way.

---

[1] http://www.ornl.gov/sci/techresources/Human_Genome/faq/snps.shtml#snps

The phrase "terminally unique" can be applied not only to those who are overly entitled, but also to many who sacrifice any chance of happiness by focusing on their differences. Sometimes the condition is literally terminal, as we conclude there is no solution and opt to end the process. More often the result is not as dramatic as suicide, but the impact can be debilitating. Early in my career there was a young boy in a treatment center where I was employed. The boy was black and his mother insisted that he have a black therapist. In response the director assigned the only black therapist on staff to the young man. This therapist was from London. She had grown up in a rather privileged family and, while a gifted therapist whom I believe overcame the cultural differences, she had no experience or knowledge of the realities of a young African American boy growing up in the United States. I remember attending staff conferences and hearing this therapist struggle with the huge cultural gap between herself and the client. The mother's focus on her son's superficial differences actually resulted in the assignment of the one therapist on staff who would have the most difficulty "relating".

From this I learned that a therapist does not have to come from the same background to be effective if they can connect as a person. This young man did wonderfully in spite of the cultural contrasts between client and therapist. I believe it was because the therapist was skilled and caring, and ignored the superficial differences of culture and gender. Instead, the therapist focused on what they had in common as people. This is one place where I began to realize the damage caused by focusing on our differences. While it is often the case that we need to have an awareness of the cultural context of another person, the moment of connection occurs only when we see each other as the same.

IT'S AS EASY AS 1, 2, 3: THREE BASIC IDEAS

Over my career I have seen many situations in which assumptions of difference resulted in less than ideal treatment. Patients leave treatment because "I need a male therapist" a female can never understand me" or because "You have never been raped, so you cannot understand my trauma" or, "Only another combat veteran can really help me." There are social service agencies that serve only certain "types" of people. In the field of mental health, we segregate people by diagnostic category, often referring to them by the category name as though they were a separate race or species. "Borderlines are hard to treat" "I cannot work with cutters." This kind of labeling is not only disrespectful and clinically unhelpful; it ironically results in our inability to see the true individuality each of us does possess. As a client I do not feel respected or understood when I am labeled in this manner.

For, while we are all the same in terms of underlying biological and psychological processes, we are also unique as individuals, every one of us. There will never be another you. No one else will have exactly the same experience of life and develop precisely the same memories, self, and perspective as you. For some, life requires much more endurance than others. For a few, abilities and skills are far above those of the rest. As momentous as these differences seem, however, they are ultimately just circumstances. Circumstances do not dictate our true worth and value, nor do they change our underlying uniformity. Martha Washington is reported to have said, "The greatest part of our happiness depends on our dispositions, not our circumstances." The trick is that we must be able to tell the difference between our circumstances and our dispositions—the basic processes that produce the unique self. Telling the difference is not always easy.

While there will never be another me, it is also true that most other people can come to understand me. No matter how different our backgrounds and knowledge, it is possible for each of us to understand one another because we are 99 percent alike. More importantly this means that I can be understood. If I insist that others cannot understand me, all I have actually done is consigned myself to hopelessness. I am not alone in my humanity, only in my experience of it. I am connected, like it or not.

This book is about the facts of life that are true for all of us, the things we all share. Specifically we are interested in the facts that impact our ability to achieve a measure of contentment in life. We are all the same, and we are all different, but it is our similarity that holds the promise of happiness and connection. So, the first fact of life that we need to acknowledge if we are to achieve peace and contentment is that, by and large, #1 All People Are People. We are human. As humans, we are alike in so many more ways than we are different. To believe otherwise is not only at odds with the facts; it is to adopt either the defeated position of a perpetual victim and abandon all hope, or that of a perpetual god living apart and above the "lesser folk." If I am totally, or even very, unique, another person cannot understand my suffering. If I alone have felt a given pain, then I cannot logically expect much help from anyone or anything else. In the case that I am completely unique, I go to therapists or sages with utter pessimism. Psychiatrists can offer no help with their potions formulated for others. Friends and family can offer no true support for emotions they cannot comprehend. I am in reality mortally unique and without faith. While this, sadly, is true for many, *it is only a choice they have made*, a belief they hold. It is not a fact. The fact is we are alike. We are all people.

> #1 All People Are People

IT'S AS EASY AS 1, 2, 3: THREE BASIC IDEAS

Over the decades of my professional life, I have seen people suffering all sorts of emotional distress. In psychiatric hospitals, residential treatment centers, jails, and private practice, I have discerned a pattern: There are generally only two reasons people become distressed enough to seek professional help—grief and shame.

Grief is the pain of loss. It does not matter the nature of the loss; the process of adapting to it is the same. And, *we all go through it.* And we all have the ability to do it with varying degrees of efficiency.

Shame is the emotional result of believing that I am different from other people in some significant way. Shame is what happens when I no longer believe that people are people and I am one of them. When I no longer believe in Fact of Life #1, I begin to doubt my value as a person, my worthiness as a member of the species. A leading researcher on shame, based on thousands of interviews, says, "Shame is the intensely painful feeling or experience of believing we are flawed and therefore unworthy of acceptance and belonging."[2] I don't believe I can overemphasize the debilitating impact of shame in our culture and in our lives. It is the most formidable foe I have faced in both my professional and personal life. It disconnects us from our own species, and that is deadly. Believing that people are people and we are all mostly alike is a basic requirement of emotional health.

If people are all pretty much the same, then we can find amazing strength in our similarity. Since we are all one as a species, our sense of meaning and purpose arises out of our connection to one another, not in the barriers of minute differences. I believe there is hope—hope for everyone. I believe that each of us has within our

---

[2] Brown (2007) page 5.

being the ability to live in contentment without rancor or drastic unhappiness. As a therapist I do not see how any other belief is possible if I am to serve my purpose. I have over the years supervised many therapists of all sorts of theoretical persuasions. Of those who were most effective, 100 percent shared this belief that clients were people, just like themselves and just as capable. In my view those therapists who perceive clients as somehow defective or "less than" or even "different from" themselves are not only less helpful but also miss out on one of the most amazing experiences possible for a human being: the experience of connection with another on a profound emotional and spiritual level. This connection to others is a biological need in all of us. There are reports and studies going back hundreds of years that document this need. If we are not able to accomplish it, we will not thrive and may not survive. This is true for everyone. To focus on difference is to focus on separation and loneliness. To understand how we are alike will lead us to an ability to achieve true happiness. Differences separate. Similarity connects. It is as simple as that.

If happiness is our goal, it is important to have some common idea of what constitutes happiness. Sometimes, when we are dominated by the need to numb our pain, we can come to believe that happiness is the same thing as fun, or pleasure. If we are after a life that consists of nothing but pleasure, I fear we will be disappointed. I have never met anyone, no matter how rich or famous, who enjoyed a life of pure pleasure. I do not think such a thing is possible. Other people come to believe that happiness can be achieved only when someone loves us. Not only do I not believe love is the answer, I believe that folks who are not already happy can never know the full experience of love. There are many possible definitions of happiness. For our purposes here, happiness is not just a state of bliss. In fact, happiness can coexist with pain

IT'S AS EASY AS 1, 2, 3: THREE BASIC IDEAS

and loss. What good is happiness if it abandons us at the first sign of adversity? Happiness must be something that stays with us and sees us through. The happiness I am speaking of is not a state of being. It is not something that happens to us; it is something we do. Or as Abraham Lincoln is reputed to have said, "Most people are about as happy as they make up their minds to be." Happiness is first a decision about how we approach life; second, it is the follow-through. Having made a decision to be happy, we must then commit to the work. Happiness can, in fact, be very hard work. I have known many people who decided that happiness was just too much trouble. Often this decision is founded on erroneous beliefs about our ability or worthiness. Even for those who attain happiness, the challenge is continuous. It never ends. Underneath, happiness is founded on the belief that it is okay for me to be me; the conviction that despite everything I do or that

> **#2 Happiness Is Not Something That Happens To Us. It Is Something We Do.**

happens to me, I am still okay as a person; that whatever happens to me does not define me. To maintain this belief in the face of our experience of life and loss is a lifelong problem. I have had clients who describe me as "…one of those people who believe you just have to decide to be happy and you will be." This misses the point entirely. What I actually believe is that we have to decide to do the ongoing work of happiness before we can discover the contentment it offers. In this book I am going to describe some principles that can lead to happiness. The principles appear simple, and they are. Do not be fooled, however, by the notion that application of these principles will be easy. If it was easy, everyone would already be happy all the time. Nobody who has ever lived has been able to do happiness perfectly all the time. This is a consequence of the second fact that happiness is something we do. There is, of course, more to it.

In my observation of humanity, I have found one thing that is present anytime people are unhappy: dissatisfaction. I refer to dissatisfaction not only with the circumstances of our existence but dissatisfaction with who and what we think we are and the way we are coping with our life. At the opposite end of dissatisfaction is contentment, with ourselves and the manner in which we acquit ourselves in our journey. We accomplish this contentment when we discover and accept our authentic self as part of the human race. This contentment is what I refer to as happiness. It is not an emotion or a phase or an accidental gift. Many people confuse happiness with various emotions such as joy, passion or love. These are emotions and are separate from contentment. We will talk about emotions in much more detail later. Happiness for me is the ability to maintain contentment in the face of life's adversities. "Life is difficult," according to M. Scott Peck,[3] and I agree. To deny the accidental nature of abundance and depravation, the arbitrary spirit of luck and misfortune, is tantamount to begrudging ourselves an authentic experience of our life. There can be no question for anyone paying attention that life is often random. A happy person is one who approaches and passes through life at peace with himself, avoiding unnecessary emotional outbursts or silent isolation. Such individuals are living in congruence. That is, these folks have determined to keep their behaviors in balance with their nature. According to Gandhi, "Happiness is when what you think, what you say, and what you do are in harmony."[4] We can all

---

[3] Peck (2003)
[4] The Collected Works of Mahatma Gandhi

have this kind of happiness. Some have even described it as a duty. Robert Louis Stevenson said, "There is no duty so underrated as the duty of being happy. By being happy we sow anonymous benefits upon the world." Of course accepting the duty to be happy is not so easy when we undermine the effort with self-defeating beliefs.

Many times, as we watch others go about their apparently happy lives, it can seem as if we are missing something. We might conclude that we don't have what it takes or maybe that we don't deserve to be happy like everyone else. These beliefs are rife with logical errors and noisy data. Nevertheless they exist, and in the face of such beliefs, many people give up and assume that the hard work it might take to be happy would be wasted, or that for some reason, they are incapable of actually accomplishing happiness. They are missing the tools or have been too damaged by trauma to ever be successfully happy for any significant length of time. This is never actually the case because every human being is capeable of the kind of contentment I refer to as happiness. So, having come to understand that happiness is something we must do, we have to then believe we are capable of doing it.

In my lifetime I have known many people who others have decided are hopeless. I remember one young lady who came into my treatment group at a residential treatment center. She had difficulty talking clearly, and the intake staff had information from her family that she may not be mentally capable of benefitting from the program. In addition, someone at admissions indicated that this person, I will call her Rebecca, appeared to be "borderline retarded" in cognitive functioning. Fortunately I did not read any of this information before Rebecca appeared in my group. I certainly noticed a slight speech problem. However, she came to the first group late, and I did not get to spend any time with her individually. This group was a psychoeducational group in which I used the A-B-C model of cognitive therapy (a lecture that was actually the genesis of this book beginning in 1975). It was my habit to present the model myself occasionally and then ask each patient, when they felt ready, to present the model for newly arriving patients. I presented the model on the day Rebecca arrived. The next day, another new patient arrived and I asked Rebecca if she wanted to take a shot at presenting the model. I fully expected that, like many other patients, she would defer and ask for more time. To my surprise Rebecca said yes and proceeded to deliver a presentation that rivaled my own, never mind her slight speech impediment. She even took questions from the group. A few days later, in preparation for the team meeting, I read her admission papers and discovered that both family and professionals believed she was intellectually impaired. For the next several weeks I fought an ongoing skirmish with everyone on the treatment team regarding Rebecca's cognitive abilities. Aftercare planners adamantly wanted her to go to programs that provided extra support for the cognitively challenged. Eventually her performance in the program convinced everyone that a more relaxed intensive outpatient option would work. Rebecca later said it was my assumption that she could that allowed her to do the presentation. There is truth to this. Eugene C. Kennedy writes "…there is a dynamic associated with believing in other persons that transforms their chances, reversing the odds in desperate situations and frequently making the difference between life and death."[5] It was also my habit of not reading admission paperwork or psychological write-ups before meeting patients that made a difference, because it made the difference in what I believed about

---

[5] Kennedy (1974)

IT'S AS EASY AS 1, 2, 3: THREE BASIC IDEAS

Rebecca. If I had been exposed to that information, I probably would have avoided putting Rebecca into the "stressful" situation of having to make a presentation that was clearly above her ability. I would not have believed in her, or believed that she could. At my last contact, Rebecca was a senior in college.

The power of our beliefs is incredible and defining. I have been told that Henry Ford said, "Whether you believe you can or you can't, you are right." One of the biggest obstacles to most people's happiness is the belief, by themselves or others, that they cannot accomplish happiness. These beliefs are almost always wrong.

Sure, there are situations where there has been physical brain damage by accident, war, or birth, so extensive that normal functioning is not possible. Again, this book is not written with those situations in mind. What is also true is that the power of the mind is astounding. It allows us to overcome seemingly insurmountable barriers. And as far as I know, every person has a mind. This means that everyone has the power to accomplish amazing things, not the least of which is to decide to be happy. Based on my decades of life and almost forty years working in behavioral health, I believe that every person has the ability to become happy. In the early part of last century Reinhold Niebuhr, a Protestant theologian, is generally credited with composing the serenity prayer now primarily associated with Alcoholics Anonymous and other twelve-step programs. It reads:

God grant me the serenity
To accept the things I cannot change,
The courage to change the things I can,
And the wisdom to know the difference.

This is a powerful statement. I have always wished, however, that it had not been formulated as a request. I believe that God, or nature, has already endowed each of us with all of these gifts. I

FACTS OF LIFE

sometimes worry when reciting this prayer at the end of recovery groups that God is going to get tired of my nagging him for something already provided. It would be much more accurate to give thanks for the fact that we all have the ability to live in this manner rather than continually pleading for something we have already been granted by virtue of being human. Regardless of whether you are a creationist or a scientist, it does not make sense to believe that we have been created or evolved as cripples. On the creationist side, one would have to believe that God set us up to be inadequate. Albert Einstein is quoted as saying, "God does not play dice with the universe." I believe also that God did not create us in order to fail. Similarly the principle of evolution can be described plainly by saying whatever works, lasts. By definition, non-working or defective organisms would not last, so people must be designed to last, to function. That means we are all born with everything necessary to cope with life without unnecessary, and possibly fatal, dysfunctional emotions. So Fact of Life #3 is that we all have everything we needto be happy—all the time. Whether I sit down in front of a client with some horrid diagnosis or my own family member in distress over a life change, I always start from the assumption that my role in the situation is to help the person come to recognize their natural ability to deal with whatever faces them. My job is to get them to believe in themselves as I do. This means I operate on the assumption that we all have everything we need to remain happy, no matter what life throws at us. It is also the case that there is no big secret we need to discover in order to be happy.

> **#3 We all have Everything We Need To Be Happy; All The Time.**

IT'S AS EASY AS 1, 2, 3: THREE BASIC IDEAS

Everything that is needed to live a life of contentment is already known. We are not waiting for some reclusive scientist to come running out of the lab with the answer. It is not waiting to be discovered in some mossy cave in the South American jungle or in the dusty basement of an Egyptian tomb. The knowledge we need is already known and is being practiced by millions of people every day. Not only does every individual have everything needed for contentment, the human race has already discovered all of the necessary principles. Everyone can be happy. All that is required is the courage to do the work. We all have what it takes.

Many people come to therapy with the idea that "I need to change myself." I am quick to dissuade this kind of thinking. I have found that the task in therapy, and in life, is to discover our true self and accept it. It is the act of not believing in fact number one that gets us into trouble.

We have now introduced three basic ideas or "facts." It is important for the reader to spend some time in serious reflection about these three facts. If you cannot wrap your head around these beliefs and embrace them to some extent, the rest of this book will be of less help than it might be. These are the foundation of what follows. Successful apprehension and application of the techniques and tips to follow requires at least an open-minded approach to, if not a belief in, these first three facts. Do not skip over or skim these. They deserve your full attention.

The rest of this book is intended as nothing less than a guide to accomplishing happiness. Some of the information is a little tedious, but necessary for a full understanding of our potential. The bottom line is that we are all alike as people; happiness is not only something we do, it is something all of us can do, without exception.

All people are people.

Happiness is not something that happens to us. It is something we do.

We all have everything we need to be happy all the time.

CHAPTER 2

It's As Easy as A, B, C: How We Work

To begin our search for happiness, I am going to employ a classic model used by counselors and psychotherapists for the last fifty years or so. It is generally referred to as the A-B-C model for reasons which quickly become obvious.[6] Imagine that Figure 1 represents a person, me for example.

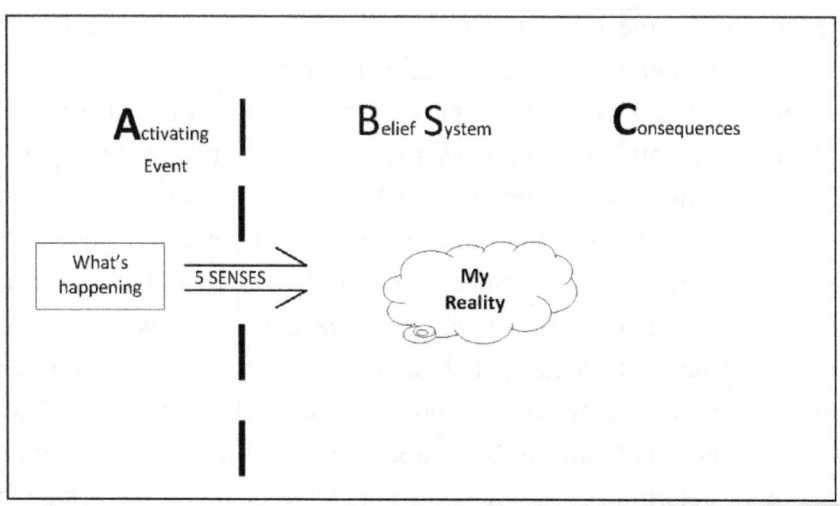

Figure 1

In this representation, the dashed line represents my skin. Everything on the left side of the line (under the A) is outside of my body, and everything on the right (under the B and C) is

---

[6] My first introduction to these principles came from the works of Albert Ellis and later David Burns and Judith Beck, all listed in the bibliography.

inside, specifically in my mind. The A-B-C represents those elements of ourselves we are most concerned with in our search for happiness.

A = Activating Event

This is the source of the data we take in from the world. It includes literally everything in the world that is not me. It can be a sunset, other people, something that happens to me or around me. An activating event can be anything and everything in the world. An activating event can also be in the past, present, or future. If I am preparing for a public presentation, this can be an activating event producing anxiety or nervousness in the present moment, even though the presentation is still in the future. Similarly, if I have done something really stupid in the past or I have offended someone, I can bring those past events into the present, creating depression now. Maybe, perhaps, possibly during a break in a workshop that I was conducting, I left the wireless microphone on when I stepped out to the restroom (not that I have ever done such a thing, no matter what someone may tell you). I can feel shame or embarrassment over this long after the event. Activating events occur in absolute reality, if there is such a thing. They can also occur in my imagination, but we will discuss those later. Activating events are usually time limited. What we know about them is determined by the kind and amount of data we take in through the keyhole of our five senses.

Thus, one of the important processes we need to understand is the one by which the data about activating events passes from the outside world into our bodies and ultimately ourselves. Generally speaking, we have five senses. I will grant that there may be individuals who have direct lines to God, possess psychic powers, or who do not share the DNA that defines human beings and therefore have different senses. As explained in the previous chapter, this book does not apply to such creatures. For most of us, the information we have about the world comes to us through our five senses: sight, hearing, touch, smell, and taste. Our five senses are powerful, but they are also limited and variable.

Our senses are limited in that there are many things going on all around us that our senses cannot detect. Many types of radiation exist which we cannot be aware of without specialized equipment. Even then our information about the radiation is only secondhand, transformed by our equipment into light or sound we can detect. X-rays, for example, or radio waves are totally out of our sensory range. All of the text messages, Facebook posts, and sports broadcasts flashing through the room right now are invisible to us unless we pick up a phone or turn on a computer. There are sounds we cannot hear and colors we cannot see, so our information about activating events, about the world, is necessarily limited. In addition, many people have differing sensory abilities.

Some of us are colorblind and see only grays. Some of us are hard of hearing. Some people (me being one) have an incurable sweet tooth, and some people do not like the taste of chocolate! Thus, everybody's experience of activating events is shaped by the limited data that is available to us. Furthermore that data can be very different from person to person. No two people perceive an event or object in precisely the same way as a result of the physical differences of our sensory organs. Nevertheless, our experience of the world is our reality. After all, it is all that we know. Reality for each of us is defined by the experiences we have and the sensations produced by our five senses, regardless of what is actually happening out in the world. It is then fair to say that everyone's reality is different and everyone's reality is valid, which is the fourth fact of life.

#4 Everyone's Reality Is Different, And Valid

This is a very significant fact of life. It means that I cannot know with complete accuracy what is going on in the world around me because I don't have all the information due to the limited range of my senses. Furthermore, I cannot ever be sure that others experience the world the same way I do. This means I cannot ever assume that another person's reality is the same as mine, even though we are watching the same events at the same time.

Years ago, television sets contained some kind of oscillator. These objects apparently emitted a very high-pitched sound. I don't know if this was a universal phenomenon or just something peculiar about our brand of TVs. The interesting thing is that my wife could hear the sound made by these devices. I could not hear it, the dog could not hear it, but my wife could. At least I don't think the dog could hear it. If he did he did not care much about it. Anytime a TV was on in the house, my wife knew it. Because of this her experience of the world was different than mine (or the dog's) beginning at this very basic sensory level. Her reality was different. This is not a particularly significant difference (except for our daughter, who must have wondered how we always knew when she turned on the TV in her room after bedtime). As these little bits of difference in the data accumulate in our perceptions, they eventually add up to meaningful differences. The bottom line is that everybody's reality is different, and valid. Think about how much time we spend trying to change each other's reality. These can be very destructive interactions when they occur in the context of intimate relationships. Think of how often we approach a sad friend and try to cheer them up with phrases amounting to "You don't have to be depressed because …" These are very disrespectful interactions because we are basically telling someone they don't know how to feel properly. These attempts to change another person's reality I refer to as "data debates." These data debates are not so bad if we are trying to build a skyscraper. In that case it is helpful if everyone involved has the same concept. Even in this situation though, 100 percent equivalence of perception never actually happens. All you have to do is talk to the architect, look at the plans, talk to the builder, and look at the result to see that different perceptions were in play. In other words we can spend impressive amounts of time and energy trying to control or manage another person's reality. When we get into these kinds of data debates, the result is a lack of the intimacy and connection we all seek. It is like the joke about teaching pigs to sing. The only result of such efforts is a pissed-off pig. We will talk about some tools to avoid this later. For now it is just important to recognize that our perceptions are not always accurate or the same as other people's perceptions, simply because our senses are limited and vary somewhat from person to person. Furthermore, there are other factors that contribute to differences in our perception of the world. That leads us to the B part of the model.

B = Belief System

Our belief system has many components. If you consult experts in various fields who concern themselves with such things, you can come up with all kinds of definitions and classifications about the contents of the belief system. They will talk to you about various types of schema, working models, templates, and connecting processes in way more enthusiastic detail than is healthy. Right now we are only going to concern ourselves with four: Core Beliefs, Memories, Values, and Automatic Thoughts. This classification of the cognitive components of our belief system is my own. It is based on my years of experience trying to explain cognitive processes to others, not on empirical studies or academic treatises. The goal of this classification is to keep things as simple as possible and still provide adequate understanding of basic processes. Let's look at each of these four components in a little more detail.

Core Beliefs

Core beliefs are fundamental beliefs we have about very basic issues such as how the world works, what it takes to get by in the world, and how I fit into the world. An example of core belief is numbers. Most of us have a belief about the meaning of the numbers one, two, et cetera. We do not have to think about their meaning very often; the concept is so basic and so much a part of our understanding of the world that it seems to be a fact, but it is not. It is an assumption; an idea. After all, when was the last time you saw a two walking down the sidewalk? The Piraha tribe in remote northwestern Brazil does not have the concept of numbers. I think they have expressions for concepts such as "some" and "many" but do not have the language for exact numbers. If we were to go there and ask someone, "What is three times three?" they would not understand the request. Numbers are not real for them. Clearly their reality is going to be different than someone raised with a belief in numbers. In fact their experience of the same stimulus, the same events in the world, will be different.

A second example of a core belief is that of object permanence. Human babies accomplish a number of cognitive tasks as part of normal early development. In the beginning, for example, babies do not differentiate themselves from the world. They have to learn where the world leaves off and their bodies begin. If you have been

IT'S AS EASY AS A, B, C: HOW WE WORK

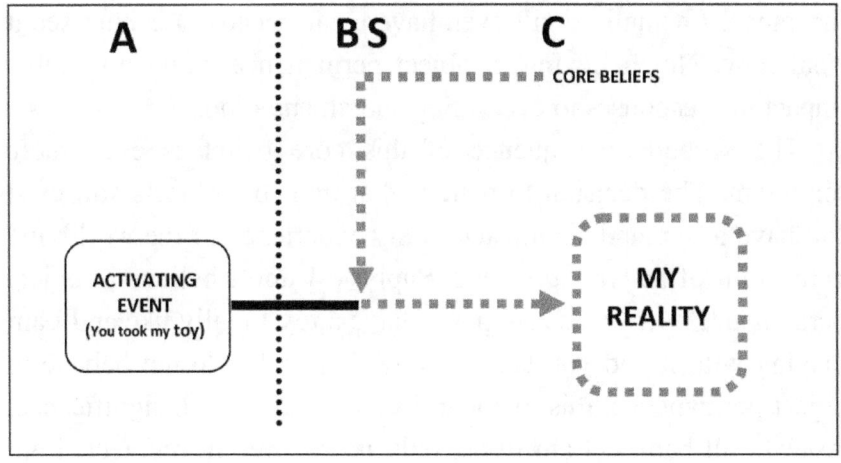

Figure 2a.

around babies, you have probably seen them discovering that their foot is a part of them (more easily figured out, apparently, with the foot in the mouth). Learning to differentiate themselves from the rest of the world is only part of the learning required. At some point in the first year or so babies also decide whether to believe that objects still exist even when they cannot be seen, touched, or sensed in any way. Again, if you have observed babies much, you may have noticed that very early on they live in the moment. Whatever they are playing with is great. When it is taken away, they don't really miss a beat; they just go on to the next thing, and that is great. If, on the other hand, you take a toy away from a baby who is over two years old, you get a whole different reaction. The baby in this case will probably pitch a fit, start looking for the toy, or try to get it away from you by resorting to crying, begging, or any of the other quite unfair tactics babies all use. The fundamental decision of whether or not to believe in object permanence determines how I, or a baby, or anyone might react to any activating event. After all, if I don't believe that things still exist when I cannot see them, I don't have to worry about paying my car insurance. I actually don't even have a car because I cannot see it right now. Not believing in object permanence could noticeably impact my responses to everything and all situations.

The second consequence of this core belief is even more important. The decision to believe that invisible objects still exist can have a tremendous impact on my experience of the world, my perception of activating events. Suppose I don't believe in object permanence. Let us also suppose I have a toy I really like and I am playing with it and you take it away. If I really do not believe in object permanence, this incident does not have much significance. As with all babies, I am living only in the present moment; I am only concerned with what is in front of me right now. If I do believe in object permanence, however, I may have a totally different experience. For one thing I can begin to ask questions that might not have otherwise occurred to me. These questions and the potential answers, imagined or actual, become a part of my experience, part of my reality. I could ask, "Where did it go?" or "Will I ever see it again?" More to the point I could ask, "Why did you take it away?" or "Are you mad at me?" or "Did I do something wrong?" Because I believe in object permanence, I can ask all of these questions and others, and the answers I take in or make up act like a filter, screening the data that is already limited by my five unique senses and totally changing the nature of my experience of the activating event—the same activating event that does not bother me at all if I don't have a core belief about object permanence. As Figure 2a shows, the data about the activating event entering through my senses, and filtered by those senses, is now further modified by my beliefs. **This is the true significance of core beliefs. They filter or modify our experience of the data coming in from activating events and thus impact the nature of our personal reality.**

Core beliefs also build on one another. In the numbers example, it is clear that if I first do not have a belief in numbers, I cannot think about multiplication. The effect is so subtle and so pervasive, it is accurate to say that core beliefs are not just what we think about—they are what we think with. This is why beliefs seem so real and why we treat them as facts. The reality is my beliefs are just ideas and not facts *no matter how real they appear*. As with the remote tribe that does not have numbers, if I do not have certain concepts already in place, there are many other concepts that are outside my ability to think.

Memories

Memories are the second component of our belief system. They are the stored record of our experience of life, our total life experience, including the good, bad, traumatic, and joyful. It is important to note here that memory is a record of our *experience,* not necessarily an accurate record of what happened, the activating events themselves. Nobody can have an accurate perception of what actually happened. Our core beliefs and memories and, as we will see, the other contents of the belief system modify the data collected by our senses. This is in addition to the modification already made by our senses (if I am colorblind or something). Thus what I store in memory may be very different than what actually occurred and is often different than the experiences recorded by other observers or participants. Furthermore, an increasing amount of research is documenting both the unreliability and malleability of memory. In fact some authors demonstrate the existence of memory as nothing more discrete than patterns and context.[7]

---

[7] Bateson (2002)

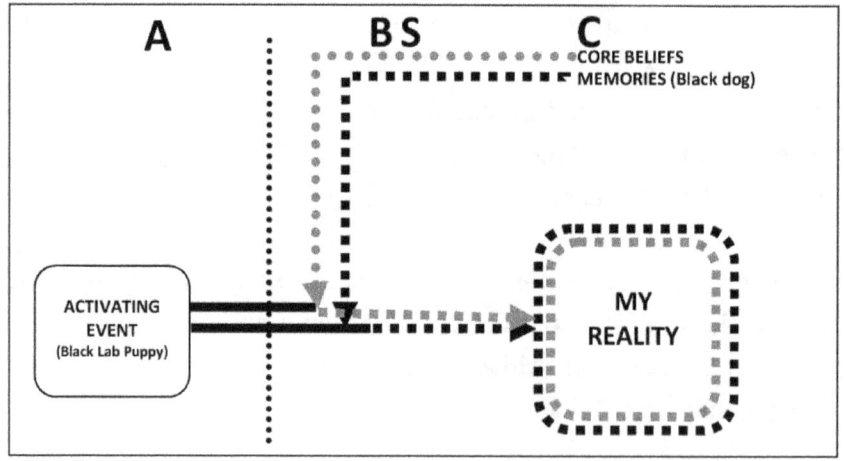

Figure 2b.

It is also worth noting that memory not only contains inaccuracies; it is also unstable. Among recent findings is the discovery that each time we call up long-term memories, when we are through with them, they have to be replaced back into long-term memory an d the process of recall and restoring *often modifies the memory*. This means that what we think we remember today may not be what we think we remember tomorrow about a particular event. Once again, this has an impact on the data coming in from an activating event because memory also filters the data as it comes in as with core beliefs. Regardless of its accuracy, however, memory always influences our perception of events.

For instance, imagine I have a memory of being bitten by a black dog when I was a child. (See Figure 2b) Further imagine the experience was painful and terrifying. That memory can influence my reaction to an obviously friendly dog jumping up for attention. Even if the dog is a black lab puppy—clearly incapable of hurting anyone (personal research over many years has demonstrated, by the way, that labs are the best pets on the planet)—my interpretation or appraisal of the present situation, and thus any additional memories recorded about it, will be different than someone whose experience of black dogs is positive. This reaction to the present-day, harmless black dog is known as a trauma reaction.

In the case of a trauma reaction, I am overreacting to the present situation because my perception of the situation is filtered by the memories of the previous situation. Because of the stored memory, my reaction to the present situation may not be appropriate or effective. Most importantly, subsequent information I place into long-term memory will also be affected by this filtering process. Thus, my later recall of the "aggressive" black dog might be puzzling to a friend who was with me but perceived no aggression on the part of the dog. Both of us were there, but our "realities" our experiences of the event, were different. My takeaway reality incorporated a little bit of "dodged a bullet that time," whereas my friend just saw a friendly puppy. The experience we each had, though different, is nevertheless our reality and is accurate for us. Again, everybody's reality is different and everybody's reality is valid.

Values

Values make up our third component of the belief system. Values are the things we consider to be important, usually taught to us by parents, churches, schools, and society in general. Once again, as with core beliefs and memories, values profoundly impact our perceptions of the world and all its activating events. Values affect perception because they control our attention. We pay attention only to what we consider important. Even though our senses provide only a bit of the total data available to us every second, it is still a flood of information. Literally billions of photons strike each eye from moment to moment. A myriad of

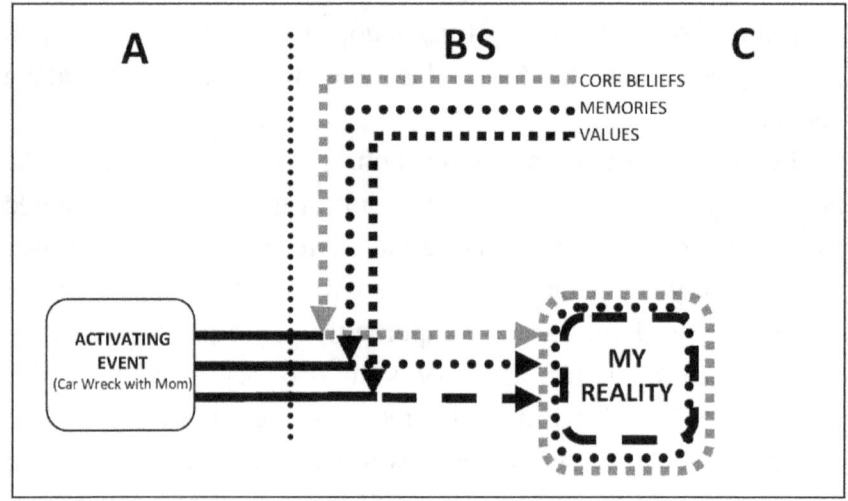

Figure 2c.

diverse sounds impinge on our ears. Our skin constitutes the largest organ in the body and is constantly taking in data from every inch of its surface. Various estimates of the amount of data sent from our bodies to the brain range between ten and twenty billion bits per second.[8] Personally I believe I can competently handle about three bits a second on a good day, assuming I don't also have to tie my shoes. So, we constantly have to decide which parts of the flood of data deserve our attention. In general, we pay attention to what is important to us, what we value. We can see the evidence of this in lots of places. As a case in point, if you have ever raised children, you might have noticed that, when they are older or grown, they will often not remember things the way you remember them. Children pay attention to different things than do

---

[8] The results of one online search led me to http://www.britannica.com/EBchecked/topic/287907/information-theory/214958/Physiology

adults. They have different values, different points of interest, and thus remember different details of the same situation.

A friend of mine was involved in a car accident. My friend, of course, remembers the accident, whose fault it was, who got a ticket, how much damage occurred to her car, and a hundred other details. Her daughter, on the other hand, remembers the day she got to play in a police car! (See Figure 2c) It is all a matter of what we value, what is important enough for us to focus our limited senses on and commit to long-term memory. Clearly then, values also filter the data we take in from activating events, like the other components of the belief system. The reliability of that data is more and more suspect, as we now have four factors which affect our perceptions: variation or limitation of senses, core beliefs, memories, and now values. But wait! There is more!

Automatic Thoughts

Automatic thoughts are the fourth component of the belief system. I am using the term "automatic thoughts" to refer to a

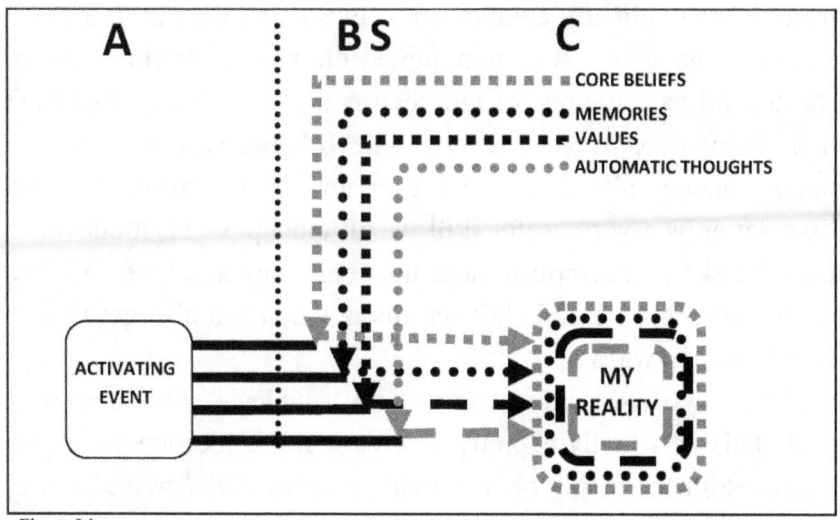

Figure 2d

variety of processes. Generally, psychologists refer to this process as dissociation. My favorite illustration of dissociation is that of driving.

If I am going to drive across town, at least in my town, it is a boring prospect. Accordingly on arrival at the end of my journey, say thirty miles, you could ask me a number of questions and I probably would not know the answer. "At 12th Street, was the light red or green when you got there?"; "At 24th Street, did you have your foot on the accelerator or the brake when you got to the intersection?"; "How about at 48th Street, was there an ambulance at that intersection or was that at 64th Street?" My answer to all of these might well be "I don't know." You could logically then ask who was driving the car. It is clear that someone had to be paying attention to driving. After all, there are thousands of decisions that have to be made regarding speed, lane selection, et cetera. The fact that I made it across town without serious consequences means someone had to be making those decisions; someone was paying attention and thinking. What has happened in this case is that I have dissociated. Facing the prospect of a boring forty-minute drive, I have split my attention into two parts. One part, a small part that I have set aside, is assigned the task of driving the car. The second part, the rest of me, then is free to do more important or at least more interesting stuff like fiddling with my iPod or making phone calls, et cetera (never texting of course.) Clearly, dissociation is a very useful skill we all must possess. It allows us to multitask, to accomplish more than one thing at a time. While a healthy and very helpful skill set, dissociation can also get us into trouble, in two ways.

One way dissociation gets us into trouble is when it is over used. This is actually a pretty rare occurrence, despite what you might see in the media or in movies such as *The Three Faces of*

Eve. This usually happens in response to early childhood trauma. The classic example would be a young girl who is sexually abused by a relative over a period of time. In response to the very painful and terrifying experience, just as we responded to the boredom of a cross-town drive, the child might set aside part of her attention to deal with the abusive situation, and leave the majority of her attention to roam elsewhere. If this occurs often enough, over time a habit is developed in which a given portion of her attention is routinely assigned the task of dealing with sexual situations. If it lasts long enough and the habit becomes very strong, we can end up with a piece of our attention more or less permanently dedicated to sexual situations and becoming in effect its own miniature personality. This is referred to as an "alter" or alternate personality. The popular literature often still refers to this condition by its previous description as multiple personality disorder. The current precise designation is dissociative identity disorder. Clearly, having multiple personalities is a problem as the self is now fractured and cannot deal with life in an integrated manner. As we will see, integration of the self, or congruence, is a major requirement for true happiness. While this situation is very serious, it is not the most common problem related to automatic thinking.

The most common problem related to automatic thinking is that it involves decision making. Since one characteristic of dissociated thinking is that it is out of our primary awareness, it is unconscious or in the background, like all of the decisions we made while driving across town. So, we have a background thought process that is a habit. In my experience, this type of automatic thinking is responsible for at least 80 percent of the decision making that keeps us involved in unfortunate relationships, or keeps us continually depressed, or renders us unable to kick an addiction.

A patient, Helen, came to group one evening and reported a relapse. When asked if she had done a thought report (see Chapter 3) she said no, that she didn't think about it. "It just sort of happened." The group began to question Helen. We learned that the incident occurred at the apartment of a friend. As details emerged, we learned that she was at her friend's apartment because earlier her friend had called and asked Helen to come over and party. When the phone call arrived, it was daylight outside. However, when Helen arrived at her friend's apartment, it was dark. A group member asked what Helen did in the time between. At first Helen could not remember doing anything. Gradually, though, we learned that Helen had gotten into her car and headed to her friend's place, but had stopped in a grocery store parking lot and sat for forty minutes, thinking. Helen was astounded to recall that she had, in fact, sat thinking about the ramifications of going to her friend's apartment, considering her probation status, possible loss of her daughter, and many other factors. This was all automatic thinking, however, and until the group pointed it out, the decision making was not in Helen's deliberate awareness.

This type of background thinking occurs automatically without serious conscious attention being paid to it. That is why we often hear those with addictions say, "I didn't even think about using; it just happened." It is also why we are surprised to find ourselves involved in a relationship with a person who is clearly not good for us, again and again and again. It is the reason I have clients in my office every week stating that "I just woke up depressed." As with Helen, the decision-making process leading to these outcomes is unconscious; it is not continuously available to our primary awareness. Lack of awareness of our internal processes is a major impediment to happiness. Of all the things we can do to maintain happiness, paying attention to ourselves is probably the most important. Automatic thoughts are a major contributor to much of the difficulty in our lives.

Taken together, our belief system can be thought of as the mechanism we use to make up meaning. It is the way we make sense of the world around us. Some have defined human beings as meaning machines, and this is not far off the mark. We assign meaning to every bit of data we process. This then constitutes our primary experience of life, our humanity.

This is a very brief description of our belief system. Any professor of psychology can go into considerable detail about the schema, attribution processes, and other mechanisms. For our purposes we have enough to understand the contribution the belief system makes to our ability to accomplish contentment in our lives or the ability to create unhappiness.

C - Consequence

Referring back to Figure 1, note that consequences appear on the right side of the dotted line. That means it is an internal consequence. There certainly are external consequences for our thoughts and behavior, but those are not our concern at this point. There are two kinds of internal consequences: physiological and emotional. First let's briefly consider physiological consequences. Physiological consequences are those physical reactions in our bodies resulting from our thoughts. If I believe I am in danger, this can trigger changes in my body designed to prepare me for fight, flight, or freezing. Often these changes involve generating or preparing to generate some form of energy. Our bodies contain two systems that regulate much of our activity. The sympathetic nervous system functions to mobilize the body's resources for action. The parasympathetic nervous system controls maintenance functions such as digestion and recuperation or rebuilding.

Believing I am in danger shuts down the parasympathetic functions and accelerates the sympathetic functions so that energy and resources are directed away from activities such as digestion and into our muscles for strength. This response is of principal importance in the instance of panic attacks. It is also a major factor in most long-term anxiety disorders. We become aware of these changes in our bodies as internal sensations that in some ways constitute a sixth sense. Perception of these internal sensations is subject to the same kind of interpretive process as the data coming in from our regular five senses. We will take a closer look at some of these physical sensations later. Emotions are the very substance of our misery and joy. For now, our main focus is on the emotional consequences of our thinking and beliefs. They are also the subject of much misinformation and downright superstition in almost all cultures. In the next chapter we examine emotions in much more detail. For now it is much more important to recognize how emotions arise. As you might guess from the model, they come strictly from our belief system. Let's look at an example.

I was raised in Texas. On my grandfather's ranch, I had multiple opportunities to become acquainted with rattlesnakes. Because of various incidents I know what rattlesnakes sound like and, I might add, what it feels like when you step on one. The hissing sort of rattling sound is a warning that the snake is feeling threatened and is poised to strike. Because of my previous experience, which resides in my memory, hearing this sound immediately causes me to experience a level of fear and to become cautious and on alert. Not everybody, it turns out, has this knowledge. Later in life I spent several years volunteering for the sheriff's office in Maricopa County, Arizona, training dogs for search and rescue. One day a colleague and I were hiking up a wash with our dogs. As we stepped into a deeper part of the wash,

IT'S AS EASY AS A, B, C: HOW WE WORK

thick with palo verde trees, I heard the sound of a rattlesnake to my left. Instantly I leapt up the opposite side of the wash to avoid being bitten. My friend heard the noise I made scurrying up the slope and turned to see what I was up to. She casually asked me what I was doing, and in order to get her out of danger, I told her to come to where I was standing, which she did. At that point my friend was calm but curious about my behavior. I was not exactly terrified, but my heart rate was elevated and my breathing was a little faster than normal. I was clearly more alert than my friend. My alarm was not extreme and lasted only a minute, but it was much different than my partner's experience to that point. I asked my friend if she could hear the sound. She listened and said, "Yes. What is it?" When I told her, she did not believe me, so we went back into the wash and I carefully exposed the snake where it was coiled in the brush. The point here is that even though both of us heard the warning sound of a rattlesnake, only one of us became alarmed. Only one of us had a belief or thought or memory telling us that the sound represents a danger. If we do not have an idea or a belief or an expectation about something, then we don't know how to feel about it. This is true even though the emotion, the fear, occurred in an instant. In a very real sense, I was a little scared, not because of the rattlesnake's racket but because of my belief that the sound represented danger. My friend heard the same sound, but because she had no prior experience with snakes, she did not become afraid. I will say it again for emphasis. *If I do not have a belief about something, I do not know how to feel about it* (the word belief is short for any and all of the contents of the belief system). This means that I cannot have feelings in the absence of some core belief or value or memory or expectation or assumption. My feelings come from my belief system, not from the world or other people.

A classic example I have used every week in our workshop at Consiliom is the parking lot example. Pretend that I am going shopping. I jump in my car and, with vigorous dissociation, drive down to the mall. When I arrive, I find the entire parking lot is full. This is disappointing. However, just as I am about to give up and leave, a car starts to pull out, in my lane, right up by the storefront. This is cool. I scoot down there and wait patiently for the parking space to clear. I have my turn signal on so anyone can see that I am waiting, patiently. Of course just as the other car clears the parking space and is backing toward me, another car comes around the corner. This other person sees the parking space, makes eye contact with me, looks down at my turn signal, then looks back up at me and *smiles* and takes my space. This then is the activating event as depicted in Figure 3.

We are going to further suppose that this incident happens, in exactly the same way, to two different people. Person #1 believes, "The other person took the space on purpose, knowing that I was waiting for it." Person #2 believes, "It was an accident." The emotional consequence for Person #1, based on the response of hundreds of workshop participants, is most likely to be anger. (I

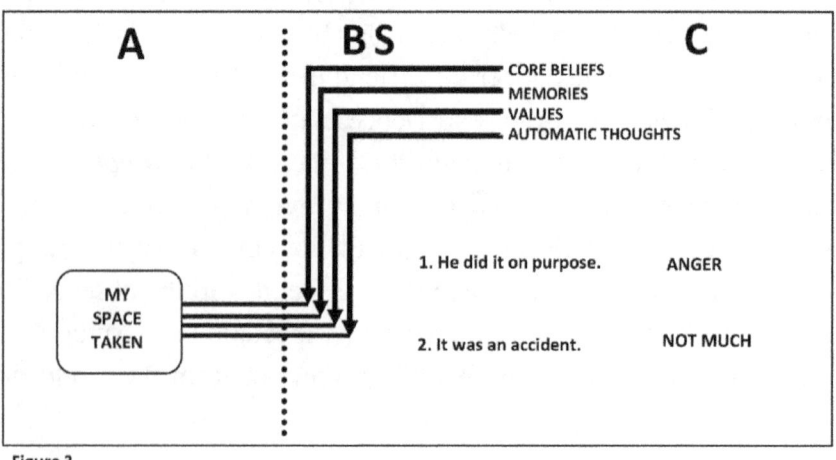

A	B S	C
	CORE BELIEFS MEMORIES VALUES AUTOMATIC THOUGHTS	
MY SPACE TAKEN	1. He did it on purpose. 2. It was an accident.	ANGER NOT MUCH

Figure 3.

am aware that this is a very simplistic example—be patient, examples will get more complex as we go. This one is intended to make one simple point.) Person #2, on the other hand, will have a comparatively mild consequence possibly some mild irritation (or possibly a daydream about some beach?), but nothing like what Person #1 will experience. So, now comes the question. What makes the difference between being the person most likely to get in a fight, or sent to jail and the person most likely to just go on with their day? As with the rattlesnake in the earlier example, the activating event is the same, so that cannot be the cause of the difference. Clearly the cause of the difference is the belief system.

It is important to emphasize that we are not concerned with the behavioral response of either Person #1 or Person #2. In fact, both may respond effectively and go on about their business. The difference on the consequence side of the model is that internally, Person #1 will have made himself emotionally upset in the process, *and he did not have to.* In fact Person #1 might very well remain upset for quite some time after the incident is over. It is this kind of unnecessary emotional distress that, if repeated consistently over enough time, will lead to serious emotional, psychological, and physical problems. This is the foundation of the model of behavioral and emotional health being described in this book. There are two enormous implications if one decides to believe this model.

First, if I believe this model to be accurate, I can never again say with any sincerity, "He (the guy who stole my parking space) made me mad." Or to take a more extreme example I can never actually believe that "she (my wife dying) made me sad." In lectures I usually get some objection to this last statement. It seems so counterintuitive. When that happens I let folks know that I only married her for her money and have been waiting twenty years for her to kick off. Furthermore it is quite a lot of money. So I could actually be pretty joyful about that activating event!

The point is *the activating event had nothing to do with my emotional experience.* The major determinant of my feelings is my thinking, my beliefs. Whether I believe that losing my parking space was an accident or I see it as having been done on purpose, this is what matters. It is what I believe about the activating event that determines what I feel. This is another fact of life that we cannot ignore if we want happiness. We never, ever have a feeling without first having a thought or belief. My feelings, or emotions, always come from my thoughts and beliefs. This is Fact of Life #5. Feelings or emotions have no independent existence. They are not imposed from the world outside of my skin. To feel them we have to create them. When I say *thought*, in this context, I am again referring to any or all of the contents of the belief system (core beliefs, memories, values, automatic thoughts, expectations, and assumptions). My feelings always come from my thoughts. This is a little bit of a downer. It is tough to accept total responsibility for all of my emotions and quit blaming life for the way I feel. Of course, to choose otherwise is to choose life as a hapless victim. If the activating events of the world actually control my emotions I have no chance for happiness on purpose. I do not have control of my own contentment. If other people control my feelings, then I am at their mercy and can never aspire to peace on my own terms. To assume the world is in charge of my emotions is to adopt the

> #5 My feelings always come from my belief system, my thoughts.

IT'S AS EASY AS A, B, C: HOW WE WORK

stance of a perpetual victim. In that case, I have no hope of happiness except through manipulation of others.

The second implication of this fact of life is a bit more uplifting. If I believe that the facts of the activating events don't have anything to do with my emotions, then I have a chance to take action and take control of my emotional experiences. Remember: Beliefs and thoughts and all of the contents of our belief system are ideas; they are not facts. The facts of an activating event cannot be changed once it has occurred. Sure, we can work to accomplish preferred outcomes in the future, but once something has happened, it is done. It is in the past and cannot be changed. This is still another important fact of life we need to consider. Everything happens exactly the way it happens. It is fair to say that once something has occurred, it happened just as it should have occurred; because that is the way it happened. So far in my life, things have always happened the way they happened. I am pretty old. Still, I have not yet come across a situation in which something happened in some way other than the way it actually occurred. This is kind of a silly statement, but it emphasizes an important fact of our existence. As soon as something has occurred, it enters the realm of fact or absolute reality (If there is such a thing.) It behooves us at that point to accept that it did happen exactly the way it *should have*. I may not like the way it happened. I might have been expecting some other outcome. Regardless of my preferences or expectations, however, things did happen exactly the way they happened. To expect otherwise is to expect the world to be different than it is. This is truly not a productive way to approach things. What is

> #6 Everything Always Happens Exactly the Way it Happens.

37

FACTS OF LIFE

> #7 The Belief System Consists of Ideas, Not Facts.

productive at this point is to recognize that there is a difference between facts and ideas.

The major difference is that ideas can be changed while facts are pretty much immutable. Knowing the difference between facts and ideas is a basic skill required to accomplish happiness. The belief system consists of ideas, not facts. Even the most basic of core beliefs are still just ideas.

Since ideas generate our emotions, and ideas can be changed, it follows that our **emotions** are ultimately under our control. That is, assuming

> #8 All Ideas Can Be Changed.

we are willing to do the work involved; and the work is difficult. Imagine how hard it would be to quit believing in object permanence. To convince myself to no longer believe that objects exist apart from our perceptions. It would be like persuading me that the door to my living room, which I cannot see from where I am working, no longer exists. Of course we probably would not want to change our belief in object permanence. It is a useful construct that generally does not lead to a lot of unnecessary emotional upset. However, the process of changing beliefs that result in depression, addictions, and other problems is just as difficult. Remember that these beliefs are what we think with, not just what we think about. They determine the shape and fabric of our experience. It is almost impossible to see around them. We are generally not even aware of them. Nevertheless, it is possible to make whatever changes are required to eliminate unnecessary stress and emotional distress. The thing is, it is not necessarily easy, nor can someone else do it for us.

Remember, too, that happiness is something we do, not something that happens to us. Many people walk around waiting for "something to happen" that will make their life complete or render them happy. They are forever looking for a lucky break in life that will make everything okay. Unfortunately, nothing will usually get better until we make a decision to do something different, to see things differently. In other words, "There is only one way to change our story, and that is by changing what we believe about ourselves."[9] Often patients in psychiatric hospitals and rehab centers come expecting that therapists can make them better or that psychiatrists can give them a pill that will somehow change their life. At Consiliom, clients often come expecting that the therapist can fix them; all they have to do is show up. I have seen people who, believing that others have the answers, go from hospital to hospital and from one therapist to the next, looking for the answer. They will never find it. The important answers we all seek already exist within ourselves, in our belief system.

All ideas can be changed. This means that we can take control of our emotional experience in life. It is not an easy task, as it involves facing, and accepting, ourselves. Finding those answers is hard work and requires a commitment to total honesty with ourselves. The process for change, on the other hand, is as simple to describe as it is difficult to implement. In our workshop at Consiliom, we emphasize that happiness is something we do, which means it is an active process, so we use the term ACT. To change cognitive distortions you have to **ACT**. This refers to the three actions that must be taken to make significant changes in our

---

[9] Ruiz (2004) page 67

beliefs and thinking: 1) Awareness, 2) Critical Thought, and 3) Training.

I want to make a very important point here about our expectations of change. In this book I describe the change process in black-and-white terms. This is for emphasis and to highlight the essential elements of the process that are simple in concept. This does not mean, however, that application of these methods is simple, or quick. It also does not mean that we are going to totally eliminate dysfunctional thinking or emotions. Much of the time the reasonable expectation is that we will only be able to reduce the intensity of dysfunctional emotions, not eliminate them. I have often had clients become frustrated because "I have been practicing and it seems like I should be done by now." In fact we may experience considerable shame because it seems as though things are not working for us like they work for others. The expectation that I can quickly, or completely, eliminate longstanding habits of thought is just not realistic. We will never "be done." I am very old as I write this. I have been working on my competence - and belonging-focused value issues for many decades. I have not conquered them or eliminated them. To this day, in attempting to do something like write this book, I will experience considerable shame and doubts about my ability. "Who do I think I am to be writing a book like this when I still struggle?" The goal, however, is not some sort of robotic elimination of all inconvenient emotions. The real goal is to understand my self and to be able to manage emotional consequences enough so that I can accept my authentic self, messed-up emotions and all, pretty quickly in all situations. If I can do this, then I am ultimately in control of my contentment, regardless of what the world is doing to me. This is not a black-and-white accomplishment but a very gray goal. We are all just people, after all, doing the best we can with what we have. And, we are always enough. With our common humanity in mind then, let's take a look at ACT.

ACT to Change Cognitive Distortions

Awareness

This is, for many people, the hardest part of the process. Precisely because so much of the belief system operates in background without conscious awareness, it is very hard to drag it into the light for rational examination. However, unless we can identify the belief, memory, value, or automatic thought that is causing the problem, it is almost impossible to do anything about it. There are many tools available to assist with the process. But what they all have in common is the expectation that we have on board an "observing self."

By observing self, I am referring to a person's habit of self-examination or introspection. It is the level of self-awareness we maintain. "Most people operate in an unstated context of conventional thought that obscures or avoids acknowledging how the world is."[10] In other words, many of us go through life never quite being aware of exactly what we are thinking. If you ask people at random times when they are sitting quietly, "What are you thinking?" a common response is "Nothing." In order to be actually not thinking at all, we have to be dead. Even when asleep, we dream. As long as we are alive, our mind is working. People will usually respond to the question with "nothing" because they don't want to share what they were thinking about or, maybe, they just don't know.

---

[10] Yontef (1993) page 126

This lack of awareness of our internal life is deadly. In order to have any hope of happiness, especially in dire circumstances, we must at least notice what is going on inside of us. We are constantly telling ourselves a story, sort of an ongoing commentary about what is going on and the meaning of things. We tell ourselves a story, and that story becomes our life. If we do not have the habit of paying attention to that story, it becomes impossible to make any significant changes in our lives. We are living in reaction to the world. There is "nobody home" watching what is going on. This is why we don't realize that our thinking causes all of our emotions. The first step in identification, then, is awareness.

Awareness can be nurtured. It is a skill, a habit. Practice in such disciplines as meditation and yoga can improve our ability to be aware of our internal processes. This is critical because, "Without awareness there is nothing we can do."[11] We cannot identify the cognitive distortions if we don't notice them.

Let me make a distinction here. There is a difference between awareness and obsession. Obsession occurs most often when our introspection involves judgment. Let's say that I notice I am anxious and, further, that I label the anxiety "bad." Now I can become concerned with all sorts of thoughts. *How do I get rid of it? I should not be anxious. It is bad to be anxious.* This kind of judgmental labeling is the exact opposite of simple awareness. Awareness means noticing, just noticing without judgment. It is awareness with acceptance that I am feeling anxious, without needing to do anything about it. This requires a willingness to accept my self, warts and all, in an effort to increase my understanding. "The most fundamental aggression to ourselves…is

---

[11] Ruiz (2004) page 76

to remain ignorant by not having the courage and the respect to look at ourselves honestly and gently."[12]

People also sometimes say they are thinking about "nothing" because they are ashamed of whatever the thoughts were; they don't think anyone will find their thoughts important; or they just don't want us to know. This does not present too much of a problem unless the person believes that whatever they were thinking was so bizarre or inappropriate that no one else could possibly understand. Or more commonly, I have come to believe that if others know about the weird thoughts floating around in here, they will recognize I am nuts and either shun me entirely or lock me up. This commonly occurs when we do not completely believe Fact of Life #1, that all people are people, and I am one of them. In one lecture, I used to ask the audience how many people ever thought about doing something suicidal. At first a predictable number of folks raised their hands. With a little self-disclosure on my part and some reminders about the time I once wondered what it would be like to swerve my car into the path of an oncoming semi, I could usually get almost everyone in the room to own up to such thoughts. Generally, however, we do not want others to know about these stray thoughts. Worse, we keep ourselves unaware of the thoughts, fantasies, and urges that are part of our inner world. If I cannot acknowledge a thought because it might be "socially unacceptable," or because it might be absolute proof that I am crazy or broken or defective, then I have little chance of learning to know my true self.

To know myself, I must listen. I must become aware of the story I am telling myself, in all its odd little details. This is not just an idle exercise. Once several years ago, I had to have a major

---

[12] Chodron (2003) page 41

surgery. The surgeon told me that, if I would start exercising, I would have a much quicker recovery and be able to leave the hospital sooner. Historically I have been opposed to exercise on quasi-religious grounds. It hurts, takes up time, makes me sweat, and is incredibly boring. On the other hand I figured that if I survived the operation, I would want out of the hospital as quickly as possible. I allowed my daughter-in-law to sign me up at a gym and begin to show me the process of "getting in shape." I had probably not been in a gym since high school, and was surprised to find that I kind of enjoyed it. I had set up a target of going to the gym four to five days a week. It was a bit of a struggle. At first I was actually getting to the gym once or twice a week. One afternoon as I was walking across campus at work, I noticed myself thinking, *it's Tuesday, I gotta go to the gym tonight.* As soon as I noticed the thought, I realized it was part of the story I was making up about my life at that point. The implications of the word "gotta" were all negative (and yes, I know it's not really a word, but it's what I was thinking). I also realized that the implied belief was a lie. In reality going to the gym was a pleasure. My daughter-in-law usually went with me, and our relationship became much richer and more interesting as a result. Of course, I also felt better when I exercised. Generally we went out for a bite after the gym. In addition, it was getting me ready for the surgery. Fortunately I noticed the lie. I was listening to myself.

It's only because I was in the habit of listening to whatever is going on in my head that I noticed the lie. So, from that point on, I changed one word of the story. When I heard that thought start to come up, I immediately stopped it and reminded myself, sometimes aloud, that no, "Tonight I <u>get</u> to go to the gym." Once I made that tiny change in my thinking, I improved my attendance to around 90 percent and was in excellent shape for the operation.

IT'S AS EASY AS A, B, C: HOW WE WORK

Getting into the habit of listening in on our internal talk is a critical skill.

One tool to aid in this process is generically referred to as a "thought report." (Figure 4)

These are exercises designed to increase our level of self-awareness. In other words, it is a tool designed to help us get in the habit of listening to our automatic thinking. In many programs and practices these have been adapted to specialized purposes, or modified to match a particular treatment terminology. The underlying process is the same in all cases. It is a practice and a discipline based on the A-B-C model of cognitive processing.

In illustration, suppose I am walking through the cafeteria at work and approaching me is a colleague. I do not know the person very well, but we are acquainted and have sat in meetings together. Being a friendly sort of person, I say, "Hey." My colleague, we will call her Sharon, ignores me. Since I really am an outgoing, friendly sort, I impose my face directly in front of her and say, "Sharon, how are you?"

Sharon still does not respond. In fact she stares straight through me and keeps on walking. I notice that I am having some feelings about this, and the feelings appear to be rather more intense than the situation calls for. This is a clue that the emotions

---

THOUGHT REPORT

NAME: _____ DATE: _____

A. WHEN I _____

B. WHAT I (THOUGHT, MADE UP, IMAGINED, BELIEVED, ASSUMED) ABOUT THAT WAS:
_____
_____

C. AND WHAT I FEEL OR FELT ABOUT THAT IS/WAS:
CIRCLE ONE – *anger, fear, pain, guilt, shame, joy, passion, lonely, love*

Figure 4.

FACTS OF LIFE

may be dysfunctional, so I decide to do a thought report. I start by entering the data, the **A**. (Figure 5) here I need to keep it simple.

Remember, the activating event, the facts, doesn't really matter much. A lot of detail is not really necessary and can get in the way. If I start specifying details, the real point can get lost. It does not matter how many times I said "hi" or how loud I said it or what sort of look she had on her face any more than it matters what color socks I was wearing. Keeping it simple, I put "Sharon ignored me."

One might assume that we then proceed to **B**. In actuality if we are just beginning to do thought reports, it is often easier and more instructive to go next to **C** because, especially in our culture, we often are aware of our feelings, but oblivious of the thoughts behind the feelings. It is best to start with what we know. So the next step is to identify what emotions came up for me regarding this activating event. In actuality, more than one feeling might come up. In that case it is best to do a separate thought report for each feeling; otherwise, the chain of events is not clear. Selecting the emotion involves some additional thought.

First, observe that the form only has nine emotions. As

THOUGHT REPORT

NAME: Mike   DATE: Today

A. WHEN Sharon ignored me

B. WHAT I (thought, made up, imagined, believed, assumed) about that was:
She does not like me

C. AND WHAT I FEEL OR FELT ABOUT THAT IS/WAS :
(CIRCLE ONE) – *anger, fear, pain, guilt, **shame**, joy, passion, lonely, love*

Figure 5.

discussed in Chapter 3, we want to avoid getting lost down rabbit trails of endless discussions about nuances of shades of various feelings. These distinctions, like the plethora of irrelevant detail in the data about the activating event, can easily confuse the issue. Notice that it is necessary to this process, however, that we must feel our emotions if we are going to make any progress at all.

Remember in our discussion of emotions that emotions will not kill you. It is very often the case that people become afraid of their own emotions. Any number of lessons from childhood can result in our discomfort with or even fear of our emotions. Perhaps we received messages such as "Big boys don't cry" or "You shouldn't feel depressed; you have so much to be thankful for" or "Nobody wants to see that. Go to your room." This is especially true with strong emotions of fear, loneliness, pain, and shame. As described in Chapter 3, we can often develop a quick response to such emotions and immediately either translate them into secondary emotions of anger or ignore them and attempt to numb them. The reality is we cannot even begin to approach the task of learning to be happy if we do not first learn to at least tolerate our feelings. We have to get our feelings up and running. Often this is the most uncomfortable part of the process and the one many people avoid. This is why therapists are often heard telling patients, "You need to get out of your head and into your feelings." They know that "healthy people face the pain and work through it. Unhealthy people lie about it, cover it up, and resort to addictive behavior to dull it or deny that pain exists for them."[13] Attempting to go directly to the thoughts and bypassing the feelings leads only to frustration and years of wasted therapy.

---

[13] Richardson (2006)

Having felt the emotion, the next observation to make is that there is nothing determinate about the relationship between the activating event and the emotion. Based on my belief system, I can come up with any of these nine emotions, or all of them, in response to any activating event. Remember, it is our thinking that causes our emotions, not what is happening in the world. So, let's suppose that the predominant feeling I experience is embarrassment, which is shame. So I put "shame" in the third category. Now I can ask the important question.

What must I have been thinking in order to feel shame about this event? Notice that I DO NOT ask how this event embarrassed me or made me feels shame. I need to acknowledge, right from the beginning of my inquiry, that I alone am responsible for my feelings. The activating event or person had nothing to do with it. After all, Sharon could be someone I detest, so I could be feeling joy that I don't have to talk to her. What I need to find out about my self is how I generate this type of feeling in this situation. What must I have been thinking in order to feel shame that someone didn't say hi to me? This is the detective work through which I will get to know my true self—the way I will become acquainted with who I actually am. It is also the first step in making any changes to behaviors that have kept me from being as happy as I can be.

There are a number of possibilities. One very frequent thought is "She does not like me." It is important here to look for logical connections. Thus, I could also imagine that she was preoccupied and did not notice me. If I actually thought that was the situation, I probably would feel little or nothing. There is no logical connection between "she didn't notice me" and shame. Because "she does not like me" would more logically produce shame, we will examine that case.

IT'S AS EASY AS A, B, C: HOW WE WORK

Having isolated the surface thought, "she doesn't like me," which is apparently producing the emotion, we need to look under it to discover the source. Here the simplistic examples are no longer adequate. The fact is that Sharon actually may not like me. That could be part of the facts and not just something I imagined. It may be part of the activating event. One technique that can be employed in such situations is the "so what" method. In this case, on discovering that Sharon might not like me, assume the worst. First, I accept that Sharon may not like me. Then I ask myself "So what does it mean to me, or about me, that Sharon doesn't like me?" As we will see in more detail in Chapter 4, the contents of our belief system are complex, and there are always layers of beliefs and automatic thoughts involved. In this case, in order to understand ourselves a little better, we need to discover the underlying thinking. This is, in part, a result of the developmental nature of the self.

At the moment of our birth, the situation we find ourselves in is pretty dire. Looking around the world as a toddler, there are a number of things I notice. I am short. I can walk but I pretty much stagger around like a drunk. I cannot talk. I cannot feed myself. I am surrounded by tall people who walk smoothly, talk endlessly, and know how to feed themselves. In this situation, I am dependent on the tall people for survival. Literally, if I do not get at least one tall person to care about me, I will die. This is partly why babies, well, most babies anyway, are cute. Cuteness enhances the probability that a tall person will care. In a normal situation, over time I develop and learn, and the changes in me result in my becoming more able to take care of myself. I start to notice that I can walk better. I gradually learn more words and can ask for my wants and needs more effectively. I become taller. At some point I am tall enough to reach up on the counter and get my own damn cereal. As the years go by, I continue to grow and develop, and at some point in adolescence, I become more or less independent. I now see myself as a fully functioning tall person.

Remember, however, the filtering effects of the belief system. If, during childhood, I experience interruptions or omissions in my development, I may not learn all the lessons that I needed to learn. In fact, unless my childhood was picture perfect, I will almost certainly have such gaps. Small gaps accumulate, and because of the influence of the belief system on our perceptions, these gaps can affect subsequent learning.

The interruptions or irregularities in development do not have to be significant to have an impact. They can be as subtle as my brother getting first choice at dinner. They can be the result of events outside my ability to understand: war, death, or the demands of a parent's work. It can be because of some perceived abandonment, or loss, or simply due to timing and other variables. In my own case, undiagnosed Attention Deficit Disorder meant my perceptions were off. Whatever the cause, I learn some lessons imperfectly or not at all. Even though later development and life experiences can compensate a great deal, some gaps still exist. In the case of needing to get tall people to like me, this can result in a residual belief about the importance of getting people to like me.

A residual belief might be something like "Everybody has to like me or I cannot like myself" or "I need everyone's approval to know I am okay." Clearly these are problematic beliefs. However, we don't usually go around saying them out loud. If we work at things like the thought report, we can uncover the underlying belief. The conversation started by the thought report may go something like this:

"Maybe Sharon doesn't like me." So what? What does that mean?

IT'S AS EASY AS A, B, C: HOW WE WORK

"Perhaps I am not good enough for her." This could be true, she may not consider you important, and so what does that actually have to do with you?

"Well, if she thinks I am not good enough for her, then maybe she sees through me and knows I am not good enough." So?

"Maybe she is not the only one. Maybe everybody can see through me, and nobody will like me." So?

"Well, if nobody likes me, it proves I am not good enough."

Or "If nobody likes me, I will die."

Pretty soon this kind of internal conversation breaks down because we begin to see the absurdity of our beliefs. After all, if Sharon does not like me, it does not automatically mean that nobody else in the world can like me. This is not even logical. Even in the event that nobody in the world likes me, it does not necessarily mean I will die. In the process of this kind of detective work, we begin to identify the beliefs or automatic thinking that is causing our dysfunctional emotions.

In my office I will often guide clients through this process until they spontaneously exclaim, "That doesn't make sense" or "That sounds stupid when I say it out loud." This is the realization, the awareness we are looking for. This is not, however, a one-time exercise. Just because we capture the thought or belief once does not mean we will remember it or remember it fast enough to intervene next time it is invoked. Because we are talking about unconscious thinking and habits of thought, it will take many repetitions to bring the issue to the forefront of our awareness. The key, again, is to develop a habit of listening to our self-talk. One thing to listen for is cognitive distortions.

Cognitive distortion is the name given to faulty thinking. In other words it is the beliefs, values, assumptions, and expectations that result in dysfunctional emotions and behaviors. Whether these

COGNITIVE DISTORTIONS	
All or Nothing Thinking (Also called Black and White Thinking)	This is our tendency to classify everything as right or wrong. Outcomes are always all or nothing. There is no grey area. We see everything as one category or another and never see a continuum.
Overgeneralization	One event is viewed as a law of nature. "I **always** lose my parking space".
Catastrophizing (Also called Jumping to Conclusions)	Predicting negative outcomes far beyond what is reasonable. Expecting the maximum worst. Generally this includes any form of 'future tripping'. "My wife is mad at me, we will probably be divorced and I will be alone."
Disqualifying the positive	Filtering, or screening, information to support negative schema. "He is only complimenting me because he feels sorry for me."
Mental Filter	The opposite of disqualifying the positive. Instead we emphasize the negative. We pay too much attention to one negative outcome or small problem.
Magnification & Minimization	Exaggerating the importance or effect of things or events, especially negative ones, or, denying the importance of things.
Emotional Reasoning	Confusing feelings with thoughts and facts with opinions. "I feel worthless, therefore I am worthless" "I made a terrible mistake therefore I am a terrible person." "I feel like...", "I feel that..."
Should statements	Expecting the world to be different than it is. Not recognizing or accepting that things happen the way they happen.
Labeling & Mislabeling	Placing absolute, universal labels on self and others ("I am a loser" "He is lazy" "She is cool") rather than less arbitrary or ridged descriptions.
Personalization	Everything is my fault. Every negative outcome is proof of my lack of value or incompetence without considering the possibility it had nothing to do with me. "My boss did not say hi to me, I am probably going to get fired".

Table 3.

thoughts are in our core beliefs or surface thoughts, they consist of faulty logic, inaccurate data, or exaggerated importance. For decades there has been a list of ten cognitive distortions circulated by a number of authors. I believe the first version of it was published by Albert Ellis, but it has been revised over the years.[14] An edited version appears in Table 3. These basically are ten types of faulty thinking. The table can be a help in deciphering our thinking and deciding if it is problematic. If the thinking is described in one of these ten types, it is more than likely a

---

[14] Ellis (1961), Beck (1995), Burns (1999)

problem. Obviously just identifying my faulty thinking or cognitive distortions is usually not enough. We have to make specific efforts to change our thinking, and that leads to step two in the ACT model, Critical Thinking.

I have used the generic form because it highlights the cognitive process as it actually occurs (Stimulus – Belief – Thought – Emotion). However, in actual practice I generally have my clients use a modified version, which I call a "Feelings Check." This format (see Figure 6) is much easier for beginners because it acknowledges that we often are aware of our feelings before we become aware of the beliefs and thoughts that generated those emotions.

Whichever format you use, I don't believe I can overemphasize the usefulness and importance of this tool. Learn to use either of these forms, and more importantly this type of thinking, effectively, and *you will be happy for the rest of your life, no matter what life throws at you.*

FEELINGS CHECK

NAME: _____ DATE: _____

A. WHEN I: (saw, heard, felt, touched, tasted or imagined): _____

C. I FELT: (CIRCLE ONE: *anger, fear, pain, guilt, lonely, sadness, joy, passion, love*)

B. BECAUSE: (I thought, I imagined, I made up, I believed, I assumed, I expected, I wanted, I hoped, I wished) _____

Figure 6.

Critical Thinking

Once identified, the problem beliefs or automatic thinking can be changed. Even if we only have an inkling of the actual belief, there are dozens of techniques available to begin to restructure our cognitive system. All of them involve the same process. I must convince myself to believe or think something different. As with unlearning any habit, it takes time and practice. In the beginning, it is possible to make a difference with some generic practices.

The most important generic practice is simply to remind myself that this emotion I am experiencing comes from me. The question always is "How am I making myself feel about what is happening?" By forcing myself to adopt the principle that my emotions come from my thinking, I am gradually changing my focus. I often simply remind myself "I don't have to feel this way right now" as a cue to interrupt the process in the moment. I am taking responsibility for my feelings, and right after taking responsibility, I accomplish the power to change. This is not an easy task because our culture, even our everyday language, argues the opposite. Phrases such as "He made me mad" or "That makes me sad" argue that my feelings come from some place outside myself. For many of us it is a huge paradigm shift to begin to believe that, perhaps, I make up or create my feelings. While this is the main change that needs to be made, there are various techniques for attacking specific thoughts and beliefs. These fall into three general categories.

I can refute my existing beliefs primarily with evidence, logic, or imagery. We will go much more into these various methods in later chapters. For now it is enough to remember, I create my own feelings, based on my thoughts, and I can change my thoughts however I like. A woman once exclaimed on hearing my lecture for the third time and finally getting it, "You want me to manage my perceptions." This is entirely correct. Since our reality is malleable, it becomes our primary responsibility to manage our perceptions in a way that connects us with others and maintains our humanity. Thus when I find myself experiencing dysfunctional emotions and identify or become aware of the problematic thinking, there are four questions I can ask that will help me to restructure the belief:

1. Is it accurate? Here I want to find out if what I believe matches available data.
2. Is it logical? In other words, does it even make sense?
3. Is it important? In other words, does it matter or is it worth worrying about?

To find out if the belief is accurate, we must gather facts. Often there are facts available which we do not notice or pay attention to. Remember, our belief system filters or screens the data coming in to match our ideas. I often have clients in my office who tell me at some point, "I can't do anything right." These folks actually believe this, usually because of some spectacular failures in business, school, or romance. This belief might also be fostered by parents' messages such as "What's the matter with you? Can't you do anything right?" In any case the individual is not paying attention to all the available data. Often my response is to point out in one way or another that they clearly can do some things right. They made it to the appointment, appear to be groomed (if that is indeed the case), and have on clothes. From this I conclude they can do a number of things correctly such as driving, dressing, and brushing their teeth. A lengthier list is usually required before people begin to notice all of the data, not just the data that fits their story of themselves. This kind of filtered or superstitious thinking occurs in many areas.

We can also challenge cognitive distortions by asking if they even make sense. For example, if someone important to me indicates they don't like me, it is entirely possible that I can become unduly upset. Depending on my specific beliefs, I can actually become depressed on discovering this. However, the fact is that someone else's beliefs have nothing to do with me at all. If my friend stated that I have twelve toes, would that make it true? No, of course not, and finding out that he thinks ill of me in some other way also does not change anything else about me either. It is not even logical to make that connection. If I can identify the thinking involved in generating my dysfunctional emotions and see that it does not even make sense, it begins to lose its power.

Finally we can challenge our thinking by deciding if it is worth worrying about. That is, what does it actually mean to me? The data may be accurate as far as I can tell and the results might affect me directly, but if there is: a) nothing I can do about it in the moment or b) only a remote probability that it will actually happen or c) no significant meaning for me, then it is really not worth worrying about. For example it is a fact that an asteroid will someday hit the earth and destroy us all in a cataclysm of fire. Thus it is possible and it will hurt me. So, should I be worried about this now? Well, the reality is, even if I knew it was going to happen in the next five minutes, there is precious little I can do about it. The fact that I don't know when it will occur argues even more strongly for not wasting "worry energy" over it. Secondly the probability that such an event is going to occur in my lifetime is pretty small. It is so small, in fact, that I personally decided that looking up the actual odds for this example was not worth the effort. Clearly something with such a low probability does not require much worry in the present. Many times, however, we expend considerable energy worrying about things about which we can do nothing and which are pretty unlikely anyway.[15]

Train

We must train our brain into new habits of thought. Common sense and some research would indicate that the longer someone practices something, the better it is learned. From typing to pistol shooting to automatic thinking, the basic principles of learning apply. Thus once I have identified my problem thinking, and found an alternative, my work is not done. In order to make long-lasting changes, I have to practice the new beliefs and thoughts until they become habits. After all, I am trying to replace long-ingrained habits of thinking, so it follows that only new fully developed habits will really do the job. Just recognizing, in a flash of insight, that the thinking is flawed does not mean I will not revert to old habits later. This is why so many insight-oriented exercises and therapies seem to be very powerful in the moment but seldom have long-lasting impact. I do not want to take on any particular procedures, but there are many that claim quick, almost magical results. What they actually deliver is some intense and pretty cool experience of emotion or flash of realization. In the long run these insights have very little impact on behavior because the new understanding is not fortified with practice or with going public.

Training ourselves into new beliefs also involves revealing ourselves to others. Changes we make in secret are more difficult to sustain because those around us will tend to reinforce our old self with the old beliefs and behaviors. This is why the twelve steps of Alcoholics Anonymous include going public as a

---

[15] See Gardner (2008)

significant step. This is also why, for example, most effective addictions programs have some sort of family involvement or family week as part of the program. Bringing in family and significant others not only makes our changes explicit, it also makes our commitment to change a matter of public record and more difficult to abandon. Any smoker who has announced to friends and family that she is quitting will understand this process. The relapsing smoker is often forced to practice the addiction in secret. Afraid to let others know.

For reasons I won't go into, I often used to walk my dogs down the alleys of my neighborhood. I have not made a count, but there are a significant number of homes behind which I would find clandestine smokers. Quite friendly people actually, but nevertheless relegated to the alley by the force of their public announcement to quit and their secret relapse. They have to struggle to maintain the addiction. Engaging this resistance to relapse can be very helpful. The same thing applies when I proclaim my intent to make changes in other areas. The peer pressure to follow through is horrid and, if I relapse, the lesson I might take in about my worth and value as a person can be debilitating. On the other hand, the chance that I will continue with and complete the change process is also much higher. Going public is worth the risk.

The processes described here are fundamental and are the same for all human beings. No matter what our experience of life has been and regardless of the cultural influences, we all learn, perceive, and believe in the same manner. The eight "facts of life" discussed so far are the same for all of us. Thus the ability to accomplish a life of contentment exists in everyone reading this, even you. The power of the mind is amazing, and one of its more amazing aspects is its ability to overcome almost any obstacle to happiness.

"Everything we hear is an opinion, not a fact. Everything we see is a perspective, not the truth." — Marcus Aurelius

---

All people are people.

Happiness is not something that happens to us. It is something we do.

We all have everything we need to be happy.

Everyone's reality is different and everyone's reality is valid.

My feelings always come from my thoughts.

The belief system consists of ideas, not facts.

Things always happen the way they happen (facts cannot be changed).

Ideas can be changed.

CHAPTER 3

Emotions

I am devoting an entire chapter to emotions because they are such an important part of the human experience. Emotions are at the core of what it is to be human. Emotions delight and depress us. They motivate and discourage. If not for emotions I am not sure we would do much of anything at all. Certainly we would not have bothered with civilization. Emotions are one of the things that distinguish us from most other creatures. They make our life infinitely more entertaining than it would otherwise be.

Emotions, usually uncomfortable emotions, are also the reason most people come to see a therapist. They are among the best and worst experiences of our lives. Generally we receive our information about emotions in our family of origin. Most families do not clearly articulate rules or information about emotions, but they all have them. Thus our education about emotions is necessarily haphazard at best.

In many families there are rules. Rules about behavior and responsibilities, such as "Be home on time" or "Don't hit your sister," are often written out and posted on the fridge. There are also other rules, however, that are usually not posted for all to see. These are the rules about emotions.

As a young boy in rural Texas, I learned well that "Big boys don't cry." At age eight or nine, while "helping" my grandfather repair a windmill, the wooden crosspiece that keeps the rod in line came loose and fell about fifteen feet before hitting me on the shoulder. Nothing I had ever experienced hurt as bad as that. I did not, however, cry out, or cry at all. Even at that age I had learned well that, as a boy, I was not allowed to express pain. Despite the fact that it had broken my collarbone, I did not cry. There are lots of examples of these kinds of rules in families. Men, in general, are allowed to be angry, while women are vilified if they display too much anger. When men are seen crying or sharing emotions such as shame or pain or loneliness, they are considered weak. Women, on the other hand, are welcome to express all of the "softer" emotions but not anger. It is not ladylike. This causes problems because the fact is, since all people are people (see Fact of Life #1 on page 4), we all can and do experience all emotions. Suppressing natural emotions consistently has predictably bad results for our ability to find happiness or sometimes even to function in society.

For our purposes, I am defining emotions as mental and physical experiences resulting from activity in our mind which occur in response to things happening in the world or in our bodies. I am not going to differentiate between emotions and feelings. For the purposes here, they are the same, although distinctions can certainly be made. Also I am excluding automatic reactions such as startle responses to loud noises and other involuntary reactions to physical stimuli. Considering emotions with these definitions and exclusions in mind, and bearing in mind the model presented in the previous chapter, I offer eight considerations about emotions.

First, emotions can be thought of as *indicators* of activity in our mind. We will look at the meanings attached to various emotions a little later. For now it is enough to recognize that each distinct emotion tells us something about what is going on in our mind, about the meaning we are attaching to our sensations. Sensations include those created by objects out in the world (what we see, hear, touch, taste, and smell) plus internal sensations created by virtue of being hot, or hungry, or the sensations which may be created by conditions such as ADHD, bipolar disorder, and other physical/medical conditions. All of these sensations reach our brain and are perceived in our mind. Based on the contents of our belief system, we ascribe meaning to this incoming data. Once meaning is ascribed to external events, emotions are created. However, the precise type of emotion created is dependent on the meaning we attach to it.

Second, all emotions include a *physical component*. This physical component is not the emotion itself, but is part of the experience of the emotion. Often, in the case of mild emotions, the physical component is barely noticeable. In the case of more intense emotions, it is quite obvious and may dominate our experience of the emotions. This physical component can be thought of as a form of energy. It is, in fact, a byproduct of the body's gathering of energy in response to what our belief system is telling us.

Third, all emotions have *benefits*. The primary benefit involves directing or channeling the energy into some form of behavior or readiness. Perhaps the most obvious example of this is fear, which channels our energy so we can deal with some sort of danger.

Fourth, emotions are *not good or bad*. They just are. There is no intrinsic moral value attached to any emotion. Emotions can, however, be classified as either functional or dysfunctional. (See Table 2) Functional emotions are a very important part of human existence. They exist for a reason and perform a function. Dysfunctional emotions can actually create whole new problems of their own. We will look at differentiating functional dysfunctional emotions in a bit. For now I want to emphasize that emotions, all emotions, are created equal. They are not good or bad; they just are. If we can come to terms with our emotions, they can tell us a great deal about our belief system and ourselves.

Fifth, all emotions occur on a *continuum of intensity*. That is, they happen with more or less intensity depending on the cause of the emotion and the beliefs that created it. The range of this continuum can be quite wide. Often, in fact, the intensity can vary so much that it almost seems as though there are two different emotions operating. Anger, for example, can be mild irritation over noticing that I missed a spot cleaning the windshield all the way to out-of-control rage. The connection between the mild irritation and the rage may not be clear, but the mechanism that creates these two forms of anger is exactly the same. Shame is another emotion that runs a gamut so large that mild embarrassment seems qualitatively different than the toxic shame that can destroy lives. All emotions exist on this kind of scale of intensity. I might feel a bit sad about the loss of a favorite car. It will not be nearly as intense or last as long as my feelings about the loss of a loved one. Again we often make a distinction between sadness and grieving. However, it is the intensity that is different. Not the underlying process. This is one reason that the feelings chart approach I will describe in a bit has been so helpful. Accepting the nine basic feelings it describes allows us to focus on the underlying processes and avoid getting lost in massive classification discussion.

Intensity is generally in sync with the situation. We will discuss this a little further when talking about discerning the difference between functional and functional emotions.

Sixth, as should be clear from the previous

EMOTIONS
- Are Indicators
- Include a Physical Component
- Have Benefits
- Are Not Good or Bad
- Occur on a continuum of intensity
- Have No Independent Existence
- Occur on three levels.
- Will not kill you

Table 1.

chapter, emotions *have no independent existence*. All emotions have to be created to be experienced. They arise out of our belief system. We cannot stumble into a puddle of shame or be hit with a handful of anxiety. Most important of all, our emotions do not come from other people or what is happening in the world, not even if it is something we believe is bad that is happening to us.

Seventh, emotions *occur on three levels*: primary, secondary, and instrumental. There are good descriptions of these in the literature, some very detailed and others very straightforward, which I prefer.[16] Primary emotions are those that occur as a result of some content in our belief system, in response to external or internal activating events. Most of the discussion in this book is about primary emotions. If there is a stimulus in the world (a snake, for example) and I have an idea about that stimulus (it is dangerous), then I will have an emotion about it (fear). If, however, in addition to the belief that snakes are dangerous I also believe that emotions such as fear are not ok for a man to feel—and, in addition, because of this additional belief, I have successfully avoided or covered up fear most of my life and thus have very little experience with it, or tolerance of it then I must find a way around or out of the fear to a more acceptable emotion. So I get angry. Anger in this case is a reaction to a primary emotion and is referred to as a secondary emotion. In other words I cover the fear with anger. Since anger is an energetic emotion, it can give me the impression that I am taking action to do something about the uncomfortable primary emotion of fear. Generally, if we cannot notice whether a feeling is primary or secondary, we will not have much success managing our emotions.

---

[16] Brent Bradley and James Furrow provide a very simple description of the levels of emotional experience.

There is also a third level called instrumental emotions. Instrumental emotions are those we manufacture in order to get a desired response from another person. So, for example, I can act hurt in order to make someone feel guilty. Perhaps I want to punish them or maybe just want some sympathy. In either case these emotions are not genuine. The importance of being able to tell the difference in the levels of emotions we are experiencing cannot be overstated. If I cannot discern what is actually going on in me, I will not be able to manage my contentment nor will I be able to achieve effective intimacy with others. Our focus in this book is on primary emotions, and that is where we can find a path to contentment. This will fail, however, if we attempt to manage secondary emotions as though they are primary. So much unhappiness and conflict is based on reactionary secondary emotions that it is no wonder we get into endless and unproductive cycles.

The eighth factoid about emotions seems almost obvious, and perhaps a little silly, but it needs to be said. *Emotions will not kill you.* Over all of my years in the helping profession, one consideration has been consistent. Especially in psychiatric hospital populations and among addicts, in all cases those seeking help are cut off from their primary emotions. Even in outpatient settings such as our current practice at Consiliom, it is very common, on asking a client what they are feeling, to receive in return a vague or elliptical response or sometimes just "Nothing" or "I don't know." Part of this avoidance of our emotional experience is the discomfort that arises with some primary emotions. This is a result of not being taught, in early childhood, how to manage our feelings. Clearly, pain, shame, loneliness, and other emotions are not comfortable. However, if we have not learned that emotions are time limited and can be managed, they will be experienced as intolerable. In that case we will engage in secondary emotions or just numb ourselves to avoid feeling at all. The truth is that emotions will not kill you, but some of the behaviors we engage in to avoid feelings can be fatal. A client with a preverbal, deeply held belief that he is different, not like and not as good as others, will experience huge shame, almost all the time. In an effort to avoid the shame, perhaps the person turns to alcohol, which, if only for a few moments, helps him to forget the agony of dealing with feelings which are not understood and for which there is no way to tolerate them. Eventually it takes more and more booze to numb the original shame. Plus the behaviors involved in drinking so much and some of the consequences for those behaviors, such as DUIs, actually add to the shame and make things worse. The shame itself will not kill this person, but the attempts to avoid the feeling with alcohol well might. The ability to tolerate and even embrace our primary emotional experience is the first step toward mental toughness and, ultimately, happiness.

One of the first skills we must learn on the road to contentment is the ability to sit with and notice primary emotions such as shame or guilt or loneliness, without trying to make them go away. If we cannot tolerate the experience of our feelings, we cannot learn what they are trying to tell us. Furthermore, we cannot tell the difference between emotions that are functional and helpful and emotions that are dysfunctional and causing additional problems. Discerning the difference between functional and dysfunctional emotions and noticing the level of emotional experience becomes very important.

EMOTIONS

TYPES OF EMOTIONS	
FUNCTIONAL	**DYSFUNCTIONAL**
Vital alert and alarm systems.	Numb or distract us from our experience.
Provide gifts to aid us in coping and adapting	Reduce our power and ability to adapt and cope.
Enrich our lives and our ability to connect.	Disconnect us from others and the cosmos
Based on truth.	Based on lies.
Vital alert and alarm systems.	Numb or distract us from our experience.

Table 2.

Emotional pain can be a helpful sign, just like physical pain. If I cut my hand, the physical pain is a signal telling me there is something I need to deal with. Similarly, if I incur some sort of emotional pain, as a result of a death or other loss, for example, the emotional pain tells me there is something I need to deal with—some cognitive work that needs to be addressed. Dysfunctional emotions, on the other hand, are problematic. Dysfunctional emotions often actually numb us, or distract us from our experience of life. Rather than help us cope with life, dysfunctional primary emotions often create whole new problems of their own. If we have not learned as children how to process and be comfortable with emotions, we may generate additional dysfunctional emotions or secondary emotions (which are almost always dysfunctional) to avoid dealing with the discomfort of the primary emotions, or the external difficulties that we face. For example, if I become embarrassed over something I have done and I am not comfortable with difficult emotions like shame, I may well cover the shame by becoming angry.

As Table 2 shows, dysfunctional emotions also reduce our ability to cope, and disconnect us from meaningful interactions with others. Most importantly, dysfunctional emotions are based on lies. That is, they are based on illogical or distorted content of our belief system—things we learn from childhood experiences which are distorted. These are the cognitive distortions or mind scars we have already discussed that are the source of almost all of our emotional misery. Dysfunctional emotions provide very good clues to these distortions. Clearly it becomes important then to be able to distinguish between functional and dysfunctional emotions. There are some guidelines to making the distinction between functional and dysfunctional emotions, and I have found four criteria especially useful, both in my own life and with many patients over the years. Functional emotions are timely, suitably intense, and contextually appropriate, and they generally produce adaptable behaviors.

First, functional emotions do not go on forever. Suppose, for example, my wife dies, again. Clearly there is going to be pain associated with this loss, pain at some level for a lifetime. Nevertheless, society generally expects us to process the major part of the trauma in as little as five days. Many companies provide five days' bereavement leave for a death, some a little more. Many times I ask folks in my workshops how much time they would allow me for such a loss. Most would give me a couple of weeks. Some begin by insisting they would allow me as much time as I needed. Of course when I suggest twenty years with pay and benefits, we soon discover there are in practice somewhat more restrictive limits. These limits represent social expectations we all share. So, what if I worked for a very understanding boss and took three months off of work? Assume also I have been back at work for three months, so we have a total of six months elapsed. If every time I heard my wife's name, or someone mentioned my wife or my loss or I tried to use this example in a lecture, I got all choked up and started crying and had to leave the room, what would you think? Most people, when asked this in

EMOTIONS

workshops, say either "You haven't dealt with it," or "You have a problem." Generally most people would agree that, even though I will never be the same after such a loss, there is a general expectation that after a couple of weeks at most, I should be able to begin to function. At least, I should be able to get out of bed, go to work, and get through the day, in spite of the pain. Grief that persists at a level that renders me nonfunctional for months or years would be called "complicated grief." Grief that is this intense for such a long time is a sign that the feelings I am experiencing are dysfunctional. I do not mean to imply that grief itself is abnormal or always complicated, but grief that is overly prolonged might be an indication of a problem. Remember, we are just looking for clues to the functionality of our emotions. I have worked with patients who had failed to process grief thirty years after a loss. Clearly this is an indication that something has gone awry. This can give us a clue to possible solutions. For sure we cannot do anything about dysfunctional emotions if we do not recognize that they are dysfunctional.

A second clue is the intensity of the emotion. This is a matter of balance and context. If my wife dies (yet again) and I have no reaction, for instance, this is too little intensity. On the other hand, if I receive a paper cut at work and run screaming hysterically to the ER for help, that is probably too intense of a reaction for the situation. Either extreme is a signal that the emotions I am experiencing may be dysfunctional. Balance is also a factor in the third indicator, appropriateness.

If my wife dies and I attend the funeral laughing and joking with no trace of grief, this is not appropriate to the situation. Again, this is a sign that the emotions I am experiencing, or the lack of emotion in this case, may be dysfunctional. I repeat, this is not definitive, but it is a strong indicator that should be taken seriously.

Perhaps more serious is the fourth indicator, repetitive behaviors I cannot seem to change. Chemical addictions, serial relationships, risk avoidance, intensity addiction, chronic enabling of loved ones, compulsive sexual behaviors, and obsessive neatness are only a few of the many types of behaviors that can be destructive. Generally we initially engage in these behaviors without recognizing the patterns or our growing dependence on the behaviors. Ultimately these are some of the behaviors that bring most people to seek the aid of a therapist or treatment center. These are also behaviors that are dependent on beliefs, and a lot of automatic thinking. Remember, this is automatic thinking, which is based on beliefs that are lies. Nevertheless, they are beliefs that have been learned early and well and can be very difficult to identify and modify. In fact all dysfunctional emotions are based on these flawed beliefs. When we hold beliefs that produce dysfunctional emotions, we refer to these as trauma-based beliefs, which we will discuss in a little more detail later. For now it is enough to be able to distinguish between functional and dysfunctional emotions.

Many people approach cognitive therapy with the idea that dealing with emotions is not going to be necessary. Nothing can be further from the truth. Cognitive therapy is all about emotions. Unfortunately, some people even go so far as to try to eliminate all emotions. As emotions are normal human experiences, this does not usually produce good results. What is needed for mental toughness and a measure of contentment is the ability to accept, or even to embrace, all of our emotions, to experience them fully. Only when they are fully experienced can we begin to explore the functionality of each. We have to accept all of our emotions as part of our essential humanity before we can gain any kind of ability to manage them. Often, based on the lack of clear teaching in our family of origin, we do not even have a practical language with which to talk about our emotional experience, much less methods for benefiting from the experience. It is difficult to manage emotions when we cannot even talk about them.

In our practice we use a rather artificial but very useful emotional vocabulary. We do this for several reasons. First, it promotes consistency, among us as therapists and among and between our clients. Second, it helps avoid semantic debates, which, when it comes to happiness, do not help at all. After all, there are probably tens of thousands of words describing emotions in the English language alone. So, if we want to, for example, we could spend considerable time discussing the difference between regret and remorse. Let us do a little bit of that now. Consulting Merriam-Webster's online dictionary, we find that one meaning of regret is "to be very sorry for." The definition for remorse includes "gnawing distress arising from a sense of guilt for past wrongs." While there may be some value in noticing the shades of meaning attached to these words, it is also true that each of them concerns, in some way, feelings about my behavior. Thus to avoid a tedious discussion about the differences, we can agree that both involve my behavior and provide an umbrella term to refer to all emotions having to do with my behavior. In our case we have selected the word "guilt." There are still many words that can be used to describe feelings about my behavior. However, agreeing to classify the emotions in this way makes it possible, with very little additional effort, to begin talking about the experience, meaning, and origins of our emotions. In other words we can begin to understand them and ourselves better. Accordingly, we have constructed a Feelings Chart (Table 4)[17].

---

[17] This chart is adapted from the work of Pia Mellody.

FEELINGS CHART

DESCRIPTION	PHYSICAL LOCATION	BENEFITS
ANGER INDICATES: injustice *irritation* *frustration* *rage* *hate*	ALL OVER BODY FACE FLUSHED	assertiveness strength energy
FEAR INDICATES: danger *concern* *nervousness* *anxiety* *overwhelmed*	STOMACH UPPER CHEST SUFFOCATION	preservation wisdom protection
PAIN INDICATES: loss *ache* *hurt* *sadness* *hopelessness*	LOWER CHEST AND HEART HURTING	healing growth awareness
GUILT INDICATES: my behavior *responsible* *regretful* *remorseful* *depressed*	GUT GNAWING	values amends containment
SHAME INDICATES: my value *embarrassed* *humble* *humiliation* *toxic shame*	FACE, NECK OR UPPER CHEST WARM/HOT/RED	humility containment accountability
JOY INDICATES: abundance *contentment* *enthusiasm* *zest* *elation*	ALL OVER BODY LIGHTNESS STRENGTH/POWER	gratitude pride energy
PASSION INDICATES: purpose *commitment* *dedication* *infatuation* *obsession*	ALL OVER BODY CHEST	focus creativity arousal
LONELY INDICATES: disconnection *isolation* *detachment* *out of place* *different*	ALL OVER BODY HOLLOWNESS IN THE CHEST	awareness consciousness involvement
LOVE INDICATES: connection *caring* *affection* *tenderness* *warmth*	HEART SWELLING WARMTH	connection life spirituality

Table 4.

You will note there are three columns of information. The first column is a description of the emotion. It includes the umbrella name, what it indicates about mental activity, and some additional, optional names. "Anger" is the first listing. You can see that anger indicates injustice. In other words, when we experience anger, it indicates that, in our belief system, our reality, we perceive there has been an injustice. We believe that something is not being done as it should be. On a continuum it runs from a low level described as frustration all the way to rage and even hate. Generally the words we use to describe emotions also indicate something about their intensity and functionality. Thus you can see that frustration is a low level of anger. This does not mean that frustration is always functional, however. Even at a low level of intensity, emotions can be dysfunctional.

For example, I have a personal expectation that tools exist to make things easier. If I have a job to do and there is a tool for it, my expectation is that, with the tool in hand, the task will be quickly dealt with. Thus anytime the tool itself becomes an additional problem, I become instantly frustrated. The frustration is due to my expectation, which is probably a little more accurately stated as "Tools should always make thing easier." Now this is a minor issue, though it has resulted in rather vitriolic reactions around the house. It is, however, an example of expecting the world to be different than it is (see Fact of Life #6, page 37). My expectation, in the face of the reality that tools sometimes create more problems than they solve, is what creates my frustration. This is an example of a pretty low level of frustration, but it is dysfunctional because it gets in the way of my being very handy around the house. Because I have made myself aware of the expectation, I can consciously prepare myself every time I set about some household chore. I remind myself that I have this unrealistic expectation. I do not know where I acquired it, but that really does not matter. I can, in the moment, change my expectation by simply reminding myself that in the world the reality is: "Tools often are broken themselves or cause additional maintenance issues, and the task before me is going to be more difficult than I expect. It will require more trips to the hardware store and more time than I planned for." If I do this well, when something does go wrong with the tool, I can actually get a sense of satisfaction. "See, I told you that would happen." This is an example of a low level of anger. The emotion can, like all emotions, run all the way from irritation to frustration to rage and even to hate (not that I have ever actually hated any tool manufacturer.) Remember, this is a characteristic of all emotions; they occur on a scale from less extreme to very extreme.

The second column describes the location in our body where we might expect to find the physical sensation associated with that emotion. In this case anger is often felt as our face becoming flushed. Some people say it starts in their face, then moves up to cover the head. Other people might experience it all over the body. This is usually in more intense situations where the anger is preparing the body for flight or fight. These locations are not derived from empirical experimentation. They are based on personal observations and observations reported by friends and family. There is nothing absolute in the location, so many people may find the physical sensations associated with a given emotion to be different than what the chart shows. This is okay. The utility of this chart arises when we feel "something" but cannot put a name to it. In that case, if we take a minute to close our eyes and do a body scan, searching for any sensation of tension or pain or warmth, the sensations we discover can be used to help us find a label for the emotion and possibly give us a starting point to discover its cause in our belief system.

The final column is labeled "Benefits." Remember, all emotions, if processed functionally, have benefits. In the case of anger, we receive the benefit of strength and energy. Anger then is a preparation for action. If we believe there has been an injustice, and then the emotion of anger helps us take some action, do something to correct the injustice or overcome the obstacle. Just do an online search for "benefits of anger" and you will find several relevant discussions.

EMOTIONS

I am not going to go over the entire chart here, believing that it is pretty self-explanatory. It is, however, worth looking at each of the main categories to get a good idea of the vocabulary.

Fear, as shown on the chart, indicates that we believe there exists some sort of danger. This can be a physical danger or a threat to our livelihood or a dream we may have been working toward. It can also include a danger to someone we care about. Remember, however, that it is our perception of danger we are talking about. It is not necessary that the danger exists in absolute reality or in the present. The perception of danger is what matters. The fear that occurs is always real for us, because as soon as we conjure it up, it becomes part of our reality. We will be talking about fear in more detail when we discuss anxiety, the most common form of dysfunctional anger.

Pain is one of two emotions that most often cause people to become so conflicted they seek the help of friends, family, or mental health professionals. I consider pain to be the emotion we experience anytime we believe we have sustained a loss of some kind. The most obvious sorts of losses occur when someone dies. The death of a family member or close friend can be extremely painful. It is also true that the loss of a dream, a fortune, a pet, a job, or our youth is painful. Grief is discussed in detail in a later chapter. For now it is important to note that life is loss, and dealing with loss is something everyone has to do.

Guilt and shame are often confused, and they are related. Guilt indicates that I believe something about my behavior. That is, "I did something wrong." It is an indicator that I think I have strayed from my moral compass. Shame, on the other hand, indicates that I believe something about my value. That is, "I *am* something wrong." The differing impact of these two is remarkable. If I believe I have done something wrong, and I feel guilt, it is possible to take this in, acknowledge my wrongdoing, make amends or reparations if appropriate, learn from it, and move on. If, on the other hand, I believe I *am* something wrong, there is little I can do. If I believe I am something wrong, then what I am telling myself, and what was probably taught to me in childhood, is that I am different from all other people. In other words, where most people believe in Fact of Life #1 and can say with conviction, "All people are people and I am one of them," a person with a serious shame core believes "all people are people, except me." This is a completely devastating belief.

This underlying belief produces depression, anxiety, addictions, relationship difficulties, perfectionism, isolation, and a host of other problems. I am aware that some writers do not classify shame as an independent emotion. They classify guilt and shame as two levels of the same emotion. In addition, some believe shame has no benefit, that it is always toxic and, in effect, it is something other than an emotion. While all of this is arbitrary and classifications of this sort are mostly academic, including mine I believe, within the scheme proposed here, it is much more consistent to view shame as "…a normal human emotion."[18] And, as an emotion, the same characteristics apply as with all other emotions—specifically, the idea that shame can have benefits when processed functionally and that shame, like all emotions, exists on a continuum of intensity.

First, if we examine the different levels of intensity, we find that on the shallow end of the shame pool is embarrassment. We have all experienced this level of shame. When I reappear on the podium after a break and someone observes that I am trailing a piece of toilet paper from my shoe, I become embarrassed. This

---

[18] Bradshaw (2005), page xvii

level of shame reminds me that I am human and humans make mistakes. It actually connects me to other people. I can say to myself, "All people are people and I am one of them with toilet paper on my shoe." At this level shame does not last very long, nor does it become debilitating. In fact this level of shame can actually connect us to others with the belief that "all people are people and we are all doing the best we can."

If, on the other hand, I harbor a shame core (a set of core beliefs that set me apart from other human beings), the experience will be much different. If the filter through which I see the world and myself already includes the belief that I am flawed, this innocuous toilet paper incident will become proof of my inadequacy, and it will set off a huge and often paralyzing episode of toxic shame. This deep end of the shame pool is much more intense than mere embarrassment. It is also more deadly.

Toxic shame is shame which arises from a core belief, often learned as very small children, before we even have language, that *I am bad. I am not a "people" like everyone else. There are things that regular people know and understand that I do not. My reactions and fundamental value are different from regular people.* What many writers call "toxic shame" equates to dysfunctional shame. That is, it is shame which has no benefit and which is probably creating problems of its own. The important thing to note is that, at this level, shame is experienced throughout our whole self. It is a filter which drastically interprets all of the data coming in through our senses in a way that results in almost total disconnection. This is why, perhaps, we tend to think of toxic or dysfunctional shame as a whole other thing than embarrassment. However, in my experience, shame is an emotion. Like the other emotions, it exists on a continuum, and it has benefits. Remember, however, that the benefits of any emotion disappear when the emotion is dysfunctional. Dysfunctional anger, what we would call rage or hate, produces little if any benefit. Dysfunctional fear prevents us from living our life, and the same is true for dysfunctional or toxic shame. So what then could be the benefit of regular or functional shame?

I believe shame functions to help us be socially accountable. Whereas guilt helps us to be accountable to our own internal moral compass, shame helps us be accountable to other people, our family and to society. We are, after all, social creatures. Something in our fundamental makeup has to work to keep us in line with social expectations.

I once heard a colleague give an example. She was scheduled to lead a group for a new program that had just been developed. Not only was it her first time facilitating it; this was the pilot group for the whole curriculum. Nobody had ever tried it out before, so there was no way to know if it would work. She had invited a number of people she knew to be in this first group, including some colleagues and friends - people she would be facing in her life outside the group. She talked very descriptively about her insecurity and how it overwhelmed her sitting her car in the parking lot trying to get up the gumption to go in to the meeting room. Her self-talk sounded almost completely negative. She almost turned around to go home. Eventually she did go in. She said, "Shame made me go in there." This, I believe, is the benefit of shame. It makes us accountable to others. In this example she could not just leave because she knew she would have to face those people later. Shame made her get out of the car and go into the building and present what turned out to be a very successful program and which was the beginning of a very successful national program.

EMOTIONS

I do not believe human beings would have developed, or been given, such a powerful motivator for no reason. Shame is powerful because our social bonds are important to us, and without it the fabric of society would be in tatters. This is tacitly acknowledged in the phrase "Have you no shame," which was used to chastise, unfairly I am sure, my behavior as a child. The implication is that a person without shame is lacking something—something important to the community. Shame demands connection. Shame is powerful because it is important to us as individuals and as a species. This power is most evident in shame gone wrong. Shame which is dysfunctional in origin or implementation has nothing good to recommend it.

The same can be said about any dysfunctional emotion. When any emotion is dysfunctional, it loses, by definition, any benefit it might otherwise provide. Shame, by the way, is the other emotion, along with pain, that most often drives us to seek the help of others. Toxic shame is also a contributing factor to complicated grief or any kind of pain that is unresolved. In my experience, shame is always involved at some level, and toxic shame is one of the most debilitating experiences we can have. Dysfunctional shame is a rampant epidemic in our society that wastes trillions of dollars and millions of lives every year.

The argument as to whether shame is an emotion like others is, as I mentioned, rather arbitrary, especially considering that we cannot even define the word "emotion" clearly. I choose to believe shame is an emotion like any other. I experience it as an emotion. Furthermore, viewing it as an emotion makes it manageable, just like other emotions. While shame is probably a factor in the majority of unhappiness, emotional distress, and psychiatric disorders, it is not the only factor. It is also not the only emotion. The earmark of emotional stability and contentment is the ability to manage all of our emotions. Shame is not the only culprit, and it is not the only emotion that allows us to be human.

The next emotion on the feelings chart is joy. Joy has to do with our belief about having enough or more than enough. The level of joy we experience indicates something about our beliefs regarding abundance. Like all emotions, joy runs on a spectrum. In the shallow end we may simply recognize that we have enough—that, in this moment and this situation, I have what I need to get by. On the other end of the joy scale we find effervescent exhilaration. Joy is probably closely related to our concept of happiness. In the deep end we find zest and excitement about our life and what we believe we have. Interestingly, not too many people arrive into counseling complaining of too much joy, though we certainly are capable of recognizing a lack of joy in our life. As with all emotions, it takes a certain level of self-awareness to recognize when we have enough or can stand what we are dealing with.

Passion can be confused with sexual passion. In this case, however, we are talking about a set of emotions that indicate our belief system currently perceives that we have purpose. The purpose can be as short term as getting laid, but it can also be as large as we want to make it. We discuss the issue of purpose or meaning in much more detail in the section on depression in Chapter 7. For now it is enough to recognize that a sense of purpose is necessary for true contentment.

The emotion of loneliness indicates that we believe ourselves to be disconnected. This can be disconnection from other people or life in general, but it usually starts with disconnection from our self. If I do not know my self or cannot accept my self as I am, there is very little likelihood that I will be successful at maintaining connections with others. Remember, connection to others is a biological need we all have as human beings. If I believe I am disconnected from humanity, in part or in whole, my first indicator will often be a sense of loneliness. The opposite of disconnection is the belief that I have connection.

Love is an indicator that I believe I have connection, that I belong and am part of something. The most basic connection is to myself. This is why it has been said that you can only love someone else to the extent you can love yourself.[19] My ability to be connected starts with knowing and accepting myself. Once that is accomplished, my awareness and acceptance can then expand to other people, all people, all life, and eventually all there is.

As I pointed out, all constructs such as this feelings chart are rather arbitrary. This convention has, nevertheless, proven very helpful. It provides a means to put semantic squabbles aside and focus on the process, which is the point. In my experience, sticking to this simple emotional shorthand facilitates the development of an understanding of self.

I now must somewhat reluctantly enter into a discussion which has occupied theorists, clinicians, lovers, and poets for as long as humankind has existed. Which comes first, the emotion or the idea?

According to my definition of emotions and the content of the previous chapter, one might conclude that I believe ideas, or concepts, or beliefs come before emotions. This is true in theory. However remember the example of the rattlesnake? In order to be useful, my reaction to the sound of the snake's rattle has to be quick. I cannot take time to stand around thinking, *Hmm that sounds like it could be a snake. Or maybe it is actually a sprinkler system coming on. They can sound very similar. Wait; there is no sprinkler system out here in the desert...* By the time this chain of

---

[19] I am pretty sure someone famous said something like this, but I got bored trying to find a good citation online.

thinking is concluded, I have already been bitten and the snake has moved on. What is needed for survival in this situation is a quick, almost instantaneous response. Our bodies possess such capacity in the form of reactions.

The reaction to a sudden loud noise is one example. This is a built-in reaction. There are also conditioned reactions based on learning. Reactions are experienced before we can complete a conscious thought. They provide a means to respond very quickly to potentially dangerous situations. The body's alarm systems activated in these situations produce a sensation very much like fear. In fact these are the same systems activated by the emotion of fear resulting from the belief that I am in danger. The fact of the matter is that, in these situations and many others, I am first aware of my reaction and only later can deduce the thoughts or beliefs that might underlie it. Thus the reaction occurs so fast, and often with such intensity, that we don't even notice what mental process produced it. So, in these situations the emotion precedes the beliefs *in our experience*. Again, I am defining emotions as experiences which occur in response to a stimulus, not because of a stimulus. The stimulus itself has little or no impact of the type or intensity of emotion experienced.

It is possible to spend way too much time teasing out the processes involved here—lengthy discussions of perceptions, sensations, apprehension, blah, blah, blah. The bottom line is that the distinction does not matter. An adequate argument can be made for the primacy of either emotions or thoughts. In a real sense, both are true. What helps us ultimately is to be able to understand the process by which we produce and manage our experience of life. I have occasionally found detailed discussions of the physiology and structure of meaning, sensation, and emotions interesting, but I have rarely found them useful in my search for contentment.

CHAPTER 4

How We Don't Work: A Model of Dysfunctional Development

So far we have considered the belief system as if it consisted of discrete beliefs and thoughts, each standing on its own. In reality, things are a bit more complicated. In general our beliefs do not stand alone. They are connected to and supported by other beliefs and values. Thus it can become difficult to undo one erroneous belief when there may be two or three other beliefs supporting it. It becomes necessary to attack the entire structure, either as a whole or piecemeal. First let us examine the structure.

Suppose I believe I am ugly. This may or may not be accurate. Regardless of whether it matches the real-world data, this belief by itself is not particularly significant. However, when this belief is accompanied by a couple of other beliefs, things become more serious. For example, I might also believe that people only care about those they find attractive. Add to that the belief that I must get people to care about me or I will die, and you can begin to see the relationships and complexity. This is why we call it a belief *system* (BS).

In terms of the belief system, many authors would classify some of these beliefs as more or less significant. I think that one is not necessarily more significant than another; what is important is how they fit together. The patterns and the ways in which they support one another and create unhappiness and resistance to change is what matters. These subcomponents of the belief system, the smaller clusters of beliefs supporting one another, are referred to as *cognitive schema* (see Figure 7). Schemas have been the subject of psychological discourse for over a hundred years. In fact, at least one writer has developed an entire approach to therapy based on cognitive schema.[20]

Schemas can be defined as "...cognitive structures within the mind, the specific content of which are core beliefs."[21] Schemas are the stories we tell ourselves about the world and our place in the world. Problematic schema, those supporting dysfunctional emotions, can be thought of as trauma-based schema. They are the schemas resulting from gaps or errors in our belief system. They are composed of one or more cognitive distortions. We will refer to these as trauma-based core issues or simply core issues. Basically these are the beliefs that keep us from being aware of Fact of Life #1: "All people are people and I am one of them" (Fact #1, page 4). These core issues can be thought of as the ways in which we lose sight of the fact that we are just like other people. We start to believe that we are different, in a fundamental way, early in childhood and then we filter our experience of life and build these dysfunctional schemas to support the belief that we are different or flawed or broken or defective. They consist of interlocking sets of core beliefs and values along with associated intermediate beliefs and automatic thoughts. All of these work in concert to support and sustain one another. The result is that changing negative habits of thinking can be very difficult. In addition, some of the contents of the schema may actually conflict with one another (remember, they are not necessarily logical), and this can cause additional distress.

---

[20] Young and Klosko (2006)
[21] Beck (1964)

MODEL OF DYSFUNCTIONAL DEVELOPMENT

COMPETENCE FOCUSED VALUE SCHEMA

Core Belief	I am not competent
Intermediate Beliefs	Compliments mean that someone feels sorry for me / If I am very careful to always do things perfectly, I can get by.
Automatic Thoughts	He is being really nice, I must be completely useless / I made a mistake! I will never be able to get by

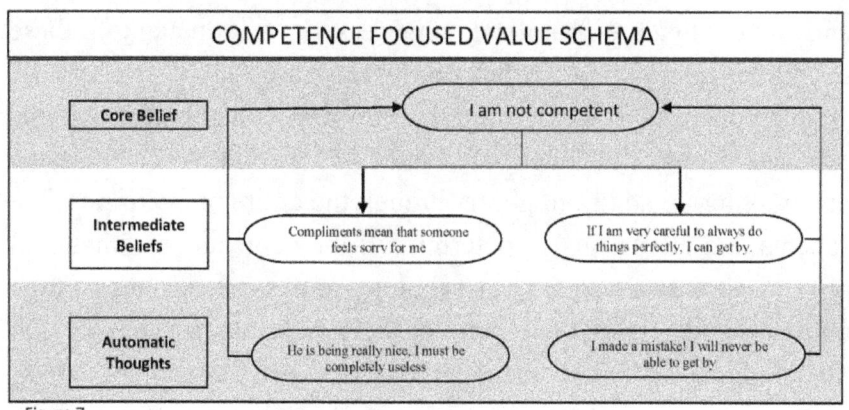

Figure 7.

Figure 7 is a representation of a cognitive schema. This schema is dysfunctional, representing a core issue of value. Notice how the core belief is supported and defended by the intermediate beliefs. This means that if my supervisor (or anyone really) tries to give me a compliment and thus disconfirms my core belief, the information will be transformed by the intermediate belief so that now it actually validates the core belief. Thus, when people start complimenting me, what I tell myself is something like "See, I knew I was incompetent. All these people feeling sorry for me prove it." In terms of behavior, this person would be quiet and unassuming, trying to stay under the radar. He would also tend to be a perfectionist and possibly phobic about maintaining order. It is likely that he would overreact to mistakes and possibly even experience panic attacks. Of course he would have trouble sleeping, spending many hours worrying about mistakes he had made and expecting the worst possible results. Again, it is important to remember that all of this does not necessarily mean this person would not be able to function. On the contrary, many people with active core issues function effectively. The real cost is the anxiety and pain they endure almost daily—pain and shame and anxiety that are completely unnecessary. As you can tell, these cognitive structures can become quite complex.

Complete analysis of the structure and content of even one schema, along the lines of Figure 7, would be a massive undertaking. In addition, going through the entire range of possible schema and attempting to determine if the contents are functional or not is strictly a task for a psychology professor with lots of time on her hands. It is also only entirely possible for the person involved, as this is necessarily a very personal activity. For those of us trying to sort out our own stuff, elaborate dissection of cognitive schema is beyond our need to know. Fortunately, such knowledge is also not necessary for a successful effort to take responsibility for our future and control of our contentment. We can take advantage of the fact that schemas, the stories of our lives, tend to organize in patterns, and these patterns are basically the same for everyone because, remember, we are all people (Fact #1 page 4). Even the patterns of our dysfunctional thinking are similar. The patterns typically revolve around some of the basic questions of life. Once we identify the pattern or core issue we are dealing with, simple tools are available to reprogram ourselves.

As described in the previous chapter, babies are precious, valuable, vulnerable, incompetent, and helpless. Since no one has a perfect childhood, we all learn the lessons of life in slightly different ways. This produces the infinite variations in beliefs and personalities that make people so interesting. The lessons of life we all must learn can be classified in various ways, and writers down through the decades have come up with all sorts of developmental systems.[22] For our purpose I believe the basic tasks

---

[22] The authors in this area are far too numerous to identify. The reader is encouraged to examine works by Maslow, Piaget, Erickson, Freud, Beck,

CORE ISSUES MODEL

DEVELOPMENTAL TASKS	CORE ISSUES	SYMPTOMS
Safety	Safe or unsafe in the world Basic needs secure or insecure World is predictable or unpredictable Helpless or powerful	Self Esteem Issues Boundary Issues Depression Anxiety
Value	Valuable vs. worthless Loveable vs. unlovable Good vs. Bad Worthy vs. Unworthy Competent vs. Incompetent Success vs. Failure	Toxic Shame Relationship Issues Addictions Personality disorders Psychiatric problems
Spirituality	Connected vs. disconnected Belonging vs. alone Aware vs. unaware	

Table 5.

we face can be subsumed under two cognitive schemas: safety and value. We are all faced with some basic decisions in each of these areas, and thus everyone creates cognitive schema around these issues. The issues, their related schema, and the symptoms associated with dysfunctional adjustment are depicted in Table 5.

Generally speaking, the precise content and architecture of these schemas are not of interest to anyone but the aforementioned underemployed psychologist. However, when the schemas are incomplete or inaccurate due to the interdiction of some kind of trauma, they become problematic, leading to dysfunctional emotions and behaviors. Schemas that incorporate trauma will be referred to as "core issues." It is important to consider what we mean by trauma in this context.

---

and Rogers, as well as more recent writings in the field of developmental psychology.

Depending on whom or what you are reading, trauma can have many definitions. Our interest here is psychological or emotional trauma. There may be various other types of trauma associated with the emotional component—physical trauma, financial trauma, et cetera—but it is the emotional/psychological aspects in which we are interested. Two soldiers can be injured by a roadside bomb blast, and both have substantially the same handicap as a result. Let's say they lose their legs. One soldier spends most of the rest of his life suffering from PTSD. The second soldier, after a period of adjustment and rehab, goes on to have a successful career and a family despite his handicap. Clearly neither the explosion nor the physical injuries were the determining factor in either situation. Something else was already different about these two soldiers as a result of their childhood, their previous experience. They entered the situation with different abilities to deal with what happened. It is the psychological trauma that can cripple our ability to cope with life. The level of psychological trauma experienced by the soldiers prior to their injuries was what determined how each man would cope. So our focus is on psychological trauma rather than the events occurring to or around us.

It is my belief that trauma is the root cause of most psychiatric diagnoses, especially mood disorders and addictions, as well as others.[23] One of the salient characteristics of psychological trauma is that the trauma is in the mind of the traumatized. Something that may be horrible to one person and result in years of emotional incapacitation may be no more than a blip in the life of another person. When something happens, the meaning we attach to it determines whether it leaves trauma or cognitive scars in the mind. People react differently to difficult situations, based on genetic or

---

[23] Ross (2000)

MODEL OF DYSFUNCTIONAL DEVELOPMENT

physiological predispositions, previous experience, what we observe about the reactions of others (especially parents), and even the state of the physical organism at the time of the incident. Most importantly of all, however, is the meaning the event has for us. By the way, the meaning we attach to an event can change later in life as we grow and develop a better understanding of life and the society in which we live.[24] The meanings we attach are generated by the beliefs contained in the cognitive schema we have developed. If our schema happens to fall in the category of core issues, these meanings will lead to dysfunctional behaviors and emotions.

Trauma can be intentional or accidental, regardless of its nature in absolute reality; it is our interpretation of the event that matters. Once, when I was in the military, stationed at Holloman Air Force Base near the White Sands of New Mexico, I found myself driving along late one night on a desolate road between Alamogordo and La Luz. With me was an acquaintance, a fellow airman. There were no other cars out that late, so we had the road to ourselves and I was probably driving way too fast. All of a sudden my friend shrieked like something in a horror movie. He threw his feet up on the dash and covered his face with his arms. In the midst of his panic, he suddenly jerked as if someone had slapped him. I spoke to him but got no response. Finally I stopped the car and he took five or ten minutes on the side of the road before he calmed down. My friend was clearly being traumatized right before my eyes. I was mystified. I had not the remotest idea of what the problem could be. The culprit, it turns out, was tumbleweed.

The lowly tumbleweed was ubiquitous in that area. If you have not seen them, they are large, generally round, dried husks of the

---

[24] Clancy (2011)

Russian thistle. They can measure three or four feet across, some larger. When I first arrived in the area, I would see them blowing across the road, and I would stop for fear of hitting them and damaging the car. Over time I learned that they are little more than air. I started to drive right through them. Even more time passed and I completely quit seeing them. Like TV commercials, which I also tune out, I no longer paid any attention to tumbleweeds and routinely drove right through them. My friend had recently been reassigned to the base and had never seen one before. His perception was *There is a large, pretty solid-looking object in the road that is as tall as this car, and Graham is not even slowing down. I am going to die!* I, on the other hand, never even saw it. Our perceptions were very different. Furthermore, my friend experienced a traumatic event while I did not. The difference was in our heads and our perceptions, not in the data available from the activating event.

Trauma, then, can be defined as the psychological damage resulting from activating events. Some events are recognizable as trauma by just about anyone; some are trauma only to an individual. Trauma can be nothing more than ordinary experience to which we attach extraordinary meaning. The exact nature of the events is not critical. What is critical is the perception of and meaning given to the event. So psychological trauma, for our purpose, is not the event but the damage resulting from the event.

When working with trauma victims, I often encounter clients who are struggling with whether events they recall actually happened the way they remember or happened at all. I tell these patients that it does not matter whether or not it actually happened, or happened exactly as they remember it; we still have to deal with the consequences. Damage in this sense is the cognitive distortions left behind in the mind. These are the scar tissue of the mind and sometimes the brain. There may be actual scar tissue in the brain in the form of diverted or disconnected neural pathways, or they may simply be ideas or habits of thinking, existing only in the mind. So long as these scars are not healed, the trauma will exert an undue influence on our emotions and behavior. In children, trauma occurs routinely. Adjusting to life outside the womb is traumatic. Given that childhood is a critical time in as much as we are all blank slates, the lessons learned here will affect us for life. Some writers define childhood trauma as anything less than nurturing.[25] That is, anything that has the effect of disturbing the optimum development of the person and results in distorted or nonfunctional schema, which we are calling core issues. So, while we tend to focus on the more striking or extreme examples of trauma, the fact is that trauma can occur in seemingly innocuous situations. It can also *not* occur in the most horrendous situations. Either way it is the emotional or psychological scars left behind that matter. It is not always clear where or when this scarring occurs. Nor does it ultimately matter.

Much attention is often paid to family-of-origin work in overcoming trauma. Many workshops and exercises focus on "inner child work" to discover and define the events that resulted in a compromised ability to cope with life situations—the actual incidents that left the cognitive scars on our mind. It is worth noting here that, while such work can facilitate recovery, it is not necessary or sufficient in and of itself. If I have trauma as we have defined it here, I have it now. The scars exist here, today; the irrational thoughts and beliefs are in play right now, in the present. I cannot change what happened to me in childhood. The benefit of such family-of-origin work is that by clarifying the origins of the

---

[25] Mellody (1989)

trauma, I can sometimes more quickly and more completely understand the structure of the existing psychological scars, the core issues, and therefore more quickly do the work that is required to change the way I respond to situations in the present. I have known many people who have gone to literally dozens of workshops and spent tens of thousands of dollars to pinpoint exactly where and how they were traumatized. Yet they still suffer from the depression or anxiety or addictions they seek to heal. We can use the past as a guide, but the restorative work must be done in the present. One cannot change what already is, only what might be.

We can, however, make changes in the present patterns of thinking that are producing suffering, with or without knowing how those patterns of thinking were learned. Family-of-origin work can be a very powerful beginning, but if it is all we do, nothing of significance will change. Family-of-origin work can help to define the problem. It, alone, does not solve the problem. Just knowing that my habit of constant anxiety originated in my chaotic childhood does not alter the fact that the beliefs still operate in me in the present. If I am feeling anxiety now, it is because I am thinking now in a way to produce that anxiety not because of something that happened in the past. If I am feeling depressed now, it is because of the core beliefs and automatic thoughts I am thinking right now. Looking only at the past in order to solve a problem in the present will not work.

On the positive side, it is completely possible to correct dysfunctional patterns of thought without ever knowing their origin. I don't have to know how I came to believe something in order to change the belief. I only have to become aware of what I believe. The beliefs, attitudes, expectations, and assumptions we hold in our belief system right now, today, make up our reality and determine our relative level of contentment. We can classify all of our beliefs as functional or dysfunctional.

With this in mind let's take a more detailed look at the two types of core issues.

Safety

Based on our experience of life in our early years, we all make an assessment of the relative safety of the world. Specifically, I determine the extent to which I am safe in the world. How much do I need to worry? How vigilant must I be in day-to-day life? What kind of precautions do I need to take? Am I powerful enough to ensure my safety or am I helpless? These assessments are founded on my experiences as a baby. If I suffer physical harm, especially in a chaotic or unpredictable manner, I may conclude that I am not safe. Having survived these experiences, I will probably also develop a number of ancillary beliefs to support that core belief. The core beliefs and the supporting beliefs comprise the safety schema I will use as an adult. If there are problems in the development of this schema, we will have core issues around safety. One reason this schema leads to many core issues is that it addresses a fundamental condition of our lives, the fact that no person is 100 percent safe, 100 percent of the time. Life is not only difficult, it is uncertain.

Regardless of our social status, wealth, and power, no one is totally safe in life. We all experience various degrees of security and safety. This is something everyone must come to grips with. We enter life with nothing and leave with nothing. What happens in between is, at best, interesting. Actual safety is an illusion. "Security is mostly a superstition. It does not exist in nature, nor do the children of men as a whole experience it. Avoiding danger is no safer in the long run than outright exposure. Life is either a daring adventure or nothing."[26]

We can never predict the next moment, other than to know that ultimately nothing ever stays the same. With ideal conditions in childhood, we develop a proficiency in realistic assessment of our surroundings and our situation. When the lessons learned in childhood go awry, we may learn to be unnecessarily cautious or reckless, unable to accurately gauge the actual risk. Perhaps we become obsessed with making sure that all bases are covered before making even the simplest decision. On the other hand, we may become careless and give little attention to the facts or details of a situation before plunging ahead. These styles of decision making and risk tolerance are the manifestations of our safety schema. The key, as in many things, is balance.

Obviously there is always some risk in life. If, however, we seek to eliminate all risk, we would have to go home and curl up in a closet and try very hard not to move. Even then, an asteroid would probably impact directly on the closet and our effort would have been wasted. Since there is nothing we can do to guarantee safety, we might conclude it's better to run around without a care for safety or consequences at all. Of course the odds are that such extreme carelessness will bring a quick end also. Somewhere there is a balance between recklessness and hypervigilance that allows us to go about our daily lives and function effectively. We have to be able to accept the risks we cannot avoid and manage those we can and be prepared to face whatever consequences life throws at us. Safety core issues result in unnecessary anxiety, difficulty with anger management, withdrawal, depression, and a host of other consequences. Sometimes the core issues are disguised by the

---

[26] Helen Keller (1957)

MODEL OF DYSFUNCTIONAL DEVELOPMENT

resulting behaviors. Often, anxiety will be displayed as anger, and the secondary emotion of anger belies the actual source of the problem.

Chuy was twenty years old when he came to my therapy group. He had been sent by the Department of Corrections following some sort of incident with guns in a mall parking lot. His initial behavior in the group was somewhat reserved. In some of the early sessions there were a couple of confrontations between Chuy and other group members that required considerable intervention to avoid violence. However, as he relaxed into the group process, Chuy showed himself to be a smart, funny, and sensitive young man. He appeared to quickly grasp the concepts being presented and often provided insightful and caring feedback to others in the group. About eight weeks into the program, Chuy's parole officer called to report that Chuy had been involved in another incident. This time Chuy had been threatening a couple in a fast-food restaurant. In the next group I inquired as to the reasons for the new charges. Chuy explained that the man had been "…dissin' me." In this particular situation it meant that the man had been staring at Chuy. It is worth noting that Chuy was a very large individual with an extreme, gangster style of clothing and associated tattoos. In addition, the man he pointed the gun at was an elderly gentleman sitting with his wife. Chuy went on to say, "You can't put up with that kind of shit. You got to show 'em or you're done" Someone in the group suggested that pulling a gun might have been a bit of an overreaction to the situation. Chuy sheepishly agreed but then went on to articulate the details of a safety core issue resulting from having been raised in a dangerous part of town, with little parental protection or guidance. Chuy believed that he was always one second from destruction and that the only protection he had was to show people that he was willing

	CHUY'S DYSFUNCTIONAL SCHEMA			
DEVELOPMENTAL ISSUES	Core Issues	Intermediate Beliefs Compensating Thoughts (Beliefs - Memories - Values – Automatic Thoughts)	Symptoms
Safety	I am not safe	If I make everyone afraid of me I will be safer. I can never show any weakness. I must respond immediately to every potential threat or sign of disrespect.	Aggressiveness Isolation Anxiety Boundary Issues Legal problems
Value	I am loveable, people like me.	I cannot trust people with my true self.	
Spirituality	I am apart I am different	This counseling stuff makes sense, but it won't work for guys like me.	

Table 6.

to respond with deadly force to the least provocation. Chuy used anger as a protective mechanism.

Over the following weeks in group, the details of Chuy's safety core issue were clarified. Chuy intellectually understood that his beliefs were causing problems. Still he would not give up carrying his gun or reacting with massive intimidation to every perceived threat or sign of disrespect. Halfway through the three-month program, there was another incident in which Chuy assaulted someone in the lobby of a movie theater. The other group members were continually befuddled by the contradiction before them. They observed Chuy to be a kind, gentle individual with genuine compassion for others. Yet, out in public, Chuy was in fact a trip-wired bomb, easily angered and clearly dangerous to others. Just before completing the group program, Chuy was arrested again. The last contact I had was a phone call after Chuy had been returned to prison. Chuy thanked me for all the help I had given him. He said that he would miss the group.

MODEL OF DYSFUNCTIONAL DEVELOPMENT

Chuy was bound into his safety core issue. In addition to the core beliefs about safety, Chuy's schema included supporting value beliefs. He believed, for example, that while the principles being taught and practiced in group could be useful and helpful for some people, they only applied to "…you white guys that go to school and stuff." This involves a value issue around being different, meaning that Chuy believed he was not the same as other people who did not live in and could not understand his world. Chuy believed he was different. (See Fact of Life #1, page 4.)

Along with the aggressive behavior in Chuy's case, his safety schema also produces chronic worry, generalized anxiety disorders, phobias, aggressiveness, legal problems, isolation, and serious control issues. As with all core issues, these runaway emotions are buttressed by numerous intermediate beliefs that seem to provide "evidence" to support the validity of the core belief. The quality of the evidence is very suspicious in most cases, but this does not weaken the core belief.

A man discovers the disposal is jammed. On investigation he discovers that there is some lettuce from a lunch salad in the unit. He frees the disposal but concludes that disposals cannot handle lettuce and, for the rest of his life, tries to prevent anyone from putting lettuce in the disposal. In this example the person's safety issues have led both to unnecessary worry and to attempts to control the behavior of others.

We have probably all heard of the fear of vaccinations as a cause of autism. Despite the total lack of scientific evidence and the fact that autism is seldom fatal, while going unvaccinated can kill, thousands of people risk their own and everyone else's health by refusing vaccination for themselves and their children.

There are people who will not drive on freeways or don't drive at all. There are people who are afraid of flying and will drive instead, even though driving is much more dangerous.[27] All of these are examples of anxiety or control issues generated by unresolved safety issues. As much as 10 percent of all Americans may suffer from one form of anxiety or another.[28] It is my experience that the majority of these are the result of unresolved safety issues.

Value

One of the most discussed topics in all of clinical psychology has to be self-esteem. The problem is that self-esteem does not actually exist. There is no thimble in the brain that contains more or less esteem fluid. There are no esteem molecules or neurons which make us feel better the more we have. Self-esteem is not in the brain at all; it is in the mind. Self-esteem is a thought process by which we rate ourselves against perceived expectations, assumptions, and standards that are as arbitrary as they are unrealistic. I like the way Sandy puts it in the weekly workshop at Consiliom: "Self-esteem is not our value. It's what we *think* about our value." The fact is, when born, we all arrive with exactly the same value as everyone else. That value is our humanity. What we are born with never changes. It cannot be increased or decreased. It is ours by right of birth. However, given any level of trauma during development, we seem to forget our birthright. Dysfunctional development can result in our perception that, somehow, my value is not the same as others. I can come to believe that I am less than or not as lovable as other people, or that my value depends on things outside myself. The patterns of this dysfunctional thinking are varied and can revolve around appearance, importance to

---

[27] Gardner (2008)
[28] The Harvard Medical School (2009)

others, how smart we are, competence in various skills and activities, our roles in life, financial success, the kind of car we drive, and many other factors—all dependent on the messages received in childhood. Regardless of the exact content of the belief, these are all lies and produce dysfunctional emotions.

Karen was an ungainly little girl. Slightly overweight and not very outgoing, she spent a great deal of time alone. Sometimes the house was loud, especially when her father came home "in a state." When this happened, if she could manage to slink out, Karen would hide under the front porch. There were occasions when this could go on for hours. Being an observant little person, Karen began to notice the comings and goings of the bugs and spiders, worms and mice. She first became fascinated with the pill bugs. Eventually the hours under the porch turned into an abiding interest in all kinds of insects. This resulted in several collections, first of the pill bugs, later of butterflies (or flutterbys). This interest in biology became a lifelong passion. If her mother spoke at all about the evening's events, and the resulting bruises, she would just refer to the need for men to sometimes "let off steam."

As she grew, Karen came to understand that her father's many hours "working late" were actually time spent with a significant string of girlfriends. On occasion she attempted to query her mother about this and how it seemed to be okay with her mom. These could not be considered to be conversations as Dorothy, Karen's mom, never actually developed conversational skills herself. Her response to Karen was some vague explanation about men having "needs." Also how there were things in life women just had to put up with in order to get by. "After all, you and me, we are not exactly lookers you know." As Karen grew older, she took in the way her father looked at other women and of course the things he would say about them. It became clear what was important to men, especially when he asked at dinner one night if Dorothy thought Karen was "...ever gonna get any decent tits." Karen's relationship with her father was distant, and the only connection he sometimes made was to comment on the fact that she made him proud with her excellent grades.

When high school came around, Karen succeeded in avoiding most social situations. Though there was interest in boys, there were few dates. One boy, Kevin, seemed really nice, but his demands for sex were insistent. Karen had no clue how to meet those "needs," so she shied away from that relationship. She focused instead on her studies and her bugs. In college she majored in biology, and she met Tom late in her sophomore year. The attention Tom paid was unprecedented in Karen's life. He seemed to actually be interested in her. They dated all the way through undergraduate school. It was the only time Karen's attention was diverted from her studies in the least. She actually got three B's during this time! Then Karen headed off to medical school while Tom went to study law. When Tom graduated from law school, they were married.

Karen's medical training took much longer than law school of course. Throughout her residency and advanced studies, Tom was unfailingly supportive. Right after she began a residency in pathology was the first time Tom hit Karen. It was an argument about when they wanted to have children. Karen wrote it off as Tom "just letting off steam." After all, it didn't hurt much, and the bruise went away quickly. Following completion of her training, Karen was very lucky to obtain a position in the pathology department of a teaching hospital. She got the position in part because a friend, a fellow student, was the daughter of a board member of the hospital. Rather quickly, as a result of some

MODEL OF DYSFUNCTIONAL DEVELOPMENT

unexpected turnover, Karen found herself appointed the department director. This was about the time she became pregnant.

The struggles of raising a child, practicing her career, and learning how to be an administrator were enormous. Karen was not sure how she managed except she knew she had no choice. It was not clear to Karen how she had ended up married to Tom. She had fully expected to live her life alone. After all, she was "no looker" as her mom had put it. She was certain that she could never be this lucky twice and so she did everything possible to make it work. This involved not only managing her career and taking care of her daughter, but arriving home early enough to have dinner ready and to "be a wife" to her husband. There was tremendous pressure, for she knew that the least mistake on her part and Tom might come to his senses, which could ruin the whole thing.

Fourteen months after their daughter was born, along came her brother. It seemed to Karen that the complication factor in her life had quadrupled, not just doubled. Still she strove to excel in every area. Shortly after their son was born, she found out about Tom's affair. This was totally devastating. All that she had done, the sacrifices and extra work had not been enough. As she stood staring at the incriminating email, she felt panic start to rise. This was clearly her fault, but she could not think of what she had done, or failed to do. Thus she did not know what to do about it. If she had let Tom down in some way, she could make it up, but not if she couldn't figure out what the negligence had been. In desperation she tried to ask Tom what she could do.

Tom interpreted her questions as blaming and flew into a rage. This was the second time he assaulted Karen, and it was much worse than the first. Recovering in the hospital, Karen could feel her anxiety beginning to overwhelm her. There was nobody she could talk to. She did not want her mother to know what a failure she had been to Tom. There were no real friends in her life. Obviously Tom was not going to be much help to her. Eventually Karen lost heart and attempted to kill herself as she lay in the hospital bed. Fortuitously a nurse tech happened by Karen's room at just the right time and intervened. A few days later, Karen was transferred to a psychiatric hospital.

Some of the admission paperwork at the psychiatric hospital described Karen as follows, "Patient is a very attractive 37-year-old pathologist from Ohio. On admission she was fully oriented and responsive. Patient appears to be outgoing and relational. Patient is an extremely successful director of the pathology department at a teaching hospital. The hospital director has contacted intake to let them know that patient is a very talented scientist and an outstanding leader and administrator. The director indicated her employer would pay all expenses and support the patient's recovery in every way possible. The intake department has also been contacted by several of the patient's employees indicating support for her. Two directors of other departments at the hospital have also contacted intake to offer their support. Patient presented with a charming sense of humor and excellent personal boundaries during the admission process."

Notice the difference in the way Karen sees herself and the way others see her? Karen has a serious value core issue. She believes that she is not lovable. She also believes she is not physically attractive and thus has little or no value to men. When her husband cheats on her or hurts her, she believes it is her fault and further proof that she has no real value. Her parents taught her that females are only valued for their appearance, and she is no looker. She even believes her professional accomplishments are due to luck and useful only to make up for all that she lacks. Generally, someone with this kind of core issue will remain with an abusive husband because it is "more than I deserve" and because they believe they cannot find anyone else. Karen is incapable of feeling anger toward her husband or anyone else. In her daily experience she probably feels very little. The fact that her employer and employees believe Karen to be extremely valuable is discounted because she sees her main function is to keep her husband happy. Work is her only means to make up for her lack of value and attractiveness. The esteem of others is important only insofar as it helps her take care of her children and her husband's "needs." It does not register in her mind that the respect and admiration expressed by her coworkers mean anything at all.

When Karen is interviewed by the counselor or psychiatrist on the hospital staff, and suggestions are made, she will discount the utility of trying any of those things believing that "those things only work for 'normal people,' not people like me." As with any core issue, the basic beliefs are supported by such ancillary beliefs, which makes it very difficult to change. In fact, judging by the frequency of suicides in this country, it is often impossible to change. Even when an early suicide does not occur and Karen is lucky enough for Tom to leave her, the pattern will continue.

As a single mother with no real value of her own, Karen begins to find her value in her role as a mother. Instead of self-esteem she develops "other esteem,"[29] devoting all of her attention to her children and receiving all of her esteem from their love and, later on, from their success. Her son becomes an attorney and is very successful. Her daughter, however, proves to be a problem. Susan never seems to quite be able to get by on her own. She struggles through school, barely making passing grades and failing completely in high school. Karen does everything possible to help

---

[29] Mellody (1989)

her daughter. In fact it becomes her life work as she continues to help her daughter out of every problem situation and to support her since Susan is unable to support herself. It is, eventually, the lone source of satisfaction to Karen that she has always been there for her daughter and has never let her down. Karen comes to believe that her only true value lies in providing for her daughter. Otherwise Karen reaches late middle age with little or no true joy in her life. Her lack of awareness of her immutable value as a human being taints Karen's entire existence. She uses her intelligence and strong work ethic to stay always focused on the task at hand, whether it is work or taking care of her daughter. Karen never looks up to notice the larger world or observe her true place in it. This precludes the possibility of any intimate relationships or appreciation of the tapestry of life. It is highly likely that Karen will wind up her days, despite any professional success and other positive accomplishments, living one of those lives of quiet desperation, always trying to make up for what she believes she lacks.

Value core issues can emerge for many reasons. It can be a straightforward belief that "I don't matter" or "I am not lovable," or it can arise because we are not good enough in some specific

KAREN'S DYSFUNCTIONAL SCHEMA

DEVELOPMENTAL ISSUES	CORE ISSUES	INTERMEDIATE BELIEFS COMPENSATING THOUGHTS	SYMPTOMS
Safety	I am safe	I have to try harder to keep men, or anyone, interested in me. I have to allow men to "let off steam" Men have 'needs' I should take care of.	Self-Esteem Issues
Value	Women must look good I am unattractive I am not loveable No man will want me I am not enough	I must take care of Tom's needs or he will leave me I can make up for being ugly if I work hard because I am smart It is my fault Tom had an affair. If I make sure I am a good mother, at least my kids will sort of love me. I must do everything possible for my kids If my kids suffer it proves I have failed	Boundary Issues Anxiety Relational Issues Control Issues Spiritual Issues
Spirituality	I am different I am apart	I cannot be understood	Over controlling Enmeshed

Table 7.

MODEL OF DYSFUNCTIONAL DEVELOPMENT

way. Perhaps, like Karen, I believe I am ugly. Or, I might believe I am not smart. In fact we can have value issues focused on just about anything. Appearance-focused value issues are common among women in western cultures. Success-focused core value issues are common among men. Some of the issues are supported publicly in the media while others go without much attention at all. Competence-focused value issues, for example, are not often discussed overtly. A competence-focused issue is not actual cognitive impairment, though there may be some present. The competence-focused value core issue is a belief that a person cannot perform as well as others, or at a basically acceptable level. It leaves a person isolated. Often it is part of what we think of as low self-esteem. In extreme cases, competence core issues result in a person's mistrust of their own perceptions. That is, if I believe myself to be completely incompetent, then how can I trust what I think I see and hear? In my own case, as a child I enjoyed an idyllic life. My parents were caring, intelligent, entertaining people who clearly loved me. I enjoyed a nearly complete set of grandparents and an extended support system of aunts, uncles, and cousins. I was young and life was good. Then I started school.

The sudden entry into the larger social arena of first grade was more than just stressful for me. I learned, seemingly within days, that out here in the world I was not the same as others. Other kids appeared to take to the academic regime with only mild stress. I could not fathom what was going on. Things came at me so quickly, I could not figure out one thing before a dozen other tasks were presented. There did not appear to be anyone else who was struggling as much as I was—nobody I could talk with. No matter how I looked at it, the inevitable conclusion was "Out here in the world, I am not good enough." This situation was exacerbated by my belief that I could not tell my mother.

In the first place, I probably did not have the vocabulary to describe what was happening or how I was experiencing it. I do not remember any specific conversations, but I do remember that it seemed as though everything, including my parents, appeared to be suddenly operating in slow motion, not quite reachable. I had the experience of noticing that my parents were not like me either. They were actually like the other kids at school and seemed to always know what was going on. This was an observation I had never made before. The result is that I perceived myself as different and utterly alone in the world. This led to difficulties in school, behavior problems throughout adolescence, and difficulty adjusting well into my late twenties. The problems, as I discovered much later, were due to undiagnosed attention deficit disorder (ADD).

I actually was a little different. I understood that I was loved and that people found me attractive, interesting, and fun to be with. I also never really thought I was not safe. After all, being brought up in middle-class America in the 1950s was about as safe as anytime, anywhere. Nevertheless, I believed as a result of the evidence I gathered that I was profoundly different and thus alone. Remember, anytime anyone believes themselves to be fundamentally different, it is a lie. Because ADD was not well recognized in those days, I had no way to put things in perspective. In order to cope with this situation, I developed a number of strategies.

I spent a great deal of time alone to avoid complicated social circumstances. I learned to lie low when entering new situations. Since it took me longer to figure things out, I made sure I did not inject myself into activities without lengthy study. I came to believe that I had to maintain control at all times, at least of my self. If I actually blurted out my perceptions, I believed the odds

MODEL OF DYSFUNCTIONAL DEVELOPMENT

were that I would only open myself up for ridicule. This eventually translated into a total inability to be spontaneous. To display surprise was, for me, tantamount to admitting that I did not know what was going on, and I believed I could not let other people see how different I actually was. I also believed that I was short tempered.

The major deficit I have to put up with is restlessness and an inability to pay attention to more than one thing at a time. I cannot multitask. For years I thought I was just mean and impatient with others. Once I figured out what was going on, I realized that, while other people could listen to TV and read at the same time, I couldn't. As soon as I began to make some changes in my situation (turn off the TV or put down the book) and told others about my situation, life became much more manageable. I gradually came to the realization that yes, I am a slow learner. It does not mean I am not smart, or that I have less value than other people. It is just a condition I have to put up with, like being left-handed.

In fact, it turns out I am very smart. I just spent almost forty years believing that I was not smart and thus not very capable. In many situations I avoided trying because I believed it would only lead to failure. I would give up too quickly on learning (took me ten years to finally get around to finishing college) because I just assumed that since I didn't get it as fast as most other people, I was just too dumb and would never get it. This schema was a devastating principle of my life for decades. It was a lie—a lie that I never questioned until a friend pointed out my probable ADD and my flawed thinking.

I still have some knee-jerk responses to certain situations that fall back on this flawed schema. I am not sure we can ever totally remove all of the cognitive scars from very early trauma. Generally, however, I have trained myself to believe differently.

As a result of modifying the schema, I have much more joy, hopefulness, and success in my life. There are, sadly, many people who remain segregated and unfulfilled due to a flawed schema developed in response to particular childhood events. Competence, appearance, success, and intelligence are only a few of the criteria we can use to hold our contentment hostage.

Spirituality

As mentioned above, the core issues or schemas we have described are intertwined. This is especially true with spirituality. This is the domain concerned with whether and to what extent we are connected to and aware of our personal existence and its relationship with others and with the universe. I may believe that I am relatively safe—that I am lovable and important to others. This is enough to provide a basic level of contentment in my life. However, it is possible to move beyond contentment and attain a measure of joy. To accomplish this requires that we grapple with profound issues of meaning and purpose. While there are many approaches to this task, I believe in the end it comes down to one. We all must address the question of belonging and connection.

Where am I? How do I fit in? To what and to whom am I related and what is the nature and pattern of that relationship? These are profound questions, and unhappily, there are no answers. It is not a matter of answers but of discernment. The goal is the transcendent experience of perceiving what is, without filters or judgment.[30] It is recognizing that "the universe and I came into being together, and I and everything therein are One."[31] The experience is, once accomplished, unspeakable. It cannot be

---

[30] Pema Chodron (2002) page 50-51
[31] Tzu, Tzu and Tzu (2007)

adequately described. It cannot be confirmed. There is no level of intimacy between two people that will permit communication or sharing of the experience, and yet it carries with it an overpowering feeling of connection. It brings an indescribable joy and incurable sense of peace. It is also fleeting. It is not accomplished once and for all but experienced in a moment, then gone. While it does not last, practice makes it possible to achieve this state repeatedly. This skill is what I mean by spirituality. It is the ability to appreciate a larger perception of existence and to have some awareness of our place in it.

Sadly, the idea of spirituality has become snarled up with notions of God, religion, cultural values, and many other interesting but unrelated questions. So much so that the whole notion was almost not included in this model at all. I was reluctant to use the word "spirituality" to name the schema because I did not want it confused with other debates. In the end it seemed more honest to use this word. It also seemed impossible to exclude it because in many ways it is the point. The whole reason we do the other work is so we can have a chance at this reward.

I believe genuine spirituality can only be addressed when we are congruent in our practice of self. It is only when we have resolved conflicts and eliminated, or at least become aware of, irrational beliefs and thoughts that we can ever focus on the larger picture. It is a matter of congruence as described by Gandhi in Chapter 1. It is when our thoughts, feelings, and actions are in alignment that we can focus on meaning, purpose, and belonging.

When we are congruent within ourselves, we are no longer as distracted by the tangled tensions and emotional discord generated by conflicted beliefs about our safety and value. This allows us to notice and appreciate the magical complexity and subtle simplicity of everything around us. Only when largely free of internal strife are we capable of apprehending the fabric of existence and recognizing something of our place in it. It is a matter of context. Generally we are focused on the details of what is around us and fail to see the larger context. Spirituality is about expanding our awareness to take in the fact that we are part of a species, of a process called life, of a world and ultimately of the universe. Observing the larger picture allows us a measure of awe and joy, for whatever suffering the immediate moments contain, the grand picture is forever beautiful. The slightest glimmer of this larger reality is the transcendent incident. One who has the fortune to accomplish this even once in life is blessed indeed. Those who practice and develop the skill to be able to do this at will find they live in a different place altogether. I am not sure if a person can live in this place all of the time, but it is certainly worth trying for, and it is something that every one of us can accomplish some of the time.

Of everything in the universe, however, the primary connection we can make is to other people. We learn how to relate to other people during childhood, and what we learn can affect our ability to connect to self and others as adults.

The patterns of relations that we observe in our parents, and experience with our parents, teach us basic concepts about how we fit into the world and how to relate to the world. We will look at some of these patterns in more detail in Chapter 5. For now it is important to recognize the determinant nature of these early attachment experiences. Many people function effectively in life, do not have any issues with safety or value, but still have difficulty with intimacy. These folks often feel as though "something is missing" in their life. The something they are missing is connection. At the most basic level, ignoring, just for now, the rest

MODEL OF DYSFUNCTIONAL DEVELOPMENT

of the universe, we all need to be able to see ourselves as connected to and part of the human race.

We are human. We belong with people. As social creatures we derive our sense of belonging from being connected to others and knowing that we are connected. Overcoming all the barriers to compassion and understanding is only possible when a measure of spirituality has been attained. A patient in a psychiatric hospital once asked me, "What does it mean when we say we have a connection?" Eventually, after a number of discussions, we came to realize that we are connected to another when we see, in the other person, our own humanity. When this happens, we are connected. Once I look at the other person and see our common humanity, I cannot hate or condemn the other person, no matter what has transpired between us. More importantly, at the instant of connection I realize my "self" again. I literally see myself in the other person. We are social creatures and we need this connection in order to overcome the tribulations of life and to share and enjoy the good experiences. When we make this connection, especially in order to help someone else, we improve our own chances.

"None of us can ever save ourselves; we are the instruments of one another's salvation, and only by the hope that we give to others do we lift ourselves out of the darkness and into the light."[32]

---

1. By and large, all people are people.
2. Happiness is not something that happens to us. It is something we do.
3. We all have everything we need to be happy, all the time.

---

[32] Koontz (2001), page 450

FACTS OF LIFE

4. Everyone's reality is different and everyone's reality is valid.
5. My feelings always come from my thoughts.
6. Things always happen the way they happen.
7. The belief system consists of ideas, not facts.
8. Ideas can be changed.

CHAPTER 5

Practical Communications and Connection Skills

Having a connection to another person requires that we communicate on some level. However, if you think about it very much, you might be tempted to conclude that accurate communication between people is impossible. Look at our situation. Let's suppose I want to tell my wife something about what is going on for me inside—a personal experience, such as how I feel about our dog that just died. I am isolated in my own skin, with my very own unique reality. I have only the limited data provided by my five senses and we already know that is different from my wife's, who can hear things I cannot.

My beliefs, memories, values, and automatic thinking around the loss of our dog are probably not that clear in my own mind. In addition I am separated by a gulf in which multiple activating events, such as the TV, barking dogs, and sirens going by outside,

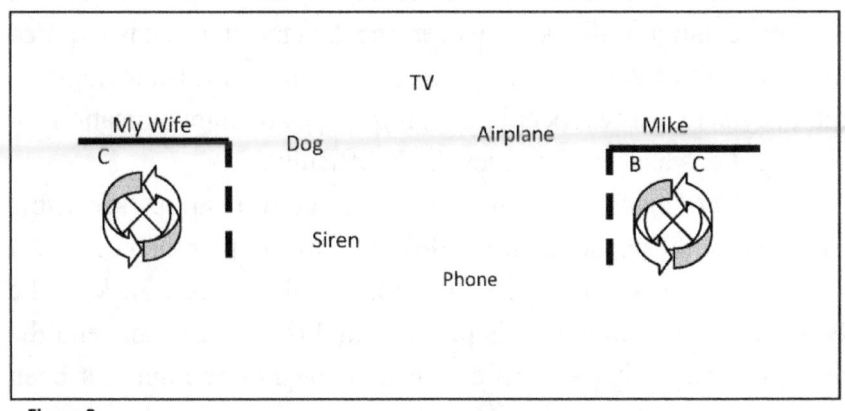

Figure 8

are occurring constantly. (See Figure 8) Here I have separated out the **A,** or activating event, to show that it is part of the world, separate from the **B** and **C,** which are me. The odds that I can accurately transfer any information between myself and my wife are not good. Now let's add that to the fact that she is in exactly the same situation. While I am involved with the whirling squirrel cage of my own reality, and limited by the capacity of my five senses, my wife is similarly preoccupied. Remember, everybody's reality is different and valid (Fact of Life #4, page 22). Plus, every second, additional activating events arise. One of the activating events of mine is actually my wife. Just as I am one of the activating events with which she has to contend.

The chances that I am going to be able to get any kind of message out about my own reality—across the cluttered landscape of all that is going on in the world, past her sensory limits, and correctly interpreted by her reality—appear improbable at best. Yet, it happens. It does not happen easily, or efficiently, but it does happen. The evidence is clear.

If we, as a species, could not communicate we would be unable to cooperate at a level that allows us to construct amazing buildings, tear up the land at a prodigious rate, and organize into groups, companies, or governments. The accomplishment that is civilization requires communications. However, the data transfer that is required to build a road is not the same as that required for achieving true intimacy between two people. Different types of communications or conversations have different levels of difficulty.

There are many types and reasons for conversations (see Table 8). Some of these, though often difficult, are simpler than others. If I am trying to communicate directions to the nearest Jack in the Box, for example, the task is pretty straightforward. I can send the data and then ask for verification that the information has been

SOME TYPES OF CONVERSATIONS	
Making Decisions	Brainstorming
Education	Planning
Sales	Debate
Entertainment	Problem solving
Connecting/Intimacy	Negotiation

Table 8.

received as I intended. The language we have developed, the words, works pretty well for this kind of information transfer. Such communication tasks are concerned mainly with the transfer of data. When I am attempting to communicate something about myself, however, something personal and intimate about what I am experiencing inside, in my reality, words alone don't work as well. The concepts are not as clear.

We have all been in situations in which "there are not words to describe..." how we feel. We are often trying to communicate not only a process we are involved in, but also the *experience of that process*. We have described in previous chapters the cognitive process—the data being acquired by the senses, filtered, analyzed, conclusions reached, and emotions produced. This process might be understood by another, with sufficient time to describe it. The person's *experience* of that process, on the other hand, is much more difficult to express because the experience has no words.

This leads us to the realm of nonverbal communications. Some research has reported that nonverbal communications are four times as important as verbal.[33] This means the words, in many cases, really don't matter very much. Generally, nonverbal communication refers to how I say things rather than what I say. In

---

[33] Argyle, Salter, Nicholson, Williams & Burgess (1970)

any case the task of transmitting information about my internal experience of things across the space between us, through the others person's filter and into the experience of another person, is difficult to say the least. To expect that I can do this with 100 percent accuracy is ludicrous. Undoubtedly the other person's experience and response to me are going to have as much to do with their own internal processes, their reality, as with the information I have attempted to transmit. We will come back to the importance of nonverbal communications in a bit.

Disregarding the interfering activating events in the world, we find that the most important activating event is other people. Because our value is in people over other things, and because the topic of conversation is probably more important to me, I will attend to the behavior of the other person rather than barking dogs and airplanes. Thus we have the simplified situation pictured in Figure 9. The most important characteristic of this is that the two people have become the primary activating event for each other.

Suppose a father and his daughter are attempting to have a conversation about the daughter's breakup with a boyfriend. The daughter, we will call Jill, and her father will be Wayne. Let us suppose that Jill has core issues of competence and value. Some of

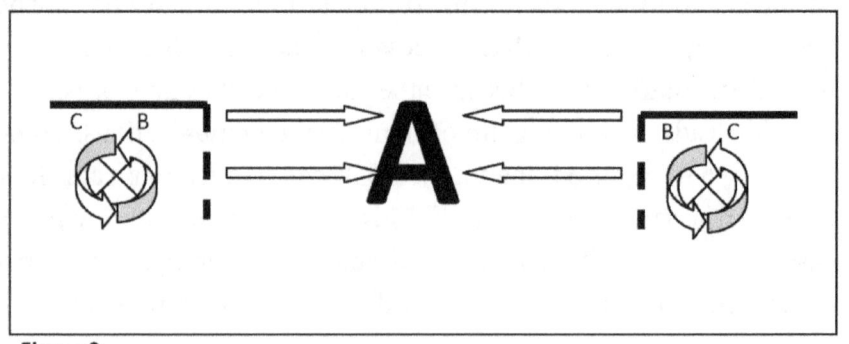

Figure 9.

the beliefs Jill has include the belief that she needs her father's approval. Of course she believes that she is generally not valuable or lovable and needs everyone's approval to some extent, but it is vital that her father approves of her. As an adolescent, believing that there is no way to get her father's approval, Jill has acted out her hopelessness through backtalk and other self-defeating behaviors. Now she is an adult but still believes that her father's approval is absolutely essential to her well-being. Presently, she also believes that her father never liked her boyfriend and that the breakup will prove to him that he was right—that Jill is somehow at fault and has failed once more.

Wayne also has issues around competence. Though he has been successful in his career, he harbors fears based on believing that he really is incompetent and most of his success has been due to luck. In fact, anytime he hears a compliment from a colleague or client, he experiences shame because he believes the only reason someone would say nice things about him is out of pity. Thus his schema is pretty well defended against positive input. Secondly, Wayne's social and relational development has been slow to nonexistent. He never learned to be relational in his family when growing up. This could be because of absent parents, parents who themselves lacked relational skills, or a host of other reasons. Wayne has been puzzled that his wife ever married him and continues to stay with him. He believes the only reason she stays is because of the income he provides. As with a lot of men he has difficulty expressing emotions, especially love. Wayne's children have been a mystery to him. He loves his family dearly but is so uncomfortable with the emotions, he tends to isolate, stay at work a lot, and avoid intimate conversations. Now, as he sits with his daughter, Wayne sees she is in distress and he immediately assumes that, due to his incompetence, he will let her down again.

He also believes the reason she is crying is because she is afraid of his reaction. He observes her eyes start to tear as she says, "He is leaving me." Seeing her tears and knowing she is in pain is almost more than Wayne can stand. He wants to figure out the right thing to say and he pauses, frowning in concentration, trying not to screw this up because she needs him so much.

Jill, on making her announcement, watches her dad closely. She notices that he frowns and that he says nothing for several seconds. Her fears are confirmed. She concludes that her father is angry and disappointed with her. Her need for Wayne's approval is so severe that she takes the least little micro expression and interprets it according to her reality, her worst expectations. She feels a huge wave of pain and shame and her tears start to fall.

The important thing to notice is that the causes of each person's behavior, more often than not, are in the stories they tell themselves, not in the behavior of the other person. The causes of the feelings and behaviors are in the beliefs they hold and the core issues that are activated. The reactions I have to some other person's behavior is as much about me and the reality I create for myself as it is about the other person's behavior.

It is <u>his fear</u> of failing her that causes Wayne to frown and pause. This is because he has a competence-focused value core issue, which is activated. Yet, she believes it is her behavior that causes him to pause and frown.

It is <u>her believing</u> that she <u>needs</u> his approval that makes his reaction so important, and painful, to her. This is because she also has a value core issue that has become activated.

It is <u>her thinking</u> his frown is about her, rather than his own internal paralysis, that results in her shame. This could be due to a spirituality core issue in addition to the value core issue.

It is him seeing the expectation on her face and <u>believing he is not capable</u> of saying the right thing that causes his frown and his hesitation. Again this is his competence core issue.

It is <u>her interpretation</u> of his silence as disapproval that results in her tears. Her activated value core issue is placing particular meaning on his behavior, and that results in shame and pain.

Whenever we have active core issues—that is, core issues that are in the foreground and dominating our perceptions—we are going to be out of touch. It will be almost impossible to relate to certain other people on an intimate basis. Remember, having an active core issue means there is significant content in our belief system that alters our perceptions of the other person (see Figure 2d). It is like a veil of preconception has been dropped between us and the other person. In the situation above, Jill literally cannot see Wayne. Instead she sees her father, who actually exists only in her mind. Wayne, the person in front of her, might as well be invisible. Especially the parts of him that are struggling with his fears of failure. Her preconceptions result in her interpretation of his behaviors rather than her actual observation of his behaviors. Often the more we know of someone, the more important their role in our life, the more difficult it is to see them clearly as people. Thus when a woman "talks down" to her husband, out of fear, he may not notice her defensiveness because his core issue is active. With the core issue filtering his experience, he perceives only that she is treating him as though he is "just a little boy." The verbal interchange that results in this situation is one of disconnection, and emotional intimacy becomes impossibility.

This kind of conversation happens constantly. In such conversations, because of activated core issues, each person is living in reaction to the other person. I am making up, in my head, that the behavior of the other person determines something about

#9 Everyone's Behavior Is Mostly About Them, Not Me.

my safety, value, competence, or purpose. In fact the behavior of the other person is mostly about that person's beliefs and values and thoughts. Jill believes her father's behavior determines her worth and value. Therefore it does, and Jill is living in reaction rather than action. Her father believes Jill's crying is proof that he is a failure as a father. Thus it becomes so and Wayne has further confirmation of his incompetence and lack of connection. Remember, we are talking primarily about our internal, emotional, reaction, not necessarily our resulting responsive behavior.

If someone says something negative about me, it does not determine anything about my safety, value, competence, or membership in the human race. If I feel pain, it is because I care. My pain is about my decision to care, not about what the other person has said to me. If I did not care, they could not hurt me. Thus, if I do care and I do feel pain, and I do react out of my pain, my reaction is about my self and my decision to care. In other words, everyone's behavior is mostly about them, not about me. Everyone's behavior is a product of their own beliefs and their unique reality. This is fact number 9. It is what I care about, or believe, that determines how I react to the world, not simply what is going on in the world. The world and whatever is happening out there provides data that I react to. It does not determine my reaction. In our culture this is not widely recognized.

Phrases such as "...you made me mad" and "that hurts my feelings" are rampant and are generally accepted at face value. If in reality, someone else is in charge of my feelings, two things follow. First, I am a complete and total victim with no ability to

PRACTICAL COMMUNICATIONS AND CONNECTION SKILLS

determine my future. Second, my happiness is now in the control of someone other than myself. I have lost the ability to do anything about my own peace and contentment. The situation gets even worse when there are more people involved. What if the conversation between Jill and her father occurred at the dinner table—with Jill's' mom, June, her brother, John, and John's friend Steve all present. Now there are five different belief systems, each taking data from the other four people, interpreting it and possibly having some feelings about it. The complexity of this conversation is colossal. In fact, one person cannot keep up with all that is going on. Jill may overhear comments made by Steve to June. This may affect Jill's response to the conversation she is carrying on with her mother. Her mother may interpret Jill's resulting behavior as a response to her. In these situations, it is even more important to keep in mind that everyone's behavior is a product of their own belief system, and that everyone's reality is different and everyone's reality is valid.

Many times in personal conversations we restrict ourselves by anticipating the impact our comments might have on the other person. "I can't say that; it will make him angry." "I can't tell her that; it will hurt her feelings." "What if I tell him and it makes him commit suicide?" It is important to stop and ask yourself if such a thing is possible. In fact, it is not. Whether he becomes angry in response to something I say is up to him and his belief system. Everyone's behavior is mostly a product of his or her own belief system. If I act as if I determine his emotions by my behavior, I am being both disrespectful and controlling. If I don't say what I think or feel, and, especially if I fail to ask for my wants and needs, because of the way I believe the other person *may* respond, I am not being true to myself. I am also preventing the other person from seeing my true self. I am being held hostage by the other person's possible behavior—behavior that doesn't even exist yet because it is only a possibility for the future.

In addition, I am not allowing the other person to choose their behavior. I have heard probably hundreds of family members use this kind of thinking as an excuse for tiptoeing around huge secrets that have dominated the family system for decades. If I believe the only reason someone loves me is because of the way I behave toward him or her, what good is that kind of love? It is like the happiness that abandons us at the first sign of pain. Most of us want a partner who will stay with us no matter what and certainly no matter what we say. Relationships built on this kind of circumscribed communication are seldom fully satisfying to either partner, so the resentment builds.

We can see from the foregoing that communication between people is fraught with obstacles and is going to be difficult in any circumstances. Yet, as stated at the beginning of this chapter, it does happen. In fact it sometimes happens in a very nearly magical way that brings two people together, almost as one. The question now is what we can do to increase the chances that our communications will be as effective as possible. There are some steps to take.

The first step is to look at, keep in mind, and believe in the facts of life we have outlined. If in fact I believe that all people are the same in their basic humanity, I will come to accept everyone, including myself. If I am sure that happiness comes from within, I will not fall into the quicksand of trying to manage the world or allowing the world to manage my emotions. When I know that everyone has everything they need to be happy, I will focus my search inward and begin to be both honest and curious about my very own self. I will allow others to find their path. When it is clear that everyone has a different yet valid picture of reality, I can start to become authentically curious about others. Understanding that things happen exactly the way they are supposed to happen, I can let go of the endless struggle to manage the world. As I begin to study my self, and learn that I am composed of countless beliefs, thoughts, fantasies, schema, urges, wants, and needs, all mutable and manageable, I can reach a tranquil, self-possessed state in which, no matter how unsafe the world and unpredictable the behavior of others, I remain content. None of the tools and techniques in this book will be effective without understanding and believing these basic facts of life. Techniques alone, no matter how cleverly described, cannot generate happiness in the face of irrational beliefs about my self and the world.

Living with the basic facts of life in mind allows us to interact with the world without taking things personally. Knowing the difference between what I can and cannot control means that ultimately I enjoy more control over myself. I can live in action and congruency rather than reaction and discord. It is only when I think other people's behavior defines me that I react. Believing my behavior is mine and everyone else's behavior is theirs, I can avoid the need to convince, manipulate, or control others in order to feel okay within my being. When everything that happens outside is personal, I have no self. When I let everyone, including me, have responsibility for their own self, we are all better off.

When I have put forth my best effort, I can be satisfied with that truth and not be overly concerned with the outcome of my actions. It is enough to know I did my best. If the vagaries of the world or the behavior of others thwarts my objective, I will be able to accept it with equanimity, remaining at ease with my self. If it sounds like this is a sort of disconnection from the world, it is not. It is our understanding the difference between the past, present and future and knowing our place in existence. This is not disconnection, but direct connection with the way things are. It is the realization that "...it is in your power to be happy while you are suffering."[34] It is knowing the difference between facts and beliefs, truth and lies.

Second, if you truly embrace the ten facts presented in this book, you will not only avoid taking things personally or becoming overly attached to outcomes; you will become curious about the other person. Curiosity fosters listening, and listening is the key to the kind of communication skills that can heal relationships.

In my clinical training, one of the first topics addressed was how to listen. It was made clear that if one learns to do this, one will become a good counselor. In my first positions in behavioral health, when I knew I was in over my head and did not know what to say to a particular client, my clinical director told me not to worry about what to say. She said my primary job was to listen. Over the years I have been fortunate enough to witness remarkable feats of recovery. Sometimes a client will acknowledge my input but far more times than anything else, they mention that it was my listening to them, and understanding them, that made the difference. Very seldom do they remember much that I said or advice that I gave. They always remember that I listened and asked questions with genuine curiosity. Eventually, I became a clinical supervisor for the first time, and therapists would come to me for consultation on cases. I began this work believing that I was supposed to have answers, that I should be able to give direction and suggestions based on my experience and knowledge. Imagine my surprise when I discovered that the real task was more listening. The best consultation services I provide are those where I simply tease out of the therapist the answers they already have.

---

[34] Adler (1952)

PRACTICAL COMMUNICATIONS AND CONNECTION SKILLS

When I have been most impressed with therapists, it is because they have found ways to fluidly and without apparent contrivance get the message across that they listen to the client.

The conclusion I reach from all of this is that the essential skill of a therapist—or sage or counselor or friend—is listening. As a professional, I am at my best when I use and exemplify basic listening skills. It follows from this that anyone wanting to improve relationships must learn to listen. This is the foundation of good communications. There are, of course, other components. Listening, however, is necessary and must come first.

In our context here, we are primarily concerned with communications between people with the purpose of improving relationships. There are many approaches to communication skills. I believe that the simpler the better, so we are going to focus on three steps to good communications:

Use active listening.
Speak for myself.
Pay attention to underlying messages.

Again, all three of these techniques are of no value unless and until we totally grasp the idea that everyone's behavior is about themselves. If I am concerned about my impact on another or the meaning their behavior has on me, I cannot let go of the outcome. Being unable to let go of the outcome prevents me from listening to the other person with curiosity. Authentic curiosity about another person is requisite for any of the following skills to be effective. If the goal of my listening is to find out something that will make me feel better, or to control or manipulate, or to do anything but find out how the other person experiences our humanity, then my effort will fail. The only reason to talk, in the context of seeking intimacy, is to be known; the only reason to listen is to know. There is a mantra to follow in this regard: "Listen to know. Share to be known."

The dictionary definition of intimacy is something "marked by very close association, contact, or familiarity."[35] It is a shared knowledge of self. When one person comes to see another person's true self, without reservation, intimacy has been achieved. The result is always the kind of connection between people described as a spiritual connection in the previous chapter. I accomplish intimacy with you, or anyone, when I share what it is like to be me, learn what it is like to be you, and accept the difference. That is my operational definition of intimacy and the definition we use for couples work at Consiliom.

Use Active Listening

This is the skill that baby counselors learn in basic training. It is also the skill that everyone needs in order to be relational and especially if the relationship is an intimate one. It is also a habit of almost all successful people. Whether you are a used car salesman or the CEO of a large corporation, how effectively you listen makes a huge difference in your ability to succeed. As the term implies, it is an active effort. The focus is taking action to insure that you are hearing everything the other person says and what they mean *and* to let the other person know you are doing so. It is not a passive pursuit. In short you must listen to know and let them know you are doing this. That is, remember you are listening to get to know the other person's reality rather than figuring out what you want to say next. There are six techniques to be used in active listening:

---

[35] Merriam-Webster online dictionary

PRACTICAL COMMUNICATIONS AND CONNECTION SKILLS

Nonverbal management
Minimal verbal responses
Paraphrasing
Reflecting
Clarifying
Summarizing

Nonverbal management

We already mentioned the importance of nonverbal communications. In the present instance we are concerned only with our own nonverbal behavior as we listen to another person. It is important to pay attention to my nonverbal behavior to be sure it is congruent with, or supports, the message I am trying to send. In this case I want to send the message that I am listening and care about what the other person is saying. Thus, I want to notice: eye contact, relative body positions, facial expressions, gestures, tone of voice, and distractions.

Eye contact can be intimidating or avoidant. It can communicate aggressiveness, interest, attraction, and aloofness. If I want to communicate my interest in what the person is saying, I must also be aware of cultural differences. In some cultures, direct or prolonged eye contact is seen as disrespectful. Generally in western cultures a lack of eye contact is considered suspicious. A person may be considered "shifty-eyed." However, in the case of Chuy, from the previous chapter, his interpretation of the eye contact of a stranger was of aggression. The important thing is to take into account possible cultural difference, pay attention to the other person's nonverbal cues, and be aware of how much eye contact I am making during the conversation.

Relative body positions are also an important but often overlooked aspect of conversations. If I am above eye level with the person I am talking to, this creates distance between us. It is literally a "one up" position. I have been employed in a number of institutions serving as a crisis counselor. In that role I would often be called to a nurse's station or an interview room to help out with a client suffering some extreme distress such as a panic attack. One of the things I always notice is the relative height of the seating. For some reason it is often the case that the chair or stool being used by the staff member is slightly elevated in relation to that being used by the client. In some cases I would find the client on the floor and the staff member sitting in a chair. Being sensitive to this makes a huge difference in the tone of my interaction with the client. If the chair I am offered turns out to be too high in relation to the client, I will adjust it. If it is not adjustable, I will get out of it and squat on the floor, below the eye level of the client. If the client is on the floor, I will get on the floor with them, and make sure that I am not taller than the client. This sends a message to the client, without words, that neutralizes whatever core issue may be activated regarding authority figures.

Once, working in the booking area of a juvenile detention center, I watched the police arrive and carry in a girl. She was limp as a rag doll and crying. The officers reported that the girl had been found wandering an alley, crying and disoriented. They had no information because the girl refused to talk to them. The officers reported the girl had been combative. The intake officer directed the police to place the girl in one of the holding rooms. These rooms had a glass wall opening onto the central booking area. As soon as the door was closed behind the girl, she began screaming, throwing furniture at the glass, and generally freaking out. I watched over the next forty-five minutes or so as several detention officers and counselors went into the room to try and help the girl. Eventually they removed all of the furniture because she was

PRACTICAL COMMUNICATIONS AND CONNECTION SKILLS

tearing it up. Only one stool was left. Whenever a staff member would enter the room, the girl would immediately retreat to the back corner and curl up, crying and sort of growling. I think about three staff went in, pulled the stool over, and sat with the girl, trying to comfort her. Nothing helped. Clearly this girl was qualifying herself for an isolation unit and eventual transfer to the State Hospital. Eventually, the detention officer whose case it was came and asked me if I would try.

To that point the girl had not spoken a word. We did not have a name or any other information about her. I did not think I would be able to do any more than anyone else, but I said I would try. When I entered the room, the girl once again stopped screaming, retreated to a back corner, slid down to the floor, and began whimpering and sort of growling at me. I walked over to her and started to sit on the stool and then realized that would put a barrier between us. Instead I moved the stool away and sat on the floor about two feet from the corner. The girl almost immediately stopped growling and just quietly whimpered. I said nothing. I just sat with her for about five minutes and she became completely quiet. She had been screaming and growling for some time and as a result had spittle and snot on her face. After a few minutes I just asked, "Thirsty?" and she nodded yes. I went and got a cup of water and a paper towel. When I came back she took the water greedily and allowed me to wipe her face off. We never did have much of a conversation using words, but we got along fine.

Her name turned out to be Alice, and she had a severe speech impediment in addition to a cognitive handicap. Imagine what that must be like, to be unable to express yourself and to be lost in totally foreign surroundings with nobody familiar. And to be twelve years old. Of course, everyone who came in and sat on that stool loomed over Alice, and she was already terrified. These looming figures must have appeared dreadfully threatening, and Alice reacted out of fear. This was one situation in which my fortuitous attention to relative body positions made all of the difference. Following strenuous detective work by the detention officer, and Alice, she was eventually returned to the facility from which she had become separated.

Facial expressions also refer not to the other person, but also to myself. Again, it is a matter of being congruent with the message I am trying to send. I need to be aware of what my face is doing. This is not a very natural habit. Generally our faces are out of our conscious control. If we focus, however, we can manage to keep a more or less neutral expression. This is important because my face might unknowingly reflect my sudden awareness that lunch is having some trouble settling in. Or, perhaps, that I forgot to make an important phone call. This has nothing to do with the conversation, but a sudden expression of discomfort or, perhaps, mild panic is not consistent with the message "I am listening to you." It can be misinterpreted. Many times I have slipped in this area and either made an unfortunate expression or looked at the clock. Often I can see instant concern on the other person's face and they ask, "Do you need to leave?" or "You are bored," or "You think this is stupid," or some other statement based on their interpretation of my expression. On the other hand, I do not want my concern with keeping a neutral expression to result in a robotic demeanor.

Sitting stone-faced while another pours out her guts is not conducive to intimacy. It is a common mistake made by rookie therapists. At times I will need to make sure that I am sending a notice that I am in fact listening. The rule here is to make some kind of gesture. Slight nods, leaning forward or backward, the raised eyebrows of understanding are all important signals to let

PRACTICAL COMMUNICATIONS AND CONNECTION SKILLS

the other person know I am still engaged in listening and have not gone off to my happy place out of boredom.

The same is true with tone of voice. Keeping my volume, cadence, and tone of speech in line with what I am trying to project will make the message "I am listening" much more convincing. I know, for example, that I have a really soft voice. People in lectures have been telling me to speak up for decades. I have to make a special effort when talking with someone intimately, or in very personal situations, not to become inaudible. Again, watching for cues that the other person is not hearing me is important. On the other hand, a booming, boisterous-voiced person might well need to tone it down in many personal conversational situations.

Finally, it is very important to be aware of the environment and possible distractions. This is why starting a conversation with my wife about our marital relationship while rolling along the freeway is not going to work. If I am doing this while my partner is driving, I clearly am not interested in real connection and, probably, I am attempting some kind of manipulative maneuver. Deliberately choosing the time and place to provide undisturbed, quiet time for a conversation is an indication we are taking it seriously. Thus, when my wife comes in saying, "We need to talk," while I am right in the middle of the most important football game ever played anywhere, the message is that she is not really interested in that conversation but is wanting something other than a intimate encounter or is making a desperate demand for immediate connection. Similarly when I say, "Okay, let's talk," but I don't turn off the TV, I am also being disingenuous, and the message that I am paying attention is lost somewhere around the twenty-yard line. Attention to the environment is a very strong message about our intentions and our sincerity.

Hopefully you can see at this point that much can be done to communicate interest and attention, without ever uttering a word. This does not mean we cannot use words at all while actively listening. In fact, verbal responses are crucial components of active listening. These begin with minimal responses.

Minimal Verbal Responses

These can be words or noises used to indicate that you are listening to the other person. Bottom line is that we do not want to just sit like a lump, gesturing and nodding. As with gestures the rule here is to make some kind of noise occasionally.

In choosing minimal verbal responses, it is important to avoid being repetitive. Try to be a little creative. The list in Table 9 is by no means exhaustive. If you make the effort to listen to what a person is saying, it is not hard to figure out what kind of response might be appropriate. Taken together, nonverbal and minimal verbal responses can send a powerful message to the other person that we are in fact interested. I have had many powerful conversations in which these are the only skills I used.

Paraphrasing

This is a verbal statement that is interchangeable with the other person's statement, but the words are different. As with all of the verbal techniques of active listening, this requires that we pay close attention to what the other person is saying.

SOME MINIMAL VERBAL RESPONSES		
I see	Oh	Really (mind your tone here)
Mm-hmmmm	How about that!	Tell me the whole story
That's hard	Been there ...	Wow, damn, or similar
Tell me more about that	You did, huh?	Interesting
Been there...	Tried that huh?	That sounds like it sucks

Table 9.

PRACTICAL COMMUNICATIONS AND CONNECTION SKILLS

Friend: "Today was very complicated."
You: "So, your day sucked." (Best to use casual, familiar language consistent with your relationship to the speaker)
Or,
"You had too much to do today."
Or,
"You had a hard time getting through the day."

It is amazing how often paraphrasing is all we need to do to let the other person know they are heard. And it is a useful tool for clearing up misunderstandings. Do not think that making a wrong guess about what was said will destroy the rapport. It turns out that the opposite is true. If I guess wrong, all that happens is that the other person will correct me. I still get credit for trying to understand, and now I actually do understand better.

Reflecting

Reflecting communicates to the other our understanding of their concerns and perspectives. You can reflect *FEELINGS* or you can reflect *THOUGHTS*.

Friend: "I don't know what he might do if I run into him."
You: "You are feeling some fear about seeing him again." (Reflecting feeling)
Or,
"You think he might hurt you?" (Reflecting thought or belief)

Friend: "I don't think I can face her."

You: "You are embarrassed for her to see you?" (Reflecting feeling)

Or

"Do you believe she will think less of you?" (Reflecting thought or belief)

Or,

"You think you might not be able to contain your anger?" (Reflecting feelings and looking for the thought behind it)

Clarifying

Clarifying is an attempt to focus on, or understand, exactly what a person is saying. It usually takes the form of a question, but *be careful with questions,* as they can be interpreted as challenges. Clarifying can be a most effective tool to communicate to another that you are listening, and you care very much about understanding exactly what they are trying to say. In order to be able to ask intelligent questions about what someone has just said, you have to pay very close attention to what is being said.

Friend: I think it will be hard to do that again."

You: "I don't understand. Will it be hard to see her, or hard to go there?"

Or

"What do you mean 'hard to do *that*'?" (Never assume you know what all the words mean.)

Friend: "My cousin Billy told my husband's brother Billy that he did not want Billy to come over."

You: "I'm lost. Tell me again who the cousin is and

who the in-law is and who was not welcome to come over where."

Friend: "I just don't know what to do with myself anymore. The kids are grown and Alan is busy all the time. Even the house gets cleaned without me."

You: "So, do you feel useless?"
Or,
"Does it seem like there is no point?"
Or,
"Does it make you angry that everyone else seems to do fine without you?"
Or,
"Ever seem like you'd be better off dead?" (Generally asking about suicidal thinking is not going to make someone decide to do it. It normally results in a realization on the part of the other person that it is okay to talk about it with you.)[36]

Summarizing

This is actually a type of clarification in which you synthesize what has been communicated during the whole conversation, or a large part of it. This is when you make sure you get the big picture about what the patient is communicating. Do not get too wordy. Try to be succinct but capture the essence of what was discussed

---

[36] Make sure you are, in fact, totally comfortable with this kind of conversation. If you are not, your discomfort will leak out nonverbally and create an awkward situation.

during the conversation. Also do not expect that you will be accurate. This skill takes some practice. At least one report on counselor behavior suggests that "senior analysts may sit for a long time and say nothing, and then come up with something at the end of the session that is so insightful the patient feel heard and understood."[37] In other words, it takes some experience to listen that long, pay attention, and then be able to sum it up. Thus, in the beginning, if you are engaged in a long conversation, it is a good idea to summarize every fifteen minutes or so rather than attempt a summary only at the end.

When it comes to listening, remember to listen with curiosity. Accept that everyone's reality is different; then the great puzzle becomes to figure out what is going on in there. What color is the sky in this person's world? How did he/she come to the emotions and opinions they experience? Remind yourself that the answers to these questions have nothing to do with you.

Speak For Myself

Sooner or later in any balanced conversation, it becomes my turn to talk. For most of us there is a powerful need to "deal with the facts." If the purpose of our conversation is to persuade others of our opinions, or convince others to some particular course of action, this is okay. This is called a debate. If we are arguing about the facts, we are attempting to change or challenge one another's perception of reality. Conversely, this is not a great leap forward for intimacy. If, on the other hand, we are in an intimate conversation in which we want to support or understand each other, then what I say, and the way I choose to say it, requires some thought. If I *listen to know* the other person with curiosity,

---

[37] Harvard Medical School (2008)

then what I offer in return is to *speak to be known*; to share myself and to provide them an opportunity to know me. This is how connection is made. This requires personal vulnerability.

If I am not willing to be seen—if I am convinced that my "self" is so damaged, different, defective, or broken that I can never be accepted by others, then taking the step to expose my inner reality can be terrifying. This vulnerability is the ultimate test of my belief that all people are people and I am one of them. It is also the only way that I can convince myself of the truth of the number one fact of life. In order to gain control of my happiness, to insure my contentment, I must first be willing to be vulnerable.[38] If our goal is to make our contentment invulnerable to outside control, then we must practice vulnerability first. It is a sort of inoculation. If I practice vulnerability on purpose, then I gain invulnerable contentment. So the first step toward connection is to practice vulnerability, being myself, with others.

The gold standard in this area, speaking for myself, is the "I statement" I am not sure where this term originated (Wikipedia was not much help), but my perception is that it has been ubiquitous in my field since around 1969, and I assume even longer. The first key is to be aware that if I am talking about myself, the sentence would logically start with the word "I." This is a good guide, but it is not foolproof. There are a couple of serious pitfalls to watch out for.

One danger arises out of the A-B-C model itself. Remember, it is important to keep our thoughts and feelings separate both in our heads and in our language. If I cannot tell the difference between my thoughts and my feelings, then the chances that I am going to be able to sort things out are pretty slim. When I make a statement

---

[38] Brown (2007)

such as "I feel like..." or "I feel that..." I have confounded my thinking and my feelings. If I am talking to myself, it is bad enough because it does not help me understand my self. If I am talking to another person, I am not taking ownership of either my thoughts or emotions. The other person now does not know whether I am talking about a feeling or a thought. When I hear the word "like" or "that" attached to "I feel," I need to stop and rephrase.

Feelings, once generated, just are. I feel shame. I feel pain. I feel fear. I feel joy. It makes no sense to say I feel that shame. It also does not make much sense to say I feel "like shame." (Unless I am a valley girl or a leftover beatnik.) Anytime I hear myself utter such nonsense, I need to stop and rethink what I am trying to say. Either I feel fear. Or I think I am in danger. These two statements go together but cannot be mixed up if we are ever going to figure ourselves out or be able to communicate effectively.

If a friend describes how he is working too much and neglecting his family and drinking a lot, to say "I think you are not taking care of yourself" may be supportive in some sense, but it reveals little about me. It is advice-giving and not the optimal way to keep the conversation going. To be intimate I don't need to be telling the other person all about themselves, which in some sense they already know. I need to be telling them about me if anything. I need to describe my current thoughts and feelings.

"When you say that, I think you are not taking care of yourself and that thought makes me sad."

Or maybe,

"Yeah I notice we don't get much time together anymore and I have wondered what is going on. That thought makes me afraid for our friendship."

PRACTICAL COMMUNICATIONS AND CONNECTION SKILLS

Now at this point it is really important to recognize that I am no longer just listening. I have interjected myself into the conversation. My friend may choose to continue talking about himself, or he might become curious about me and shift the direction of the conversation. The important thing is that I have not said anything to him about his self, or his reality, in either response. What I have done is incorporate the A-B-C model into what I say.

In the first response I have identified the data (when you say that), shared my thoughts or beliefs about it (I think you are not taking care of yourself), and let him know the emotions my thoughts lead me to (and that thought makes me sad).

With the second response I have chosen to not to repeat his data exactly but to insert my perceptions in a way that both corroborates his observation and also lets him know what the data looks like to me. (Yeah, I notice we don't get much time together anymore.) This will either confirm his perception or add new data to his perception. It carries some small risk that he might start a data debate about how much we are seeing each other. In that case

---

THOUGHT REPORT

NAME: Mike DATE: Today

A: WHEN You say that.

B. WHAT I: (thought, made up, imagined, believed, assumed) about that was:
You are not taking care of yourself

C. AND WHAT I FEEL (OR FELT) ABOUT THAT IS (WAS):
(CHOOSE ONE OF THE FOLLOWING – Anger, Fear, Pain, Guilt, Shame, Joy, Passion, Lonely, Love)
sad; and it hurts

Figure 10.

he is not being relational any longer and I should just revert to active listening. After all, he may be indicating that he is not interested in me at this point and just wants to vent. Assuming that is not the case, I go on to share my thought or beliefs (I have wondered what is going on) and finally I let him know what thinking my feelings are causing (makes me afraid). Notice that what I am actually doing in both responses is a verbal Thought Report.

If you have ever been to couples counseling, or a family week in a residential or in-patient program, or perhaps couples groups at your church or local counseling center, you should recognize some elements of these conversations. You may find the process in those sessions similar but somewhat altered, and a very rigid approach to the exercises might be employed. I want to emphasize that it is critical to follow all such exercises exactly as presented in whatever program you are attending. There are good reasons why various aspects of personal communications are emphasized differently in different programs. These may seem stilted and not very applicable to everyday life. Remember, the formats used in all such exercises, and those used here in this book, are classroom models that are exaggerated in nature and designed to help foster different habits. Please, I ask that nobody show up to a counselor's office and point out that Graham says to do this differently. The odds are that the professionals you are working with know what they are doing and have good reasons for it and will not appreciate having a "one up" client announce themselves at the start. In fact, I believe it is best not to mention me at all.

Pay Attention to Underlying Messages

So, now you may ask what are underlying messages and what do they lie under? I refer back to the importance of nonverbal communications and to the discussion of primary and secondary emotions. By underlying messages I mean not only the fact that these messages are generally nonverbal but that, as it happens, all behavior is communication. In actuality it is impossible to not communicate.[39] Everything I do—from where I stand to whether I choose to talk or not, what I wear, and what kind of work I do—even if I am dead on the sidewalk, communication is still occurring. An observer can gather information such as "Graham is dead" as well as other data about the circumstances of my demise (quite a lot of data, in fact, if your name is Dr. Brennan or Inspector Linley). This contextual information constitutes a second level of communication that accompanies every statement we make. We began this chapter by asserting that accurate communications is difficult at best but that it occurs anyway. Now we learn that in all communications there are at least two levels.

Each piece of human communication can be thought of as a transmission. A transmission is an attempt to transfer something from my mind into the mind of another person. When another person responds to my transmission, a transaction has occurred. The transaction involves error checking to make sure the data sent and received was accurate. It also involves context checking to be sure the meaning of the data is the same for both participants. Context is addressed in a different level of communication altogether. So, now we have two levels of communication occurring in every transmission. One we will call the content level; the second level we are going to call the relationship level. Other writers have used different labels, but these seem somewhat more intuitive in my perspective.

---

[39] Watzlawick, Beavin, Helmick and Jackson (1967)

The content level of communication generally deals with the transfer of data, while the relationship level is concerned with the context of the message. All messages occur in some sort of context. The context is what gives meaning, to everything. The social context is the critical part of the context when we try to communicate intimately with others. A major part of that social context is the nature and extent of the relationship between people who are attempting to communicate. Thus the relationship level of communication is concerned with the definition and description of the nature and type of the relationship that exists between two people. For example, suppose I tell my daughter, "Please take out the trash." This is the data. The assumed context is the nature of the relationship I believe I have with my daughter, which in this case is apparently one in which I get to tell her what to do.

The content data is pretty clear; I want her to take out the trash. The definition of the relationship, being communicated in nonverbal, analog data, is not quite so clear. The lack of clarity occurs for three reasons. First, nonverbal communications are not as precise or specific as verbal communications. Everything is open to interpretation to a much greater degree than with words. Second, relationships themselves are rather complex, multifaceted processes that address a number of dimensions, such as the various degrees of intimacy, trust, power, affection, respect, and other characteristics. Third, relationships are not things. They are processes and, as such, they are not static. Relationships change from moment to moment depending on the larger context in which they exist, as well as other factors. So, when I asked my daughter to take out the trash, along with that request went a number of pieces of information about the type of relationship I believe we have. My daughter's response will let me know if we share the same definition of the relationship.

My daughter might respond with "Fine" and flounce out of the room to complete the chore with clear indications that she does not necessarily accept the definition of the relationship despite her compliance. Or she might look over at me and suggest I do it myself, a probable indication that we are now negotiating on whether either of us gets to tell anyone what to do. Or she might respond with "Excuse me?" along with an arched eyebrow. Or she might say, "Okay," and jump up to carry out my request. (Since she is a teenager, this is the least likely result of course.) The meaning may not be as clear as the content level of communication, but the reality is that with every transmission, there is an implied message about the type and strength of relationship assumed by the speaker. If there is dispute between the parties on this level, nothing else matters.

We have to be able to decode this information or we will not be able to function in society. The information is always there in every conversation. What is important is that we become sensitive to it and do not ignore the information. Most successful people pay attention to these underlying messages without thought. A good car salesman, for example, knows intuitively that he makes a sale based on the relationship he establishes with a customer. It is not the features of the car but the perception of the customer of the nature of the relationship with the salesman. There are six principles of persuasion that have been identified by researchers. Thus the effective salesperson employs six principles of persuasion[40] in all conversations in order to establish trust and respect. It is the relationship that will close the deal.

---

[40] You can review these six principles online if you search for "Six principles of persuasion" or "Robert Cialdini."

The important point for us to remember is that relationship conflicts, personality conflicts at work, and, in fact, all serious conflict between human beings occurs at the relationship level of communication. This is information about how to interpret the information. In other words, we must describe the context in which to interpret the words being sent. Even conversations that appear to be about data can be affected by the relationship level of communication. If a team of architects are discussing the design of a bridge, and cannot seem to get the job done, the problem is most likely in the relationships between the team members. Remember, all meaning comes from context, so the data alone is not a complete message. Attention to these underlying messages, the messages lying under the words, is critical if satisfactory relationships are to be maintained.

One of my most memorable professional experiences occurred during the first week of my first job as a counselor. It is not a particularly exciting story. It does not involve sex, drugs, rock and roll, or bizarre pathology. As a memory though, this incident stands as a poignant episode in my professional development. The feelings and some of the images are as clear today as when they happened almost forty years ago. In fact, as I type this, a photograph of the child involved is tacked to the wall above my computer.

I was employed at the time in a residential treatment center in the central Texas hill country. The program served adolescent girls. My group consisted of eight girls, most of whom were experiencing serious emotional problems as a result of a background of some type of abuse. They were very manipulative, especially with male staff members. A "work detail" was a form of discipline in which the child had to forego her free time and was required to perform some menial task under the direction of the

PRACTICAL COMMUNICATIONS AND CONNECTION SKILLS

shift supervisor. The real significance of the work detail was not the work itself, but the impact on the child's status on the level system employed by the program. On each level there were a maximum number of work details one could receive and still maintain the level.

Mandy was a twelve-year-old girl whose father had died and whose mother was unable or unwilling to provide consistent limits. Thus Mandy was a persistent management problem. Over the months at the center, Mandy taught me many lessons about myself and my work. This was the first.

We were at dinner. Next to the cafeteria was the swimming pool. It was prohibited for kids to be in or near the pool, except when scheduled. My eight kids and I exited the cafeteria and waited on the patio between the cafeteria and the pool. As I recall, we were waiting for another group to finish dinner so we could go on a joint activity. One of the girls, Mandy, asked if she could sit on the diving board. I said no. She renewed the request and the battle was on. I again replied no. Resorting to a time-honored limit-testing technique which, when used by a clinical psychologist or therapist might be referred to as successive approximation or perhaps systematic desensitization, Mandy said, "Well, can I just sit on the back end of the board? There isn't anyplace else to sit." I acquiesced and the result was predictable. Within minutes Mandy was seated out on the very end of the board with her feet dangling inches above the water. I knew I was in trouble and was desperately trying not to let it show.

"What would happen if I fell in?" she asked.

Strangely enough I don't recall my reply to this question. I was undoubtedly fighting an internal battle to avoid complete panic.

"Can I just put my feet in the water?"

"No." I think my voice was still fairly calm.

"Why not?" At this point Mandy knew full well that she had the upper hand. She was bouncing lightly on the board, smiling and clearly at ease.

"Because I said so." *Wow, I thought, is that the best I could come up with? I sound like my mother.* I am sure there was a little squeak to my voice by now.

"What will you do if I just stick my toe in the water?"

I thought my panic must now have been apparent to everyone. A coworker later told me that she and the supervisor had been listening to the interaction through the dining room window. She said my response was quick if not very firm. My own perception was that at least ten years went by while I scoured my memory of rules and the level system and treatment plans and the entire contents of my textbook from psychology 101 for the correct response. Incredibly I could not recall any policy or procedure or psychological intervention that described the appropriate response for a staff member to make to a twelve-year-old sticking her toe in the water. I was on my own. Somehow, after laborious calculations, I settled on the dreaded work detail as an appropriate response.

"I will give you a work detail." Mandy's face dropped in disbelief and my self-doubt redoubled. How stupid could I be? I could tell from the look on her face that a work detail was way out of proportion. *This isn't going to work. She knows I won't really do it. I should have picked something else.*

"Just for sticking my toe in the water?"

"That's right."

"I don't believe you."

My worst fears now confirmed, I watched in horror as her toe descended delicately, slowly toward the water. At that point in time nothing else existed for me. I have no recollection of the other kids, or anything else except Mandy's toe. Finally, gently it touched the water, sending out the barest ripple. I doubt if even her toenail got wet.

"I did it," she said.

"You got it," I said and my guts churned.

Mandy immediately began to whine, I think. I don't remember her exact words. I was concentrating on standing up and walking to meet the shift supervisor, who, mercifully, was coming toward me. Work details were not considered official until reported to the supervisor. If I could get that far, it would be out of my hands. Mandy was determined to keep me from it and used all sorts of tactics they never taught me in college. She used reason, "I didn't really get wet"; guilt, "I didn't think you were serious"; compassion, "I will lose my level"; and many other weapons, all of which worked. Each statement staggered me. By the time I was within talking distance of the supervisor, I knew the whole damn thing was my fault.

Mandy was crying now and pleading, and I didn't understand how I could have gotten so carried away as to think that I should give this poor child a work detail. As she pointed out, it would result in a level drop for her and that meant she could not go on the off-campus activity that night or the following Saturday. In addition, I experienced a massive sense of failure. If I had done the "right thing," then Mandy would not have called my bluff. If I was any good, I would have been able to keep her from sticking her stupid toe in the water.

To this day I do not know what prompted me to follow through. I certainly had no confidence that I was doing the right thing. At that point I even became unsure of my authority and approached the supervisor with some trepidation. I am sure, however, that all child care workers and counselors go through this type of experience. If we are any good, milder forms are also repeated throughout our careers. At least they are for me. This is how I stay on my toes and avoid slipping into robotic therapeutic routines. Whatever the reason, I did follow through and announced my decision to the supervisor, who provided both support and criticism when she replied, "'Bout time. I was beginning to wonder when you would wake up," as she noted the action on her clipboard.

This was my first opportunity to observe an amazing phenomenon. The sweet little child, who I had but moments before been so conflicted about, suddenly disappeared. In her place was a foul-mouthed, demonic little creature displaying such hostility that much of my guilt vanished, eventually to be replaced with anger. Clearly there was no excuse for such verbal abuse of a staff member, especially me! Had not the supervisor been present I have no doubt that I would have had a major containment failure and responded in kind to her anger. I won't repeat the names she called me. We have all heard them. I also can't say that all my doubts disappeared when Mandy became angry and I followed suit. The doubts remained and the lesson began.

The lesson has continued now for almost four decades and there have been many instructors. Mandy taught me much in just this one episode. The lesson continues today and I hope it continues as long as I am. No matter how many clients I meet or programs I work in, I will always remember Mandy and her toe and how I missed the underlying messages.

The entire conversation was not about the pool or Mandy's toe or where she should sit. It was also not about work details. The conversation was a negotiation between us about the nature of the relationship we were going to have. In addition, the context included the rest of the kids in the group, so it also included a negotiation about the nature of the relationship between the group and me. I was a new counselor, and the nature of our future relationship with the kids was the point of this conversation. My hesitation and lack of confidence were communicated nonverbally in the beginning of the conversation. Weeks later, with the same group, if someone asked if they could sit on the diving board, I would say no, and that would be the end of the conversation. At this early point, however, due to my activated competence core issue, I experienced one boundary failure after another, all leaking out nonverbally and all giving Mandy the message that I might not be serious or I might not follow through.

Many times negotiations or nonverbal discussions about the nature of a relationship turn up in the form of questions, especially using the word "why." There was an IT specialist at a company I worked with who kept getting poor evaluations for customer service. I will call him Jim. This was as part of an internal survey conducted by the company on almost all staff and all function groups. Finally Jim came to me for some advice on how he could improve his scores. In talking with him I found him to be personable, a good listener, and possessed of a great sense of humor. I could offer no advice, so I asked to accompany him the next time he was called for service. This person's actual job was to design, or redesign, the software interface being used by programmers and others in a software company. Thus, users of the company's enterprise software application would call and ask to have a screen designed differently, or the database modified in some way, to make it more functional for them. I observed about two minutes of the first interview and could see the problem.

Each time a customer would ask to have something done, say move an icon from the bottom to the top of the screen, Jim would immediately ask, "Why?" If we just consider the words, there does not seem to be much of a problem. The accompanying nonverbal behavior displayed by Jim made it clear, however, that there was an immediate relationship problem. Let's look at the sequence of events and possible meaning at the relationship level in Table 10.

ACTION	RELATIONSHIP IMPLICATION
Jim arrives in response to a request for help.	Jims function is to meet the customer's needs.
Jim asks what the customer wants	Customer gets to say what he wants and Jim's job is to do it.
Customer specifies his desires	Same as above
Jim asks "Why"	Jim will only do the task if the customer can explain the request to Jim's satisfaction?

Table 10.

Even the word "why" carries an implication that the customer must provide a satisfactory explanation. What is not apparent in the figure is the nonverbal component of Jim's communication. My interpretation of what I saw and heard is in line 3. The customer has a similar perception, which led to the customer's belief that Jim was not being particularly helpful. In fact, the customer described it as resistance. On the other hand, Jim's stated intention for asking why was so that he could better understand the customer's needs. Unhappily, Jim had some core issues of his own, and these leaked out nonverbally and contaminated the conversation. There is no need to go into Jim's issues, and in actuality I did not. I talked with Jim a bit about his issues but then simply suggested that he stop asking customers "why'" as a means of clarification. I offered several alternative phrases he could use. Jim later reported much better interactions with his customers.

PRACTICAL COMMUNICATIONS AND CONNECTION SKILLS

I cannot overemphasize that messages at the relationship level of communication go on all the time, and many, if not all, of our conflicts and interpersonal difficulties stem from a failure to address or even be aware of them. During the Vietnam conflict, I was sent to a yearlong technical school. This was a massive operation with thousands of airmen being trained in many highly technical specialties. The management issues must have been monumental. On arrival at the base, as was the custom, the regular drill instructors divided the soldiers into groups and picked someone out of each group as "squad leader." This was not an official position, and the usual criterion was to find someone with "prior service." Prior service could be anything from a whole career to the guy who happened to join up a few days earlier than the rest. At this particular base I was chosen as the squad leader.

For months things went along swimmingly. Tech school was interesting, if a little tedious, and because of the demands of the curriculum, some of the military sternness was relaxed. Then one day some of the members of my squad were caught shooting craps during a break between classes. In the process of his investigation, the drill instructor asked if I knew what was going on. I, of course, said yes. I actually had no idea, but I said yes because that is what a leader is supposed to do, right? A leader takes care of his guys and is responsible for the squad's behavior. We saw it in all the movies when growing up. I learned it from lots of great soldiers like Jimmy Stewart, John Wayne, and Audie Murphy. On hearing this, the drill instructor excused the rest of the squad, chewed me out, relieved me of my position as squad leader, and gave me some sort of punishment. I think I had to guard the mess hall for a few nights instead of sleeping. The drill instructor also replaced me with one of the other squad members. Almost right away a curious thing happened.

The new squad leader took charge immediately, but every time he would give an order, the entire squad would look over at me to see if it was okay. I would nod in the affirmative and then the order would be carried out. The new squad leader understandably became frustrated with this behavior and chewed me out and several other individuals to no avail. He even attempted to report squad members to the drill instructors but nothing changed. Finally, after a week or two, we were cleaning up after class and the squad leader ordered the squad to "fall in." Everyone looked at me and I nodded and they lined up. A nearby drill instructor noticed this behavior. The squad leader noticed that the situation had been noticed and addressed the drill instructor about it. I did not hear exactly what was said, but I heard the word "defiant" from the squad leader. The drill instructor responded clearly with "No, soldier, you have failed to earn the respect of your men. That is what is going on here." The drill instructor was correct.

Nothing the substitute squad leader ever said was technically out of line or incorrect. He was clearly going to do things by the book and was determined to do a good job. However, nonverbally it was clear that he was getting a lot of mileage out of "being in charge." He saw himself as better than the rest of the squad members. This nonverbal behavior was obvious to the rest of the squad, even though nobody ever talked about it. The squad's decision was made quickly and unanimously without any verbal discussion. In addition, when the drill instructor asked about the curious behavior he observed with the squad, the new squad leader blamed it on his men instead of taking responsibility himself. If he had covered for his men, he might have begun to earn some respect. In the military, as in lots of other relationships, knowing someone has your back and will cover it is pretty important.

Again, the total significance of all of the conversations involved in this incident was in the underlying messages. The context and the nonverbal signals define the context and therefore the true meaning of every conversation. Failure to attend to these messages is a sure way to mess up even the best relationships and make any chance of teamwork or intimacy very difficult.

In this chapter we have attempted to cover the basics of the kind of communications that lead to more satisfying, intimate relationships. In summary, we have covered these five areas:

It is impossible not to communicate.
People's behavior is mostly about them, not me.
Use active listening skills *(listen to know)*.
Speak for myself (speak to be known).
Pay attention to underlying messages.

A very important consideration is that using any of these techniques *in order to improve our relationship* with someone will not work. These are techniques for how to be intimate—how to share myself and come to know another. These are best used regarding primary and secondary emotions in an attempt to understand ourselves or to have others understand us. They are not techniques designed to get someone else to behave differently. The purpose of including these techniques in this book, my lectures or workshops, and many of the couples, marriage, and family workshops available is ultimately to help us be more connected. It is about helping to resolve spiritual core issues and learning to notice those around us in a different way. Connection cannot be about manipulation on instrumental emotions. I once gave a book on communications to a friend who was having difficulty finding a sense of purpose in her life. The book covered many of the topics we have discussed here. My hope was that she would try some of these things out as a means to finding more connection and meaning and putting an end to her isolation. When I saw her a week or two later and asked what she thought of the book, her comment was, "You don't talk this way. Why do you think I should?" This was a very sad outcome.

The point of that book, and this one, is to help find ways to improve myself and to share myself with others. Even writing this book has been as much about clarifying some of my own thinking and issues as about telling others anything. It is very important to approach these techniques, not as tools to change others or our lot in life, but as tools to help discover our authentic selves and how we are profoundly and eternally connected.

All people are people.
Happiness is not something that happens to us. It is something we do.
We all have everything we need to be happy.
Everyone's reality is different and everyone's reality is valid.
My feelings always come from my thoughts.
Things always happen the way they happen.
The belief system consists of ideas, not facts.
Ideas can be changed.
Everyone's behavior is mostly about them, not me.

CHAPTER 6

Relationships and Roles

We have talked about the necessity of becoming aware of the patterns of our own thoughts, feelings, and behaviors. As mentioned in the description of spirituality, there are, however, patterns larger than our own. We are part of these larger patterns. As human beings we are a thread in the tapestry of human existence. We play a part in the patterns of interaction, connection and belonging that make up the human species. An understanding of these patterns of interaction is necessary in order to realize that we all have a spiritual existence. The first-level pattern, or context, outside ourselves involves our relationships with other people beginning with our family of origin; thus the topics of this chapter. The lack of functional personal boundaries is a recurring pattern in almost all relationship difficulties. We will begin with a brief overview of boundaries and then look at codependence as a model for patterns in relational issues. Finally, we will look at some patterns frequently developed in our family of origin. These patterns can often stay with us for life, cutting us off from genuinely intimate and meaningful relations with ourselves, other people, and the world in general. Relational issues are combined in this chapter with boundaries, codependence, enabling, and family of origin roles because they are all inextricably intertwined.

Personal Boundaries

Personal boundaries have come to be defined as the patterns of behaviors we employ when interacting with others. In other words boundaries are the parts of our belief system which determine how we protect our reality and how we respect the reality of others. Boundaries can also be thought of as the rules of interaction we use in our relationships. Personal boundaries are primarily internal, thus the inclusion of the word "personal" in the nomenclature. They function to define, contain, and protect our sense of self.[41] Imagine if I ask several friends to take a set of chessmen out to a football field and play a game of tennis. What would happen? A couple of things clearly would not happen very easily, namely a game of tennis or football or chess, because those games and sports are defined by their rules, procedures, roles and boundaries. Change the rules and you change the game.

The same is true for people. A major part of my definition of self is the rules I use in my relationships. If I change my rules for interacting with others, it can be said I have changed my self. Haven't we all heard someone assert that "You are not yourself today" in response to some temporary change in the pattern of our behavior? This is because, ultimately, *my self* is a construct inferred from my patterns of behavior and experienced by my ability to notice those internal and external behavior patterns. There is no actual "self" as a static object within my physical body. The self resides only in the mind and its ability to observe the brain-body interactions. These patterns of behavior originate from the cognitive schema we have developed as a result of addressing the four primary tasks of psychological development. Most of

---

[41] The definitions of boundaries, though somewhat different, were extrapolated from Pia Mellody's work in *Facing Codependence*.

these are functional and some, as we have defined it, are dysfunctional and referred to as the core issues most often arising around safety, value, competence, and spirituality.

Personal boundaries then are the patterns of behavior that define, contain, and protect our sense of self. These patterns of behavior arise out of the beliefs, memories, values, and automatic thinking that make up our reality. Taken together, boundaries help us to avoid harming others and protect us from being harmed. Without functional boundaries, society as we know it would not be possible.

There are three types of boundaries we may employ (see Figure 11): functional boundaries, walls, and no boundaries.

Note, in Figure 11, that a dashed line denotes functional boundaries and. This is used to indicate that the boundary is semi permeable and subject to my control. In other words, it is capable of performing both the function of containment and the function of protection, but it is a matter of my choice. Thus, I can choose to listen or to be intimate. On the other hand, I can choose not to allow other people's behavior or life's vicissitudes to enter. I do not lose my sense of self or my ability to cope, regardless of what is happening outside of me. I have a clear sense of where the world leaves off and where I begin, and I can maintain that definition of self, that boundary, no matter what happens. This allows me to perceive both my own internal patterns of being and meaning, and to notice and appreciate the ways in which they are part of a larger reality outside of my self. Thus, connection to other people and intimate relationships are possible. Also possible is the ability to notice that individual patterns fit into the context of larger patterns that encompass all life and, ultimately, the universe.

The second representation is labeled "walls." In this situation the individual has completely disconnected from meaningful interaction with the world. Crippled by one or more serious core issues, this person does not believe herself to be safe, valued, or competent to a degree that almost any interaction is seen as dangerous and thus to be avoided. Spirituality is, of course, not even approachable in this condition. There are many types of walls. Almost any behavior can be used to distract ourselves and others from getting to know us and therefore to learn the awful truth about our supposed inadequacies. The primary function of walls is to avoid intimacy at all costs. Often we are unaware that we are using walls in our relationships. The patterns of our usual behavior are somewhat invisible unless there is some unusual occurrence to bring them to our attention. Many people spend the majority of their lives living behind these types of defensive patterns of relating to others.

The third type of boundary is none at all. This person has little or no awareness of their patterns of thinking and the sources of their emotions or behavior. If asked to define or describe their beliefs, they are at a loss. This person goes through life at the mercy of whatever or whoever happens to influence them at the moment. They cannot tell when they are the ultimate victims. They have no ability to contain their own behavior or to protect themselves from the behavior and emotions of others. Again, spiritual connection is absent and genuine relationships are nonexistent.

Our boundaries, like many other aspects of our personality, adapt to context. Different times, different people, different situations all result in our use of different types of boundaries. If I am with someone with whom I am in an intimate relationship, the distance I will allow them to approach me is way smaller than the distance I will allow for a stranger. If I find a stranger to be attractive, I will allow them closer than another stranger I find disgusting. In addition, if I am with even the most intimate of people, my spouse for example, there are circumstances which cause me to alter how close I will let them come. If my spouse decides to be frisky but has morning breath, I might adjust the distance…until alterations are made anyway. Or, if I am experiencing an upset stomach, amorous approaches will probably be repulsed or delayed. In these cases, I am adjusting my boundaries to meet my current needs.

There are two purposes for boundaries: containment and protection. Common instances of failures of both types are shown in Table 10. Any time we lose either containment or protection, we

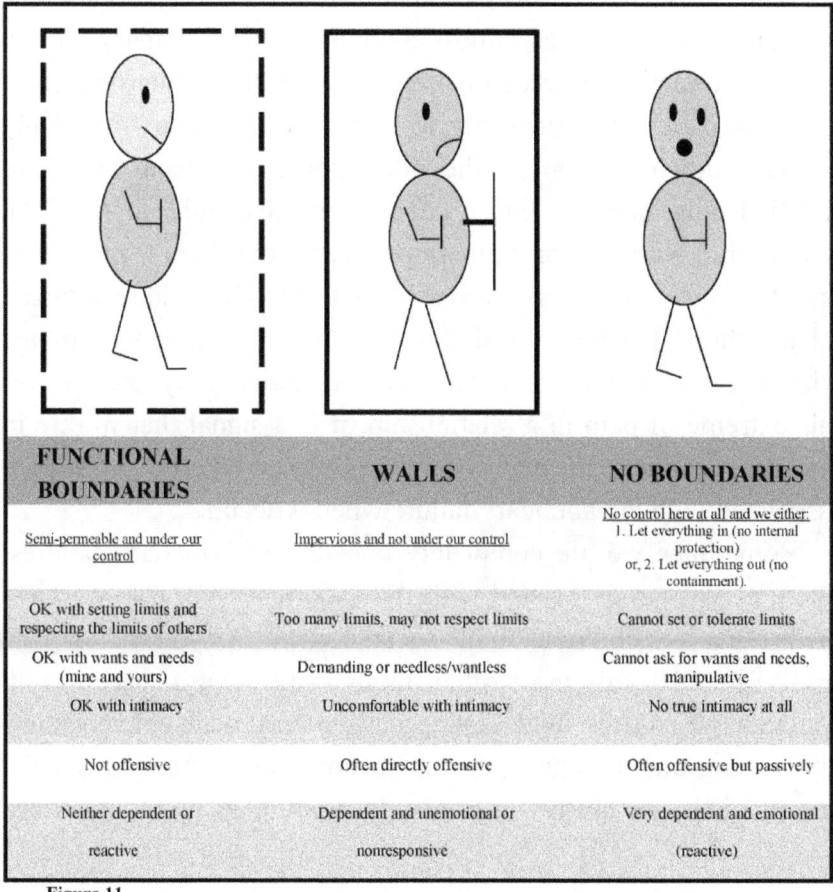

FUNCTIONAL BOUNDARIES	WALLS	NO BOUNDARIES
Semi-permeable and under our control	Impervious and not under our control	No control here at all and we either: 1. Let everything in (no internal protection) or, 2. Let everything out (no containment).
OK with setting limits and respecting the limits of others	Too many limits, may not respect limits	Cannot set or tolerate limits
OK with wants and needs (mine and yours)	Demanding or needless/wantless	Cannot ask for wants and needs, manipulative
OK with intimacy	Uncomfortable with intimacy	No true intimacy at all
Not offensive	Often directly offensive	Often offensive but passively
Neither dependent or reactive	Dependent and unemotional or nonresponsive	Very dependent and emotional (reactive)

Figure 11.

are in boundary failure. Sometimes boundary failures are painful. I have found this is usually the case with a loss of protection. When I lose protection I become a victim, and that is a painful condition. When I was young and so codependent I could hardly walk by myself, I found it hard to understand how someone could turn away from a friendship or a lover as though the connection and feelings had meant nothing. I remember struggling to understand how a relationship that had been so intense and fraught with meaning on one day could mean nothing to the other person the very next day. How could she let it go that easily? Did it mean nothing? Was I that far off base that it meant so much to me? The problem was that I lived almost continuously in boundary failure, with no protection. I needed the relationship, the demonstration of love from the other, in order to feel okay about myself. Only constant demonstration of the other person's esteem and love satisfied this need. It must have been miserable to be in a relationship with me during that time. Turns out there is more than one kind of protection needed when we enter into intimate relationships! The reality is that we cannot be functionally intimate without the protection of functional boundaries. Anytime we feel this extreme of pain in a relationship, it is a signal that we are in boundary failure. In many cases, however, there is no pain associated with the boundary failure when it occurs.

Sometimes we are completely unaware of boundary failures. There is no pain associated with the experience because we have made ourselves oblivious to the social context. As you can surmise from Table 10, this most often, though not always, occurs with containment failures. When I am interrupting private conversations or blabbing way too much personal information in the wrong social context, it is not always immediately painful. In these situations,

COMMON CONTAINMENT FAILURES	COMMON PROTECTION FAILURES
Screaming or yelling at others	Unable to say no to physical contact
Helping others when not asked or needed.	Taking on other peoples responsibilities
Answering or speaking for other people.	Taking on other peoples emotional pain
Helping others break rules or avoid responsibility	Allowing someone to stand in my space
Touching someone without permission	Not noticing others containment failures/offensiveness
Standing in others personal space without permission	Allowing myself to be abused.
Reading or looking at others mail, email, etc.	Allowing others to speak for me.
Mind reading	Needing to explain my behavior or justify my feelings
Revealing way too much personal information	Needing other people to demonstrate their love
Interrupting other people's conversations	Not seeing others as functionally separate

Table 11.

the pain of embarrassment comes later, when we evaluate our behavior from a distance.

As mentioned above, boundaries are a product of the definition of self. Having functional boundaries means that I am definite about where I end and the world begins. I do not confuse the emotions of others with my own, and I am clear about the difference between my interests and the interests of others. Since boundaries are a reflection of the definition of self, it follows that when I have a good definition of self, and no core issues are activated, functional boundaries are automatic. In this situation I do not have to think about "putting up my boundaries"; they just are, as a result of my sense of self. It also means that boundaries are an internal process; thus nobody outside of me can "violate my boundaries." This is a common misconception.

This misconception arises from confusion between personal boundaries and personal limits. Limits are external. They are restrictions I place on other people's behavior in relation to me. Personal space is again a good example. There is an area close to me that I do not allow people to violate. If someone enters this space, against my wishes, they are violating the limits I have set. Personal boundaries are completely internal. They are about my containment and my protection. If I allow someone into my personal space when it is not comfortable for me, I am having a boundary failure. The other person may be having a containment failure, but that is their business. Just because someone else has a containment failure and defies the limits I have set, it does not mean that I automatically have to have a protection failure. In other words I don't have to feel bad about my self. Even in the case of physical assault, I have a choice about how I am going to feel about the event. I have known many people who were victims of rape and other physical assaults. The difference in people's responses is sometimes remarkable. Some people have huge boundary failures in the face of assaults. They suffer from PTSD for months or years afterward. They may require years of therapy to fully recover. Others seem almost to take it in stride. Still others seem to grow from the experience and become mentally and emotionally tougher. These folks seem to live out the old adage that what doesn't kill you makes you stronger.

I remember conducting a group in a hospital years ago. It was all female and two of the women had recounted rape incidents from their recent past. They were very distraught and the rest of us in the group were very sympathetic, except for one woman. I noticed that her nonverbal expression was different than the rest of the group and asked what she was thinking. She was very hesitant and did not want to comment. I was pretty insistent and finally she said something like, "I just don't think this stuff has to be such a big deal." You could hear the shock among the rest of the group. How could she say that being raped was not that big of a deal? I asked for clarification. The woman first revealed her own rape story, and it was much worse than the other ladies'. Then she said, "It sucks, but it didn't change anything important."

At the time I did not have a clear concept of personal boundaries and had to really think about this woman's statements. Now it seems clear that she had very functional personal boundaries. Her sense of self was well defined and she did not have an active safety core issue operating at all. In fact, she probably did not have any issues with safety or value. I do not remember why she was in the hospital, but I will never forget the matter-of-fact attitude she had about being raped. Clearly she was victimized under the law, but emotionally she did not surrender her self, no matter what someone did to her. She understood the difference between things that happen to us and things that are us. She understood that people's innate value never changes. We are not what we do, and we are certainly not what happens to us. I cannot remember this woman's name, but I will never forget the lesson she taught.

Because boundaries are part and parcel with our definition of self, they will be a factor in most of our relationship issues. Patterns of boundary failures are driven by core issues and thus are a significant clue in our efforts to uncover and correct the problematic beliefs associated with our core issues. As we look at some of the typical relationship problems, the solutions often involve improvement of a person's boundaries. An important point here is that maintaining boundaries is a skill that anyone can practice and improve. I have never met anyone who had permanently damaged boundaries. Like typing or swimming, it is just a skill that can be taught and learned by anyone often in spite of the active core issue driving it. In fact, purposefully practicing boundaries is one powerful technique for chipping away at core issues. By repeatedly acting as if I have functional boundaries, I can actually begin to restructure faulty core beliefs. For example, I simply ask myself, "What would I be doing, or how would I be acting if I had functional boundaries?" then act that way regardless of how I am feeling. We almost always can figure out what the functional response would be in a given situation, but habits of automatic thought prevent us from being aware of it. We generally avoid this response, also, because it is not familiar or we are not sure we can pull it off. One way to do this is to begin to notice some of our surface thoughts and behaviors that are founded on faulty core beliefs. When I read things into other people's behavior, for example, I am presuming that their behavior in some way defines me or determines my worth.

"He slammed the door; he must be disappointed in me. It must be something I did." This is an assumption. It denies the other person the right to determine their own emotions, meaning, and behavior, and it prevents me from maintaining my own peace. A functional response might well be no response at all. After all, the other person is the one with the door issue. Let him and the door work it out. If for some reason I am that interested, I might inquire as to what is going on, but to assume I know, and further to assume it is about me, is just not functional. In this case I can act as if I believe there is no connection between the slamming door and my safety, value, competence, or spirituality.

"If I tell her what I think, she will hate me." This is not a functional response in that I am now predicting the future. I cannot actually do that, but I can make myself miserable with the illusion. I can make myself really miserable by taking on the onus of controlling the future so that "she" will always like me no matter what I do. The functional response is to manage my behavior congruently, speak my truth, and deal with the future when it happens. Stifling my self because of something that might happen later just insures my needs won't be known and my anxiety will rise. In this case I can act as if it does not matter to me what her response might someday be.

Every time we admit we know what the functional response would be, and make a commitment to behave as though we had that boundary in place, we wear down the core issue causing the problem. Eventually we don't have to keep acting as if; we just act. This effort quickly becomes a significant component of the effort to convince myself to believe something different.

Codependence

This is a relationship pattern that appears in most of our relationships from time to time. It is a result of a lack of functional boundaries on the part of one or both parties to a relationship. There are at least three definitions of codependence in pretty wide use:

> The dependence of one person on a second person's addiction or emotional difficulty
> The dependence of one person's sense of value and worth on another person's behavior
> The lack of a relationship with self

In the first instance let's assume a husband is alcoholic. The wife has core issues of value and competence. While believing she is valueless and incompetent, she also believes that she can make up for these deficiencies by taking care of others, especially her husband, who, in her mind at least, needs her so much. Remember, the wife's beliefs are unconscious habits of thought. Because they are unconscious or automatic, she is not even aware of the basis for the experience she is having. She copes with her core issues with compensatory intermediate beliefs, which are also mostly automatic, dissociated thinking. In the absence of extraordinary effort, she will remain in the delusional system, which appears to be the only way to preserve a sense of worth. However, in this situation the wife's value and competence are only assured so long as her husband needs her. If he were to suddenly not need her so much, because he recovers from his drinking for instance, then she is left with a diminished sense of self. She no longer has any purpose or function in life. And, she will not even understand why, because so much of her assumptions and expectations are out of her awareness. So, while she works diligently to take care of her husband, she also covertly assures that he does not actually get into sobriety. She cannot allow it, consciously or unconsciously; she would then have to face the pain of her dysfunctional core beliefs, and that is something she believes is impossible. The wife is codependent on her husband's alcoholism to meet her need for value and competence. She does this not even aware of the core issues and irrational beliefs involved. It is automatic thinking and unconscious.

In the second instance, one person does not believe himself or herself to be valuable or lovable or desirable. However, they have intermediate beliefs that if they can get certain significant people to respect them, or love them, then they can get by. This person is totally dependent on someone else's behavior for their internal sense of well-being. Many people take this to the extent that they end up with no life outside of taking care of others. Such a person may even repress their own emotions for fear that others may become upset. Serious grief issues and other needs may not be addressed because it would be stressful for others. They are the one at family dinners who is always the last one to sit at the dinner table, making sure everyone else comes first. They spend free time and weekends doing things that other people want to do, perhaps going shopping with a daughter-in-law when they really don't want to. As a grandparent this person can't just have her grandson and his wife over for dinner but will end up inviting her son, his wife, her daughter and husband and their kids and every other available family member for fear that someone will get their feelings hurt. More commonly, this person is the one in the family whose job it is to keep everyone happy. He or she cannot tolerate any discord in the family because it activates their core issues.

In the last instance, codependency is a lack of relationship with self. That is, a lack of awareness of the patterns of thoughts, emotions, and behaviors that constitute who I am. It results from the inability or unwillingness, and often the lack of awareness of our ability, to drag our direst thought out into the light for examination. We lose sight of the fact that our worst thoughts are still just ideas (Fact of Life #7, page 38). Thinking something, whatever it may be, does not necessarily cause it to occur. When we refuse to examine our most horrid and feared thoughts, our core issues persist and prevent us from recognizing meaning and purpose. Sadly, this disconnection from ourselves also prevents us from the realization that we are part of a greater whole. With no active self, I am totally dependent on external events to tell me who I am and where I belong.

These are three traditional ways of thinking about codependence. For our purposes here we will define codependence as relational patterns which are based on a set of beliefs (thoughts, values, memories, assumptions, expectations, etc.) in which our own worth and value are dependent on the perceptions and behavior of others. This can take many forms as we have seen. In addition to the situations already discussed, codependence includes situations in which, in order to maintain my worth and value, I need you to agree with me. In the extreme this includes people who are not only "one up" in their relationships, but when confronted with disagreement, believe they are justified in judging, blaming, or criticizing. This is in opposition to, but no less nonfunctional than, one who, on encountering disagreement, retreats into a "one down" shell. Codependence is almost always at the root of relational distress.

Like boundary failures, codependence is important as a tool for identification of core issues. Anytime there is codependent behavior, it is driven by a core issue. If there is persistent codependence maintained by both parties to a relationship, then the odds are very good that both people have core issues, which the codependent relationship relieves in some manner. Noticing patterns of codependence in our behavior can give us a huge advantage in figuring out the specific beliefs and values that make up my core issues and drive me away from happiness. The boundary failures associated with codependence many times involve a basic conundrum of human existence.

I have said we are all connected by our humanity and I believe this is true. It is also the case that we are all individuals and thus different. That presents us with an almost paradoxical situation. We are all connected, and we are all alone. We are connected by our common humanity but alone in our experience of that humanity (Fact #1, People are people, page 4). Losing sight of this leads to huge boundary failures and a level of codependence that is difficult for others to appreciate. Until this basic condition of human existence is embraced, I believe we will experience difficulty resolving many of the problems of meaning and relationship that complicate our lives.

There are many patterns of codependence that have been defined. We are not going to go into an exhaustive exploration of them. Several, however, are worth note.

Enabling/Caretaking

Enabling or caretaking is doing things for other people that they can do for themselves, without being asked. These behaviors are almost always present to some extent in codependent relationships. It can be overt or covert in nature and it can be done consciously or out of the enabler's awareness. Enabling is an epidemic among American families as far as I can tell. It appears to be part of the overall transformation of the United States into a nation of victims. I have met very few families, on a professional or personal basis, that do not engage in this behavior. Moreover, most families do so at a pathological level. I have many good friends and family members trapped in this wretched behavior pattern and it is painful.

Well-established enabling behaviors are also very difficult to change, because the enabling person believes that what they are doing is good for the other person and, usually, they believe they are *supposed to* be doing the caretaking. More importantly, the enabling person usually has a core issue around value or competence, and they actually need the caretaking activity in order to feel good about themselves. Because the behavior involves the enabler's core issues, they often are not even aware of the true reasons for it or the actual impact of the behavior on the object of their care. Generally, the enabler sees no option and will frequently report that they "have no choice; after all, I am his father" (or mother or whatever). The relationship will be symmetrical with regard to the dimension of power and helplessness. That is, the child will accept the definition the he or she is not capable because it means they do not have to face the hard part of life, and since the behavior starts early, it is all they know. After all, if a parent or happenstance of life tells me that I am incompetent, or valueless from the moment of birth, what else am I to believe?

Parents define the majority of an infant's world, and the underlying messages and nonverbal behaviors of parents during these formative years cannot be ignored. Children are not born with adult boundaries in place. If a parent begins obsessive caretaking during infancy, due to the parent's core issue, the baby cannot discount the input. It is simply taken in. I have known a father who purchased twelve cars for his son and spent well over a hundred thousand dollars in legal fees in less than two years, as a result of his son's repeated DUI offenses and continuous substance abuse. "What else can I do?" the gentleman asked in a group session. "I am his father. He has to have a car to be able to get to work." As long as I was acquainted with this family, the father never saw any options and especially never saw the damage he was doing to his son. He believed he was being a good father; he was doing what he was *supposed* to do. This father was trapped in the belief he had no choice. Of course, we always have choices. Our "supposed to's" are self-imposed limits. We invent them in order to help us cope, but they end up restricting our ability to be authentic. The veil of this father's beliefs kept him from noticing the fact that his behavior made his son into a cripple. Even though wealth would mean the son might never suffer physically or financially, the chances of developing an authentic life are pretty slim. We see the effects of enabling and caretaking in a variety of areas: financial, emotional, and spiritual. Most of the time, no matter how flagrant the behavior, those involved do not perceive any problem.

RELATIONSHIPS AND ROLES

A 42-year-old man has an accident on slippery roads and ends up in a ditch, with his wife unconscious next to him. He grabs his phone and calls his father. He does not call 911. He calls his father. His father calls 911 for the man and then arrives on the scene ahead of the police and paramedics to manage the situation. Clearly, calling his father instead of 911 in this situation endangers his wife as well as himself. It is not a functional response. More than likely, however, neither the father nor the man sees anything problematic with this behavior.

A 40-year-old woman experiences dizziness and falls in the shower, striking her head hard enough to knock her out. When she wakes up, in a pool of blood on the bathroom floor, she manages to crawl to get her cell phone out of her pocket. She does not call 911, however. She does not even call her husband, who is working out in the garage. She calls her mother. Her mother calls her husband, who then walks from one end of the house to the other to see how serious the situation might be. In this case the enmeshment between mother and daughter not only affects them, but interferes with the marriage. The mother has interjected herself into the marital relationship. The mother has become the third party in a triangular relationship in which the daughter talks to her mother about her relationship issues, rather than talking to her husband. At the same time the husband talks to his wife's mother as though she is an extension of his wife.

An elderly man, who has managed to save up for a marginal retirement after decades of hard work, spends most of his savings to support his daughter following her third divorce. He does this despite the fact that his daughter refuses to get a job or make any efforts to support herself. She is thirty-seven and perfectly healthy but bleeds her parents' retirement until their deaths, then goes on disability for the rest of her life.

Many, many families have several kids who are functional, self-supporting members of the community, but also have one child who is supported to an extent that deprives the parents of their retirement and builds resentment among the other siblings. When I have asked such parents why they provide this level of support to the one child and nothing to the others, the response I usually get is something like "The other kids can take care of themselves, Johnny cannot." Thus it is clear in the minds of the parents and the particular child, a role has been established—a role that requires the child to be unable or incompetent and that further requires the parents to provide lifetime support. The "child" in this case can be fifty or sixty years old. Age does not matter. The child can also have college degrees and other accomplishments that would seem to indicate at least an average ability to function. None of this matters either. The roles result from our definition of self.

Susan comes to an inpatient facility when she is twenty-nine. The immediate impetus for her admission is her mother, a prominent physician. The mother reports Susan has a persistent history of drug abuse, intermittently disordered eating, poor relationships, especially with men, and failure in school and work usually due to lack of attention or interest. Susan's mother reports that there have been several suicide attempts and numerous threats of suicide. Susan also engages in occasional self-mutilation. Her mother provides all available medical records and a list of current medications and makes arrangements for an intake interview for Susan with the understanding that if she is considered appropriate for the program at the facility, she will be admitted immediately. There is only one advance phone conversation with Susan in which she indicates she is willing to come to treatment but does not think it will do much good.

RELATIONSHIPS AND ROLES

On admission to the facility, Susan presents as withdrawn. She is an attractive young woman who dresses unfortunately and who has multicolored hair with numerous piercings on her face and body. She offers minimal responses to questions from intake workers and counselors. Her initial psychiatric interview produces lots of NOS (not otherwise specified) and "rule out" findings due to lack of input from Susan. In her group therapy Susan is almost non relational and only slowly begins to interact. As she begins to develop trust in the counselor and other group members, Susan completes exercises designed to develop a picture of her childhood and adolescent years.

The counselor learns that Susan's father was a non-participant in Susan's life. He was often working and her parents divorced before Susan was ten. Susan describes her father as distant, powerful, strange, and dangerous. Susan describes her mother as serious, competent, controlling, caring, and needy. From an early age Susan recalls being aware that she cannot function or perform at a level equal to, or expected by, her mother or others. When asked how she came to the conclusion that she was not capable, Susan replies, "Because she has to do things for me—things I should be able to do for myself." With a very brief flash of anger she continues, "…like getting me in this place. Apparently she doesn't even think I can sign myself into the insane asylum on my own…" The flash is quickly replaced with resignation as Susan continues, "I guess she is probably right. I never have done anything much for myself."

As Susan works her way through treatment, she describes a "suffocating" relationship with her mother but professes profound appreciation for the support her mother provides. Susan relates that she has a hard time with things like school and even everyday life skills, and "If it wasn't for my mother, I probably would be dead."

She also describes how her mother prevents her from trying anything on her own. Susan describes her mother's overprotective behavior as embarrassing and overpowering.

Gradually Susan and the counselors begin to decode Susan's competence core issue. In addition to basic incompetence Susan has also come to believe that she is not smart. Despite scoring in the 90th percentile on several assessments, she believes she cannot learn complex material at all and what she does learn takes her much longer than most people. This is associated with a set of beliefs about being lazy. Susan's laziness is a result of her beliefs that, since she is incompetent and not very smart, almost anything is going to be very hard for her and the chances of success minimal. Since failure is the probable outcome, she decides trying is not worth the trouble.

There are a whole set of automatic thoughts that keep Susan from performing even simple daily chores on a regular basis. A task such as washing the dishes and cleaning the kitchen begins to feel to Susan like an impossible mountain to climb—a crushing cloud of defeat. She thinks things like, "Damn, look at that mess; it will take forever to clean it up," and "I don't feel like it now, maybe later when I am in the mood," and "I don't really have enough time right now to do a good job of it, so I will just wait." All of these thoughts are based on lies, of course, but the effect is to render even the simplest tasks insurmountable. Let's examine the lies.

First, there is no indication that cleaning even the filthiest kitchen will take forever—maybe an hour. Using the word "forever" in her thinking portrays the task in a whole different light. This kind of catastrophic language makes the task seem much larger than it is. Next, there is no indication that putting off a task like washing the dishes makes it any easier. If anything it will actually make things more difficult since, with the passage of time, more dishes accumulate. Of course in Susan's case, her mother's periodic appearance at the apartment and subsequent cleanup of the mess tends to prove to Susan both that things will get easier (because someone else will take care of it) and that Susan herself is not only unwilling, but unable to take care of herself. The belief that there is an easy way around most boring tasks is also instilled and perpetuated. This leads Susan on a lifelong quest to find the easy way around things, rather than just dealing with what is in front of her. So Susan's mother colludes in maintaining the faulty automatic thoughts as well as Susan's competence core issue. The idea of waiting until she is in the mood is also faulty automatic thinking.

Let me speak for myself here. There never has been and never will be a time when I will feel like doing the dishes. There are a lot of things that I will be in the mood for from time to time: sex, ice cream, tamales, or training dogs. At no time, however, will I ever be in the mood to wash dishes. The same is true for Susan, but she allows the faulty thinking to convince her to put off something that is more easily done on a routine basis. The notion of not having enough time assumes that the whole job must be done at once, and making a dent is not advantageous. The bottom line is the dishes don't get done; neither does the laundry, nor many other domestic tasks. So the mess gets worse and her procrastination serves as proof of her beliefs about the difficulty of the task and, more importantly, her general incompetence and laziness. This kind of thinking extends to all Susan's efforts, in school, work, relationships, everything. Some of this thinking is made obvious in treatment with Susan's procrastinating on homework assignments and failure to keep up with her laundry. The thinking behind these

Susan's Dysfunctional Schema

Developmental Issues	Core Issues	Intermediate Beliefs Compensating Thoughts	Symptoms
Safety	I am safe enough	I am not able to take care of myself. I am too lazy to accomplish anything. Life is too hard for me. My mother has to work very hard just to take care of me. It is a good thing I am loveable and pretty, or nobody would take care of me. I can make up for being incompetent by being attractive.	Self-Esteem Issues
Value	I am loveable		Boundary Issues
			Anxiety
			Relational Issues
Competence	I am not competent		Control Issues
			Spiritual Issues
Spirituality	I am alone I am different		

Table 12.

behaviors is explored by counselors and Susan, but progress is slow.

As the family week program approaches, Susan makes herself very anxious, certain that she will once again disappoint her mother with her poor performance in treatment. Susan does begin to display more frequent flashes of anger toward her mother's behaviors during group sessions and is encouraged to explore this anger. Her competence issue is so deep, however, that her sense of reality is impaired and she does not trust her own perceptions regarding her emotions. She recounts many times when her mother would tell her she should not be discouraged or should not "feel like a failure." This convinced Susan that she could not even accurately describe her own emotional experiences. Susan has no protection boundary and a wall of containment. Susan and her mother are enmeshed, both codependent on one another. When family week arrives, Susan and her mother present a classical case of codependence to the staff.

Arriving on campus for family week, Susan's mother immediately asks for consultations with Susan's psychiatrist and key counselors, neither of which are part of the family week program. She demands to review the chart and see what additional assistance Susan is going to need. She also wants to review all medication decisions. She is willing to participate in the family sessions, focused on increasing communication effectiveness, but does not think it is an important factor in treatment. She has always done everything possible for Susan and knows what is best for her daughter. Susan's mother does not see any problems in the relationship with her daughter and believes they communicate effectively. For the entire first day, Susan's mother engages in a power struggle with facility staff over the meetings and discussions she wants.

In initial meetings with counselors, Susan's mother relegates Susan to the sidelines of the conversation, constantly answering questions that were directed at Susan and ignoring Susan's attempts to speak for herself. The same thing happens in family groups, and counselors struggle to get Susan's mother to exercise some containment. The mother's core issues drive the behavior of course. Susan's mother is Karen from Chapter 3 and, as we know, she has significant issues around value. Karen needs to believe she is doing everything she can for Susan. After all, she believes that "...her only true value lies in providing for her daughter." Thus for Karen, there is no choice. She sees it as her responsibility, and it is the only thing from which she derives value in her life. She cannot see that her behavior has contributed to Susan's ongoing incapacity.

In situations such as Susan and Karen's, effective communication becomes extremely difficult if not impossible. Blame and shame play large roles in every interaction. Very seldom, if ever, do people in these circumstances find a way to communicate on an intimate level. Instead of listening to know, or sharing to be known, we listen to discover if we are okay (which is codependency) and share to explain or excuse. There is the magical belief that if I can successfully blame someone else, then things will somehow be better. Unfortunately, fixing the blame does not alter present circumstances. Discovering that I was abused as a child does not have to have an impact on my present behavior. Excuses are defenses of core issues, attempts to hang on to the distorted beliefs. Thus, we generally filter the available data in conversations to confirm our own suspicions about ourselves and about others. When I work with people suffering these kinds of relationship problems, I suggest four things to focus on.

Accept responsibility for my emotions
Let go of the outcome
Share to be known, listen to know
Neutralize core issues

Accepting responsibility for my emotions is accomplished by believing, or constantly reminding myself, that my feelings come from my thoughts, and my thoughts can be identified and managed (Fact #2: Happiness is not something that happens to us. It is something we do. Fact #3: We all have everything we need to be happy Fact #5: My feelings always come from my thoughts. Fact #7: The belief system consists of ideas, not facts. And Fact #8: Ideas can be changed). Furthermore, our happiness is contingent on our willingness to manage this process. Thus our emotional consequences are our responsibility and we do not have to react to what the other person is doing or saying. This means it is possible to sit and listen to almost anything and not lose the protective function of our boundaries. My protective boundary will stay in place because I recognize that the other person's behavior is mostly about them, and offers clues to their reality. People generally do not want to accept responsibility for emotions because it is hard. Also because it requires self-reflection and we don't always like what we see in the mirror, especially if we believe we are "not enough" or incompetent.

Letting go of the outcome involves understanding that the world is not under my control (Fact #1: All people are people. Fact #6: Things always happen the way they happen. And fact #9: Everyone's behavior is mostly about them, not me). While I am in control of my self; I cannot control the behavior of others, or the consequences of my behaviors. We cannot predict the future because we have excluded psychics from this discussion. Not only is the world not under my control, it is also not about me. Powerful as I can be in determining my own personal consequences, the universe does not center on me (never mind what I may have said to my kids and coworkers on a number of occasions about being the center of the universe). Meaning that whatever happens, however other people choose to behave, their behavior is not up to me, nor is it about me. That is, whatever someone else says, even if it is directed at me, it does not necessarily mean anything to me or about me. Just because my son says I am a lousy person does not make it so. Just because I have been a lousy parent does not change my basic humanity or my ability to become a better parent. I may have to acknowledge that some of my behaviors in the past had a negative effect on my son and others, but it does not change who I am in the present. This is an extremely difficult concept to grasp and a difficult skill to build into our conversations. All we can do is our best, and then wait for the results.

When coaching people through couples work or family communications exercises, I often encounter folks who have made themselves absolutely terrified. Like Susan, they generate massive anxiety in anticipation of the session. Sometimes they arrive for the session in a near panic state, requiring de-escalation before being able to begin. Often I suggest to clients that the possible outcomes of the session do not justify the level of anxiety they are generating. I encourage them to examine the outcomes they are anticipating and point out that most of the possible consequences have either happened many times before (my father will get really angry with me) or that bad as they may be, they will not change anything important. Sometimes I have people count their fingers and toes; I tell them that we will take a similar inventory after the session and that I am betting the count will be the same. In other words, I am trying to help them see that they are catastrophizing the outcome.

Number 3—share to be known and listen to know—really means to practice using appropriate containment and protection boundaries. Remember, the reason to listen to the other person is not to find out if I am okay, or to find out who I am, or to get ammunition with which to manipulate them. It is to learn about the other person. I will frequently give folks the assignment to listen closely and, after the sessions tell me something about the other person they did not already know. The best way to do this is to practice and use all of the listening and talking skills discussed in the previous chapter. Those communication techniques are actually practical ways to make sure I am in appropriate containment and have adequate emotional protection. If I do not have any core issues activated, it is not necessary to even think about these communications techniques because they proceed from my internal congruency. Most of us, though, have some core issues that have not been completely resolved or we lack personal insight. Consciously practicing the communications techniques helps us to nullify the effects of activated core issues. It is a way to act as if I have no core issues and thus perfectly functional personal boundaries. Of course, the ideal is not to have any active core issues but that never happens to actual people.

If I have serious core issues that are activated, it is extraordinarily difficult to be relational at an intimate level. You will notice that Number 4—neutralize core issues—does not require that we resolve core issues. That may or may not be possible prior to a particular conversation. It may be that core issues imprinted in very early childhood may never be eradicated or totally resolved. However, it is necessary to at least nullify the effects of core issues. We do this first by becoming aware of what our core issues are, and secondly by sharing them with others.[42] Knowing I have a given core issue makes me more immediately responsive with countermeasures. It allows me to be alert to the nonfunctional beliefs and faulty automatic thoughts. This awareness makes it possible to accomplish the other three tasks and behave relationally in situations that might otherwise end up badly. Notice that I have just implied that Number 4 has to be done first. In reality there is no order.

All four of these tasks must be addressed if we are to be intimate with another intellectually, emotionally, physically, and spiritually. Intimacy is sharing my true self with another person. I cannot put off Number 4 and be intimate. If, however, I can actually resolve core issues, or at least marginalize them, I do not really have to worry about the four items on this list. All four items will occur automatically as a result of my integrated and

---

[42] Brene Brown (2007)

uncomplicated self. I also cannot just practice communication skills in accordance with Number 3 and expect that alone will result in satisfactory communications or more functional relationships. All four items have to be in play to assure a positive outcome. In family sessions the function of counselors and coaches is to assure these four items are addressed.

For Karen and Susan the task in the treatment program's family week is huge. Both have constantly activated and mostly unaddressed core issues. As Karen sits to listen to her daughter, her sense of value is at stake. She has lost touch with the fact that all people are human beings and as such have exactly the same value. (Fact #1: All people are people.) Because she believes herself to be valueless, she will attempt to deflect issues toward her area of strength: competence. This obviously is exactly the area in which Susan is least well defended since her core issue is competence. For either of them to hear the other person without becoming defensive requires setting aside their most sacred core beliefs about themselves and the world. I have known many people who struggled for decades trying to accomplish this. With adequate coaching and considerable luck, Susan may be able to see and hear her mother and know, for one brief minute at least, that all of the messages of incompetence Susan received were in fact expressions of her mother's struggle with her own core issue of value. Her mother's behavior was mostly about her mother. It is only when Susan can actually learn about Karen that this can happen. Karen also has an opportunity to see her daughter and herself in a new light.

Karen must be able to listen to her daughter talk about the ways in which Karen's well-meaning efforts have crippled Susan. For someone like Karen, who has no sense of value beyond her ability to take care of her daughter, this information can be devastating.

RELATIONSHIPS AND ROLES

There is the risk that she will conclude as a result of the new information that she has been right all along. She is worthless and her entire life has been a wasted effort to make up for what she lacks. On the other hand, Karen has the opportunity to begin to see her previous behaviors from a different perspective. She can learn that she is valuable in spite of her mistakes and past behaviors. I cannot recall all of the details of their core issues, but I will never forget one statement made by the daughter. Her mother had just realized the meaning of her daughter's comments; that is, that the daughter had been rendered helpless and dependent by the mother's efforts. At the end of the session when asked if there was anything else anyone wanted to say, the daughter told the mother, "I love you." The mother was stunned speechless. She looked at me with total incomprehension on her face. On questioning, she explained that she could not see how such a thing was possible after the way she had failed as a parent. I suggested she ask her daughter how it was possible. I never found out, but I would still like to know if the mother ever understood the profound truth expressed in her daughter's simple response. "I don't love what you do. I love you."

Enabling, caretaking, enmeshment, and other terms all describe patterns of boundary failures. Usually the failures are a combination of protection and containment failures. As with all persistent boundary failures, these involve active core issues. That is, when there is a pattern involved, our boundary failures are a signal of deeper problems. These deeper problems can only be resolved by looking to the belief system. An awareness of the facts of life can help us detect where our beliefs and thinking have gone wrong. The essential requirement is the willingness to face ourselves, as we are, completely, without omission.

Rules & Roles in the Family of Origin

As mentioned before, the patterns of our lives do not exist only in our mind. There are larger patterns that exist in our relations with other people, with life in general, and, ultimately, with the universe. The first of these in our experience of life are the relationships in childhood with our family. We have seen with Karen and Susan how core issues are passed down through generations. The issues may change, as in the case of Susan, or remain the same, as in the case with Karen and her parents. Susan's core issues arose in the context of her relationship with her mother's over involvement. Karen's core issues developed in the context of her family and the abandoning father and sexualized view of women. These family roles define our function and purpose in the earliest social unit of our experience. If we are to understand ourselves, and the patterns of our behavior, it is very helpful to first understand the context in which they developed. "The family is the external context in which a person…develops."[43]

Fact #10, meaning depends on context. Victor Frankl gives an example of the chess move.[44] If we ask, "What is the best possible chess move?" we discover the only possible answer is "It depends." There is no value of any move except in the context of a particular game. If we define the situation and our goal of the moment, then we can determine which move will be effective. The same is true in life. There is no meaning outside of the context of our existence. Just as the meaning or

> #10 Meaning Depends On Context

---

[43] Satir (1988)
[44] Frankl (2006) page 131

value of a chess move depends on the context of that particular game, the meaning of our life depends on our particular context, which is itself a product of our perceived reality. In other words, meaning depends on context, and context is a function of our reality. The scope of the context may vary, based on our awareness, but any meaning can only be drawn from the context in which we find ourselves. Our context is our reality.

The first context in which we find ourselves in this life is our family of origin, whether it is a nuclear family or an orphanage. The people and patterns of these early relations instill in our minds our initial set of core beliefs, memories, and values. As with anything else, we find there are patterns to the ways families operate and train children. These patterns have been described as family rules and roles.

Families can be classified as functional or dysfunctional, just as we classified emotions. Functional families are characteristically open to emotions and changes, support the development of the individual, and are flexible with regard to roles and rules (see Table 13). Dysfunctional families are rigid, secretive, and do not allow individuals to choose their own roles. Usually, dysfunctional families are also shaming and blaming in their approach to discipline.

As a result of the dysfunctional environment, children grow to adulthood with a number of irrational or faulty beliefs about themselves as well as a lack of information about how to be relational. The relationships with parents in particular can set a pattern for future relationships.

Relationships with parents can be healthy, enmeshing, or abandoning. In a healthy relationship the child is taught how to be relational and intimate while maintaining functional boundaries and a sense of self. In the early years, attention is directed almost

FUNCTIONAL FAMILIES	DYSFUNCTIONAL FAMILIES
Open system, evolving and expansive	Rigid, closed and secretive
Mistakes are addressed and forgiven	Mistakes are judged and punished
Emotions are allowed and shared	Emotions are controlled and avoided
Roles are negotiated	Roles are assigned and do not change
System supports the individual	Individuals support the system
Parents model relational skills	Parents are enmeshing or abandoning
Individual boundaries taught & modeled	Individual boundaries are not taught or modeled

Table 13.

completely from the parent toward the child. As the child grows, the parents facilitate independence, and attention is gradually shifted so neither person is dependent on the other. In many cases this is not what happens. In many families the child is subjected to abandonment or enmeshment.

In the case of abandonment, the parent's attention is directed away from the child. This can be due to divorce, death, the parent's addiction, or many other reasons. The causes of the abandonment do not matter; the impact on the child is the same. The child has no model for relating to people of the same gender as the abandoning parent. There is associated grief for the loss of the important relationship. When the grief is not resolved and there is no alternative role model for the missing parent, the child comes to adulthood believing he or she needs the love and attention of another person in order to matter. This neediness has been referred to as love addiction and dependent personality.[45] Someone with this background will be consistently afraid of abandonment, and this fear governs their every move. The result is that to be in relationship with them is a lot of work. This excessive neediness ultimately drives the other person away thus reinforcing the fear of abandonment. This fear involves a number of erroneous beliefs,

---

[45] American Psychiatric Association (2000), Mellody (2003)

the basic one being "I need…" This person has lost sight of, or never learned, the basic Fact of Life #2 15 (Happiness is not something that happens to us. It is something we do) and Fact of Life #3 (We all have everything we need to be happy. There is nothing else any of us need.) They also are not in touch with Fact #5 (My feelings always come from my thoughts) because they believe their feelings come from others—that they cannot be happy unless the other person loves them. This is the opposite of a person raised by an enmeshing parent.

When parents take more from their kids than they give, this is enmeshment. The child becomes the caregiver. The attention is all directed at the parent's needs, and the child has to become a small grown-up way before his time. This can occur because the parent has a chronic illness, mental health issues, or an addiction, or just because the parent is emotionally immature. Sometimes a parent whose marriage is not working out will use the child as a surrogate spouse. As with abandonment, the reason for the enmeshment is irrelevant, but the impact is the same. The impact in this case is that the child experiences the relationship as suffocating. The child learns that intimate relationships are painful. This person grows up with a fear of intimacy. The condition is referred to as an avoidant personality or love avoidant. Like all human beings she or he needs connection with others and yearns for intimate, meaningful relationships. However, each time such a connection begins to develop, the avoidant person begins to feel stifled and draws away. This creates an endless cycle of seduction, followed by rejection, followed by seduction. This pattern, like the love addiction cycle, is debilitating and unsatisfactory. With both abandonment and enmeshment, the context teaches the child how to be in relationships. Beyond these general patterns, there are often specific roles assigned to family members in dysfunctional families.

There are many roles that have been defined by various writers. Table 13 is a compilation of some of the various roles that have been observed in dysfunctional families. In dysfunctional families, these roles are assigned to the individual and can be extremely rigid. This is because the family system organizes itself around particular problems, and any change in the role of an individual challenges that organization.

A classic scenario is the philandering father whose sexual escapades are an open secret in the family. Like the proverbial giant elephant in the middle of the room that nobody talks about but everyone has to skirt carefully around, this secret and its protection become an organizing principle. The mother is incapacitated by various core issues and abdicates her role as protector of the children. In fact she becomes needy and enmeshed with at least one of the children. The child who is enmeshed with the mother is assigned the role of placater or caretaker. This child often becomes a surrogate spouse. Another child may be assigned the role of hero. It is this person's responsibility to "fix" things. She cleans up after the mother and father, sometimes making sure that bills are paid and no untoward damage to the family's reputation in the community occurs. Still another child may become the mascot. This role is kind of like a court jester, providing comic relief to everyone. Meanwhile the scapegoat has the task of acting out the pain of the family system. The scapegoat often becomes the "identified patient," kind of a designated hitter for the family who acts out to take the focus off of the real problems. The emergency quality of the problems created by the scapegoat means they have to take precedence over other issues, and thus the system is preserved without secrets being

RELATIONSHIPS AND ROLES

compromised or real problems addressed. You will also often find a people pleaser among the crowd. This person takes on the task of making everyone feel better, regardless of what is going on. Each of these roles carries with it a burden of cognitive distortion (ill-founded beliefs about the individual and the meaning of that person's life). Very often these roles, or significant components of them, live on into adulthood in the form of core issues. When this happens the individual can be stuck in a lifelong pattern of relationships that strive to recreate the situation in the family of origin.

If the meaning of a child's existence is defined by the context, by the assigned role, the person has a very painful time finding meaning outside of that role. Thus we will have a need to find relationships in which we can continue to play the familiar role and have some sense of purpose and belonging. Being trapped in a role assigned by the family of origin can cripple a person for life. It is very difficult to break out of these patterns because we believe that we risk losing our sense of self and our tenuous sense of value. In fact, no such risk exists.

The difficulty arises out of the fact that we do not recognize the

ROLE	BEHAVIORS	FUNCTION
PLACATOR	Always agrees with everyone. Never says no. Mediates problems. Perfectionist, unable to relax, never ask for help, never make mistakes.	Reduces conflict. May be surrogate spouse or sibling.
HERO	Solves problems, manages families business	Keeps things working no matter what problems there may be.
MASCOT	Never serious, always joking and makes others laugh. Attention seeking, poor decision maker.	Stress relief. Shift focus
SCAPEGOAT	Inappropriate expression of anger, self-destructive, defiant, rebellious.	Identified patient. Distraction from dysfunction in the family.
PEOPLE PLEASER	Always nice, no matter what is going on. Sees only the bright side. Always cheering up everyone else.	Soothes and suppresses

Table 14.

roles for what they are. We are immersed in the situation. If you grow up knowing only your role, and only your family system, you do not have the data available to notice what is going on. It is only as we grow older and become exposed to other family systems and the larger social system that we can begin to gather comparative data. When this happens the child becomes aware of the role they have been playing. "Awareness of your own role is the turning point."[46] Once we have this awareness it becomes possible to deconstruct the core issue into its component beliefs and make changes. This core work, the investigation and restructuring of our belief system, is what will eventually set us free. Living in the quagmire of assigned roles, with the attendant enabling, dependencies, denial, and isolation, reduces us to something less than our human potential. While many of the patterns developed in our family of origin become lifelong habits, they need not be. Not only family roles, but everything we have discussed in this chapter has this one thing in common.

While it may feel as if the roles we are assigned, and the rules and marching orders of the family of origin, are laws of nature, they are not. They are just ideas. Dysfunctional boundaries, codependence, dependent personality, enabling, and caretaking and many other patterns of behavior are all based on faulty thinking. These insidious patterns of behavior can all be changed once we recognize their basic nature. Making ourselves aware of the ten facts of life and developing a habit of self-exploration can break any of the cycles, no matter how well entrenched. No unhealthy habit or pattern of relating can stand under the light of self-awareness.

---

[46] Black (1999)

Ten Facts of Life Summary

At this point we have discussed all of the ten facts of life. Below is a list of all ten facts together with some of the associated factoids.

1. **All people are people.**
    Everyone is human.
    All humans have exactly the same value.
    All people make mistakes, fight, fart, fuck, forget and are generally messy.
    All people are connected to all other people.
    All people need meaning in their lives.
    What I do is different from what I am.
    What happens to me is different from what I am.
2. **Happiness is not something that happens to us. It is something we do.**
    Sometimes happiness requires hard work.
    Many people decide it is not worth the effort. That is their choice.
    Happiness can coexist with suffering.
3. **We all have everything we need to be happy; all the time.**
    Nobody else can do it for us. (No guru, priest, therapist, shaman has the answers I need)
    I only need to pay attention to my self with total honesty.
4. **Everyone's reality is different and everyone's reality is valid.**
    Intimacy requires accepting each other's reality no matter how divergent.
    Another person's reality or perception of me does not define me.
    Everyone's reality, especially mine, changes from minute to minute.
    My reality is the context of my life.
5. **My feelings always come from my belief system, my thoughts.**
    I cannot blame my feelings on the behavior of others.
    I cannot be responsible for, or cause other people's happiness or pain.
6. **Everything always happens exactly the way it happens.**
    Once something happens it becomes a fact.
    Facts cannot be changed.
    Facts are exactly as they should be because that is the way they are.
    Life is not fair. Life is not unfair.
    Life is uncertain.
    Excuses do not alter consequences.
    Bad thing happen to good people and good things happen to bad people all the time.
7. **The belief system consists of ideas, not facts.**
    Facts include everything that is and everything that has already happened (See number six above).
    The ideas in the belief system include beliefs, memories, values, expectations, assumptions, opinions, etc.
8. **All ideas can be changed.**
9. **Everyone's behavior is mostly about them, not me.**
10. **Meaning depends on context.**
    My perceptions determine the context – not some absolute reality (See number 4d above).

CHAPTER 7

Mood Disorders and Grief

In the previous chapters, we have described the ten facts of life that we believe are important for a life of contentment and happiness. In the next two chapters, we will take a look at how these principles operate in the real world. It is ignorance or lack of acceptance of the ten facts that results in distress and misery. This distress does not necessarily reach the severity that requires formal therapy or psychiatric diagnosis. Common, everyday depression, anxiety attacks, and phobias may go untreated or even unacknowledged. Nevertheless, they account for the vast majority of all human suffering. This chapter will discuss the application of the ten facts of life to the mood disorders of anxiety, panic attacks, phobias, depression, as well as grief.

Before we begin these discussions, there is a point that needs to be made. Recall from Chapter 3 that one characteristic of emotions is that they all have a physical component (page 62). The human body contains systems designed to mobilize energy to respond to emergencies and other needs. This system involves pretty much the entire body when fully activated. There is much we could describe about this, but we are just going to refer to it as the body's alarm system. This alarm system is part of the 99 percent of us that is the same person to person. What is not the same is how finely tuned the alarm system is for each of us. For some people, for whatever reason, the alarm system is set to a hair-trigger status. Thus it can be activated for very little reason or no reason at all. In the absence of an actual threat, we may find ourselves experiencing sensations such as racing heart, changes in breathing, sweaty palms, even changes in vision. These and a host of other possible sensations can be puzzling, even frightening. This can be interpreted as a heart attack, stroke, or other life-threatening condition. It is also likely that this will be interpreted as some sort of emotion such as anxiety. When I feel certain sensations, it is natural to look around for some threat or danger. Finding none I make the best interpretation I can and call it anxiety or fear. Actually it is not an emotion as we have defined it (see page 61)—the sensations start in our body, not in our mind. We often become genuinely worried or anxious about the sensations because we interpret them as a sign of something wrong, and this complicates the picture.

There is not a name for this situation. Much of the time these purely physical sensations are labeled as anxiety or depression, as a panic attack or even mania. However, this is not simple anxiety as we are discussing below. It is a physical problem and requires the intervention of a physician. There are medications that can regulate various aspects of the alarm system and without them no amount of talking therapy or positive thinking will help. If the sensations have become identified in such a way as to result in actual anxiety, then both medical and psychological intervention may be required. In either case it is important to rule out medical conditions as causes before we rush to the judgment that we are experiencing a purely emotional problem. Effective mindfulness includes an awareness of the origins of such sensations and thus a more accurate assignment of meaning. That said, I now return to the regular, dogmatic, black and white discussion of mood disorders.

Anxiety

There is no such *thing* as anxiety. (Told you I was going to be dogmatic.) As with self-esteem and other concepts, it is not a thing like a shoe or a kitten. It is a process. There are also no somatic or physical manifestations of anxiety. You cannot have a manifestation of something that does not exist. Anxiety does not accumulate in the body until it bubbles over in various sorts of symptoms. It is not a liquid, solid, gas, or anything else. "…anxiety is a conscious experience…"[47] of a person's perception of vulnerability and the resulting marshaling of resources to deal with that vulnerability. Let me hasten to add for those affected by chronic somatic symptoms of anxiety that what I am talking about here is not the continuously activated alarm system that is characteristic of several disorders. These processes do not have a cognitive component and thus, in my definition, they do not fall into the category of anxiety proper. They can be debilitating, and no amount of talking therapy will alleviate those symptoms. I am referring to anxiety as an emotion which therefore has a cognitive process. The process involves first the perception or appraisal of a threat. This can be an accurate perception or a misperception. Regardless of the accuracy of the perception, once a threat is perceived, several of the body's systems are activated. Notably the sympathetic and parasympathetic nervous systems prepare the body to cope with the perceived crisis. This activation involves a number of changes in the body such as heart rate, sweating, etc. These are real, physical processes that affect the body; collectively these processes are sometimes referred to as the stress response. These physical processes produce sensations in our body that the conscious mind perceives. Our belief system is then used to

---

[47] Beck (1985) page 51

ANXIETY/STRESS PROCESS
Stimulus > body's physical response > sensations > beliefs > perception/interpretation of sensations

Table 15.

interpret or give meaning to the sensations. This is the point at which a threat is perceived.

Stress, as the term is commonly used, also does not exist. Most of us know, at some level, that stress and anxiety are processes rather than things. We then go on, however, in daily discourse to talk about being "under a lot of stress" as though it is an actual physical object mashing us down. This is just not the case. Being "under stress" is again the sensation of having our alarm systems activated for some reason. Again, this can be a result of a purely physical process which is miserable and often diagnosed as anxiety. I am going to use the terms *stress* and *anxiety* rather interchangeably in order to focus on the process. The reasons for stress or anxiety can be physical, physiological, or mental. That is, my body's systems can be activated by an induced chemical stimulus, like an injection of adrenaline, for example, or something I eat or inhale; or the same systems can be activated as a result of internal physical processes producing hormones and other chemical stimuli which cause sensations in my body. Finally, these very same systems can be activated by an idea or belief that I am in danger or about to engage in some exciting activity such as sex. Fear and excitement both incorporate arousal, and the physical sensations are almost exactly alike. It is the function that is different, and the function is determined by my perception of the situation. If I perceive that I am about to be killed by a tumbleweed, the exact same sensations in my body are activated as if I perceive a tiger is about to kill me. Furthermore, many of those same sensations are activated if I perceive that I am about to have sex. The actual intentions or capacities of the tiger or the tumbleweed are irrelevant. It is my perception that can start the process. In the end anxiety is still a process and not a thing.

I want to emphasize here that while the process of generating anxiety is primarily one of perception and beliefs, the experience of anxiety is something quite different. When the alarm systems are set off, the process becomes organic. It does not seem like something I am doing. It seems as though it is something that is happening to me, and it can be terrifying. This is because, once the mind has done its job of perception and interpretation, the process is handed off to the sympathetic and parasympathetic nervous systems, and at that point, the process does become organic and somewhat automatic. Once it becomes an organic process, it is hard to recognize or to interrupt. Despite the realistic nature of the experience, however, it is still a process in which I am engaged. It does not come from outside, and the solution to the problem does not lie in the immediate external experience but in the internal origins of the process, in our beliefs, expectations, assumptions, and automatic thinking.

Since it is a process and not a thing, I cannot accumulate stress or anxiety. There is no savings and loan for storing anxiety. If there was, we would no doubt have a government agency to regulate it. I cannot make periodic deposits of anxiety to be drawn on at a later date. It is a process that I am either engaged in or I am not engaged in. I may have a very strong habit of thinking and reacting that engages the stress response quickly in a specific situation as a result of previous experiences. This we would refer to as a trauma reaction, the psychological residue or emotional scars we remember from accumulated life experience.

To be sure, continuous activation of the alarm systems can have deleterious effects on the body. Continuous activation of the body's alarm system takes a huge toll. The effects of these processes can accumulate over time, resulting in actual physical scars, inflammation, cellular deformities, etc. Furthermore the location and nature of that toll can be determined by what we believe or think about the situation. This can result in physical scars that accompany the emotional damage. This is what lends to the perception that anxiety or stress has "settled" in a particular part of the body. If I play tennis, I can get "tennis elbow". This is the effect of repetition of a series of actions. There is no "tennis elbow" as a separate thing that has landed on my arm like a dragonfly or raindrop. You cannot pick up one in the pro shop. It is damage resulting from repetitive use in a particular pattern. I can treat the symptoms—take anti-inflammatory drugs, apply heat or cold, or wear braces, etc.—to treat the problem. This might make my elbow feel better and possibly, over time, improve the condition somewhat. If I keep playing tennis in the same way, however, I will never get rid of the tennis elbow. Tennis elbow is the result of repetitively engaging in a particular activity in a particular pattern. If I want to stop having tennis elbow, I have to stop playing tennis, or change the way I play tennis. Anxiety is the same and so is trauma. These are the results of repetitively engaging in activation of the body's alarm system in a particular pattern and in response to particular stimuli. They are habits of thought, feeling, and behavior. Since they are habits, they can be changed.

 To say that anxiety is a process means that anxiety is something I do, like tennis; it is a behavior. It is not something I caught off a toilet seat in Thailand. Since anxiety is something I do, the cure for anxiety is to stop doing it. I will not cure anxiety with antibiotics or other substances. I can certainly interrupt the anxiety process by introducing various chemicals, but that does not mean I will stop the behavior or the thoughts generating the anxiety. It just changes, or reduces, the sensations associated with engaging in the behavior of anxiety. Let me repeat myself: If I want to cure anxiety, I have to stop doing it. Unfortunately, most of us concentrate on reducing the sensations associated with anxiety rather than examining or looking at the activity producing those emotions.

Remember that anxiety is pretty much the same as fear, which has a function like every other emotion. The distinction is that fear is usually a response to a specific threatening object, whereas anxiety is a response to an anticipated or imaginary threat. I have fear when confronted by a snake, or nuns. These pose, or may pose, an immediate threat. I have anxiety when I anticipate or imagine a future threat, though there is not a physical materialization before me at the moment. The function of anxiety is to warn us there is something we need to deal with. It is like the fire alarm system of our body. When the fire alarm goes off, the functional response is to first look to see what the reason for the alarm might be. Is it an actual fire or cooking smoke or a malfunction in the system? If we determine it is a malfunction in the system, we correct it either by repairing the equipment or buying a new alarm.

Unfortunately for many of us, when our somatic alarm system goes off, the first thing we do is turn off the alarm, except for those who are addicted to intensity as a way to distract from the pain of core issues (we will discuss that in Chapter 7 though). This is especially true with what we consider to be clinical or pathological anxiety. Generally this is done through the use of some kind of chemical intervention, street drugs, alcohol, or prescription medication. This is the equivalent to shutting down the fire alarm without checking to see whether there might be a real problem. We might get away with it a few times, maybe many times if we have a poorly designed system, but sooner or later it will have catastrophic results. Don't forget that our emotions exist for reasons. The reason for, or function of, anxiety or fear is to warn us of a potential or immediate danger. The question often is "What is the danger?" In many cases the danger which anxiety warns us about is the result of problems in our thinking rather than actual danger in the world.

We have already described that problems with our thinking can be faulty logic, inaccurate perceptions of danger, exaggeration of the importance of the situation, or misperception of bodily sensations. Many of us are chronic worriers, constantly on alert for potential danger. As a result of some sort of safety issue, we cannot let our guard down. Reality seldom supports such concerns. As a good friend puts it, "The things we worry about most hardly ever happen, while the things that do happen are worse, but we cope." In addition to anxiety produced by unrealistic assessment of danger, there is also anxiety produced because some of our beliefs are contradictory or incongruent. They don't fit with each other.

There are many ways our beliefs can become incongruent or contradict one another. They also can be incongruent with our behavior. Such is the case of a person who professes to be religious but never attends church and does not follow any of the precepts of the church. I can believe that smoking pot should be illegal but also believe vehemently that the government should not control our personal behavior.

Anxiety can be a warning of emotional pain. Like physical pain associated with a cut on my hand, it can be telling me that I should look at my thinking, to listen to myself. Once again the need to listen to ourselves is the critical factor. "The obedience of faith, like that of friends to each other, asks us to listen to and respond to the depths of our honest experience. ...It is obedience to the truth of ourselves and our lives that is the essential psychological note of the true believer."[48] It is only when we are willing to be honest in this way that we can begin to unravel the sources of our generalized anxiety. The first step in this process, however, is just to believe in the facts of life we have already discussed. If I believe in the facts and respond to the "depths of (my) honest experience," I have done all I need to do. I will eventually resolve internal conflicts, become grounded in reality, as I know it, and eliminate unnecessary anxiety.

Unfortunately, many of us avoid this level of self-awareness at all costs and go on believing that we are defective or broken or substantively different from others. We often avoid looking into the core of our selves. To look into those depths provokes fear— the fear that we are, in fact, going to discover that we are monsters of some sort and have no hope for improvement.

I remember a patient who came into treatment following years of drinking and sexual acting out. As treatment proceeded the patient became more and more depressed and hopeless. In a conversation with her one day, I realized that she was doing everything she could to avoid considering the actual state of her being. Much of her acting out had been a way to numb herself from the pain inside, the pain of her core issues. On top of that, the behaviors she had been involved in during this time were truly disgusting to her. I asked if she ever thought, "What kind of person must I be to have done that?" The result was a small panic attack that took several minutes for her to overcome. She finally calmed down and we talked about her fear of finding out what she is really like. The idea that she and I were pretty much the same was totally

---

[48] Kennedy (1974), page 45

incomprehensible to her. She was convinced that at the core of her being there must be a grotesque and disgusting troll that truly did not deserve life. That fear was the pain she had spent years avoiding. Rather than experience the pain to the fullest possible extent, and then explore its origins, its fallacies, and its truths, she had numbed herself with sex, drugs and intensity seeking behaviors (I am not willing to blame rock and roll). I suggested to her that her pain was, in fact, her best friend. All I could say to her was the thing she feared was the source of her salvation. I said, "That pain is your best friend and, if you are willing to embrace it, you will find a way out." I do not know if she eventually did find a way out. She seemed to improve in mood after our talk and was much more active in treatment but was discharged to another program soon after I talked with her. I do know that this "fear of self" can be a most debilitating trepidation.

By "fear of self," I refer to the core belief that there is something so defective, broken, or evil about my essential being that to comprehend it would bring the equivalent of total annihilation. This belief is a type of cognitive distortion. It is catastrophizing an outcome. The result is that I can become terrified of examining myself and thus be cut off from the very activity that is my salvation. The fact is, whatever I discover about myself is not going to change me. I have been existing and getting by, whatever I am made of, and that won't change just because I come to consciously know what I am. This is in addition to the fact of life that I am probably a human, so it is very doubtful that I am going to be significantly different from others.

Nevertheless, I have seen men come into my office in a tortuous state of anxiety, convinced there is something wrong with them because they found themselves, at some point, attracted to someone other than their wife. This seemed to them to be so wrong and different from others that it would destroy them and their relationships to even talk about it to their wife or a friend. This results in horrible isolation from others and precludes the possibility of relational or spiritual connection. It is excruciating. It is also ludicrous. Men are attracted to women, by and large, and woman to men, unless you are gay. The basic mechanisms of physical attraction operate regardless of promises made or of marriage vows taken. To deny this is to deny our humanity. To assume that we are different than others cuts us off from the shared experience of our humanity. Differences of gender and sexuality or gender identity are trivial in the context of our common humanity. Further, not to allow discussion or exploration of the sexual nature of our humanity increases the chances that we will act on the repressed and unexamined impulses. In other words, if we don't talk about it, we are more likely to do it. Remember, all people are people (Fact #1, page 4). Anytime we begin to operate on the assumption that we are significantly different, we are creating an insurmountable obstacle.

If I am afraid of my self, and I believe I am different from others, I have nowhere to turn. I cannot approach others, because I am so different that nobody will understand and I run the risk of being ostracized. I cannot even explore my own experience because I am too afraid of what I will find. In this situation, sex, drugs, and intensity make as much sense as anything. Intensity seeking and distracting ourselves from the pain and the problem seems the only way out. But, of course, there is always another way.

If I have placed myself in a situation where I believe there are only two options and both are unacceptable, what I need to do is return to the facts of life. I do this by reminding myself that everything in my mind is a thought or a belief, and thoughts and beliefs can be changed; they are not facts. Just because I think something does not mean it is factual. Thoughts are merely ideas. Even if I did act on it, that does not mean I am doomed beyond recall. People are people. We all make mistakes (Fact #1: All people are people). Sometimes our mistakes result in horrible consequences. This does not change the basic facts. What we do does not define us. If I begin to remind myself of these facts of life, I will come to believe them. Once I believe in the facts of life, I will eliminate all sorts of unnecessary anxiety. This starts with the willingness to look at my self, warts and all, to be totally honest and curious about myself and what is going on in there.

Panic Attacks

Panic cannot attack us. In order for that to happen, panic would have to be a thing. It is not. Like anxiety and self-esteem and many other concepts in this book, panic is something we do to ourselves. Panic is a form of anxiety, and as such it conforms to all of my comments about anxiety. Nevertheless, the American Psychiatric Association (APA)[49] considers it a separate process, and most people who have experienced one consider it to be a significant event, so we will take a look at it. Remember that anxiety is a process that involves somatic sensations in our body. In the case of panic attacks, these sensations are extreme and become the focus of additional anxiety. Many people have experienced a small panic attack and don't even realize what's happened.

---

[49] American Psychiatric Association (2013). The DSM-5, on page 214, indicates that "panic attack is not a mental disorder and cannot be coded. Panic attacks can occur in the context of any anxiety disorder as well as other mental disorders" Thus, while listed as a separate classification, it appears to be more accurately considered a feature of other actual disorders.

Have you ever laid awake at night and begun to notice your heartbeat? At some point it turns to an obsession. It may seem as if a beat was skipped or, perhaps, the beats are coming faster. You can't be sure because at first you were not paying close attention. Now you focus. You convince yourself that it is true and your heartbeat does seem to be louder and a little faster than is normal. Perhaps it is even a little irregular. As you focus your attention on your heart, you begin to worry. This worry is a form of fear and anxiety. This begins to start up the body's alarm system. Of course when the alarm system is activated, there are a number of physical changes, and suddenly you notice that you have begun sweating, just a little. Many of us at this point "shake it off." We get up and watch TV, do something to distract from the troubling sensations, hoping they will pass. These sensations and thoughts usually do pass. If they do not and they begin to get worse, perhaps because there is a physical problem, the functional response is to investigate and deal with the problem. In a "panic attack" we do not do this. We just continue to focus on the sensations. If we do not stop focusing and catastrophizing about these sensations, we can end up with a feedback loop in which our physical sensations lead to catastrophic thinking ("I am having a heart attack" or "I am going to die") which increases the fear. This in turn produces more physical sensations and, just like audio feedback from a rock band, the whole process can get out of control. Hope is not totally lost though. There are several steps to take when in the throes of a panic attack. They are the same things a therapist will often do to help someone out of a panic state.

<u>Breathe</u>. Focusing on our breathing distracts us from the focus on the "symptoms." It also alters body rhythms and invokes a relaxation response.

MOOD DISORDERS AND GRIEF

<u>Orient</u>. Again, this is an attempt to distract from obsession with the sensations in our body. If I count the tiles in the ceiling, or make myself notice other details in the immediate environment, I will, again, not be so focused on my panic.

Learn to <u>recognize sensations</u> in my body as what they are. Don't assume every twinge is a sign of impending death. Get used to knowing my body.

Learn to <u>recognize the thoughts</u> that occurred immediately preceding the symptoms. In this way you can identify any fears leading to the physical sensations.

<u>It cannot last forever</u>. Remember, panic is a feeling, an emotion, not a fact. Wait it out. Nobody can remain in a state of terror for very long.

There are also some things you can do between panic attacks to reduce the impact or learn about the causes. If you are having frequent attacks, consult with a medical doctor. There are medical conditions such as hypoglycemia that can produce the same sensations. Any medical issues should either be ruled out or dealt with. You can also inoculate yourself against misinterpretation of physical sensations. That is, when you are not having symptoms, engage in some mild exercise and raise your heart rate. As you do this notice the details of what it feels like. Check out the way your heart feels beating at this quicker rate. Observe the way your breath becomes a little labored and you begin to sweat. Also becoming familiar with these symptoms places them into a category of normal, rather than life threatening. Then, when the symptoms occur in the context of a panic attack, you can more easily break the anxiety process. Plus you will be better able to identify the thoughts producing the symptoms. This is called panic induction and should be done with someone else present if you are prone to severe panic attacks.

Phobias

Phobias can be defined as obsessive fears of specific objects or situations. They are a form of anxiety, and all of the previous comments apply. Additionally, phobias are susceptible to being changed by a specific set of techniques that are rather straightforward in application. Because of this straightforward approach we will take a quick look at how these things work.

A phobia is an irrational fear. Fear is an emotion. All emotions start with beliefs. Therefore, phobias start with beliefs. Generally our phobic beliefs are lies. For example, a fear of flying is not based on the data regarding the safety of flight. Folks who are afraid of flying usually have no problem riding around in cars. The data is clear that cars are a much more dangerous way to travel than planes. The fear of flying or eggs or anything else is a phobia when it is an irrational fear. A phobia can be innocuous and not a problem. When a phobia begins to interfere with our ability to function, it can become a serious problem. This means we are operating on faulty beliefs about the object of our fear. In addition, our fear-based behavior means we have no way to gather real data to challenge the false belief. In other words, because I avoid the object or activity of my fear, I have no way to find out what the actual danger might be.

The solution is to collect enough data so that the belief is no longer supported. There are various techniques therapists use to help change phobic beliefs. All have one thing in common. They provide a means for gathering information, in the form of data or experience, which contradicts the false belief. As with any false belief, there are two primary methods we can use: We can use logic and external data or we can gather experiential data.

Many irrational or false beliefs are not even logical. This is especially the case if we keep the facts of life in mind. That is, the beliefs do not make much sense if we stop to really think about them. Suppose I discover that someone at work does not like me. Many of us will start to have some feelings about this. Some of us will actually begin to feel shame or some level of embarrassment. Perhaps we will feel anger. In the case of shame we know the belief is that we are "less than" or inadequate in some way. This is not logical. Somebody else's behavior or opinion is about them and does not determine my worth and value (Fact #9: Everyone's behavior is mostly about them, not me. Page 120). There is no logical connection between someone else's behavior or feelings and mine. If that were the case, then my feelings would be affected whether or not I knew about the other person's behavior. In reality it is only because I know about the other person's behavior that I am affected. Thus the difference is in me. The fact that someone else is mad at me, or disappointed with me, does not change me. In fact it says nothing at all about me. It is not logical if we bear in mind that people's behavior is mostly about them. The question that needs to be asked at this point is "How am I making myself feel embarrassed or shame over the fact that she does like me?" Notice that I do not ask, "How does this make me feel embarrassed?" The second question presumes that my feelings result from what is happening in the world, the activating event. Since my feelings do not come from the event, this question cannot produce a useful answer. If instead I ask how I am making myself so embarrassed, then there is a greater chance that I will discover what component of my belief system is causing the problem. My attention is directed at the actual source of my shame, my thoughts.

If I look here I can discover my internal workings. In other words, I will come to know myself and how I operate. I may even begin to see the patterns in my beliefs and emotions and gain control over them. I can use thought reports to help with this process. In many situations, though, logical analysis alone may not suffice, especially in the face of an entrenched phobia. In these cases I may need to gather real-world experiential data in order to modify an irrational fear.

If, for example, I am afraid of spiders, part of my irrational thinking can be due to a lack of experience with or data about spiders. I can gather data, from books or other sources, about spiders and the dangers they may pose. This is seldom enough to reduce or eliminate a phobia, though it can help. What I really need is experience with spiders. I need to go consort with the actual, living creature. Personal experiential data is much more powerful than static facts drawn from other people's experience. The trick is to make sure I do not create additional spider trauma by trying to overexpose myself or expose myself too quickly. Generally, with a deep-rooted phobia, it is best to seek the help of a therapist. A behaviorist can assist in desensitization or help you develop a program of graduated exposure. With such a properly designed program, most phobias can be eliminated in very short order. This is one area of psychology in which we do have pretty good science and very good results.

Depression

Depression is a malady of the spirit. Sure there are physical concomitants, just as there are with chemical addictions. It is my perception, however, that some of what the Diagnostic Statistical Manual, $5t^h$ Edition lists as symptoms are actually the causes of depression. Of the symptoms listed for Major Depressive Episode

MOOD DISORDERS AND GRIEF

in the DSM-5,[50] four of them are emotions or thoughts; that is, lack of interest, sadness, feelings of worthlessness, and thoughts of death or suicide. In addition, for a diagnosis, at least one symptom must be either depressed mood or loss of interest or pleasure. These are basically mood issues, rather than behavioral (insomnia) or physical (weight loss). Mood means feelings, and we should know by now where feelings come from—and it's not from storks. Feelings come from our belief system. While there may be some situations in which depression begins with some sort of chemical imbalance, I suspect these are somewhat rare. What is not rare is coming face-to-face with the facts of human existence and the lies we believe about life and ourselves.

Like anxiety, depression is not a thing. However, unlike anxiety, it is not something we do; it is instead something we fail to do. Depression occurs when we fail to construct any meaning in our life. Or when we construct false meanings based on irrational beliefs about our worth and value or our place in the world. False meaning, based on core issue beliefs, will in fact lead to the most intransigent kind of depression. Whether it's caused by a total lack of meaning or false meaning, depression is a state of mind. In my experience, depression can be considered almost normal when we observe the frequency of its occurrence in the population. Sooner or later almost everyone experiences a period where they lose all sense of meaning—and this is depression. The physical correlates to depression can turn up anywhere in the body, but are mostly in the brain. A quick review online shows research indicating that the subgenual cingulate, the parahippocampus, the visual cortex, and other brain centers are involved in some way in depression. In

---

[50] American Psychiatric Association (2013) page 160. The DSM-5 is the "bible" that psychologists and psychiatrists use to diagnose their patients.

addition, there are many chemicals that can cause or alleviate the symptoms of depression to some extent. In my opinion and experience, however, these factors are not determinate. I believe depression proceeds from, and is maintained by, our thinking. Like anxiety and many other processes, it results in and involves physical correlates. Nevertheless, it is in the mind that we find the origins.

Believing that my existence has to be somehow justified or that I somehow have to "deserve" or "earn" the right to live is a common and heartbreaking source of depression. Believing that I "should" be somehow different, or better, that I should "make up for" my difference from others in order to qualify for continuation puts us on an excruciating and possibly endless treadmill of despair. When my mind holds these kinds of assumptions about my worth, value, and membership in the human race, hopelessness, exhaustion, and depression follow.

Depression, then, is a loss of meaning. From previous chapters we know a couple of things about "meaning." First, meaning depends on the context. Second, our perceptions of things around us determine the context. Third, our perceptions are limited to our five senses, filtered by our belief system. If I am not aware of certain aspects of the world in which I live, for whatever reason, then for me, those factors are not part of the context in which I construct meaning. The broader and more detailed my understanding of the context of my life, the more useful and enduring will be the meaning in my life.

Meaning for people has two components: place and purpose. Human beings need to know they belong and they need to have a reason or purpose. These two components comprise the meaning of our lives. When either of these is missing, we are depressed. When both are missing for a significant length of time, we die. Notice that I did not say losing our sense of purpose and place causes depression. It is more fundamental. Loss of these two drivers of our lives is depression itself. While these concepts are in the mind, the mind-brain connection is important to understand. I believe our need for meaning arises out of the development of the brain in the areas of causal reasoning and pattern recognition.

Causal reasoning refers to the ability, actually the need, for us to figure out the chain of cause and effect for as many things as possible. Understanding the chain of cause and effect is what allows us to predict outcomes. Clearly this is an advantageous faculty. Many animals have a similar ability. I cannot deny this when I watch my cat leap up and try to turn the doorknob. Clearly at some level he has figured out that activity around the doorknob is related to or "causes" the door to open. It can be argued that people have developed this skill much further than any other creatures on this planet. How often and how well we use this faculty is another matter.

This is how human beings could figure out that a seed placed in the ground would produce a wheat plant. It is how we noticed that if we water the seed and seedling, the resulting plant is more likely to reach maturity and bear fruit. Billions of these kinds of observations about our world and the things in it result in civilization. It is because of our innate, hardwired need to understand the causes of everything that we have come to dominate this world so completely. Our lines of inquiry include everything we can detect with our senses, and many things that are beyond our senses. The systems of our brain strive to insure that everything around us must have an understood cause. Our brains have been designed for this kind of reasoning. There are areas of the brain concerned with cause-and-effect relations. When there are things that occur without explanation, an imbalance is created.

When there is no adequate empirical information on a cause, we will make one up and operate on that assumption until further evidence demands that we change it. If we are driven to understand the causes of everything, sooner or later we must ask, "What caused me?" and "What do I cause?" In other words, "Where did I come from and what is my purpose?" I believe this forms the biological basis for the human drive to find purpose and meaning in life. The second biological mechanism, pattern recognition, is just as important.

In order to discern cause and effect, I must be able to recognize patterns in my environment. In fact, all animals must be able to do so. Pattern recognition is a basic capacity wired into the sensory organs and brains of any creature that survives. Being unable to recognize many basic patterns renders an organism unable to organize data into useful information. Such organisms would be unable to function in the world. Thus pattern recognition underlies the ability to construct cause-and-effect relations, and all of this together allows, or requires us, as a biological mandate, to have meaning in our lives. So the question arises, how do I construct meaning for myself?

Probably thousands of books have been written addressing the meaning and purpose of human existence. Many of these inquiries are philosophical or theological in nature and have only limited value to a person who has lost her way. Depression is a personal experience and requires a personal solution. That is, we all must have a personal reason to live. The general tenets of philosophers and religious leaders do not help much when one is facing the loss of all meaning in one's life. When we are just going through the motions of our life, a more personal approach is required for meaning. That personal approach revolves around the twin components of purpose and place.

Purpose does not have to be a big deal. I once heard someone, somewhere; say that the secret to life was to always have something to which they could look forward. That is a pretty good guide. My purpose can also be a duty or an obligation that must be fulfilled. That could include making sure that everyone in my family, those I am responsible for, always has something to look forward to. It could be suffering in place of another person. Whatever the purpose, we must recognize that it comes from within. While there may be larger purposes for me, decreed by God or the universe, I cannot know what they are. That particular context is far beyond my ability to comprehend.

Remember that all meaning comes from context, and my context is a function of my personal reality, my direct experience of the world. My context then will always be limited, a small subset of whatever the universe or God has going on. So, I cannot know God's purpose for me. That is a matter of faith. What I can do is come up with my own purpose within the context that is my experience of life, which is relatively simple to describe but can be hard to accomplish.

It is important to realize three things in our pursuit of purpose. First, that purpose is not something that necessarily remains the same for a lifetime. Things change. Our purpose today may not make sense in the new context of tomorrow. I have to accept that developing a purpose is a skill that I may have to employ continuously in my life. Second, I cannot find my purpose; I have to make it up. My purpose is not hiding in the grass somewhere like an Easter egg. The task is more like selecting a purpose, or making up a purpose. Knowing that all purpose is temporary, however, I do not have to get too worked up over finding the right purpose. There is no right purpose; there is only my purpose now. If I have a purpose just for today, that is good enough. Third, my true purpose, in a spiritual sense, cannot be driven by a core issue. Remember Karen in Chapters 3 and 5. She had a purpose. Her purpose was to take care of her daughter. The caretaking was driven by Karen's core issue around her own personal value. When we develop a purpose that is a disguised attempt to compensate for a deficit in our perception of safety or value or competence, it is not a true purpose. In this case, whatever the purported purpose, the real purpose is to make up for our core issue, and this will not only fail to alleviate depression; it will make it worse. It will make it worse because we know that we are, in effect, tricking ourselves. It is like the person who manipulates a spouse into behaviors designed to "prove" their love. When the spouse complies, there is no satisfaction, because the actuality is that the behavior was requested, or demanded, and it is proof of nothing. If I attempt to construct a purpose in order to make up for my perceived faults, all the purpose can accomplish is to demonstrate how lacking I am. It is like a gift given with expectations and strings attached. A true purpose must take into account all of the facts of life we have described.

In the case of Karen and Susan, several facts of life are ignored. First, Karen sees it as her purpose to make Susan happy. This is not consistent with facts 2 and 3 (happiness is not something that happens to us; it is something we do, and we all have everything we need to be happy). Nobody can make someone else happy. We all have that to do for ourselves. In Karen's case, she not only fails to have a legitimate purpose of her own, she helps Susan stay helpless and prevents her daughter from finding true happiness.

A true purpose has to occur at a spiritual level. There is no sure-fire formula for coming up with a purpose, but there are some guidelines.

MOOD DISORDERS AND GRIEF

1.	What kinds of things are easy for me? (Things that just seem to come naturally).
2.	For what do other people most often compliment me?
3.	What do other people often ask me to do for them?
4.	What do I enjoy doing, just because I enjoy the activity, regardless of whether or not it is productive or anybody else knows?
5.	When I have no demands (work, school, parenting, etc.) what do I generally do with my time?
6.	What kinds of things are <u>always</u> interesting to me?
7.	What kinds of things make me cry (other than my own personal tragedies)?
8.	What do other people need from me?
9.	Who do I admire and why? Who are my heroes?

Table 16.

In order to know my purpose, I first have to know myself. This echoes a theme the astute reader may have noticed in every chapter. One major key to happiness is to know myself as thoroughly as possible. If I have active core issues, and we all do, the probability of being able to develop a sense of purpose that will work is pretty small. Knowing myself, the patterns of my thoughts and feelings, I can then start the process of constructing a purpose by noticing the patterns in my behavior and life in general.

There are things we are good at. There are things we just enjoy, for no particular reason but the joy of it. There are things we care about and value. To help sort out these three areas, you might try asking yourself some of the questions in Table 14. Note that the nine questions are focused in the three areas mentioned above. The first three questions concern my talents and strengths—what am I good at. The second three questions are about what I enjoy—what I am passionate about. The final questions concern what I value—what are the causes to which I can devote my attention and energy.

When I know these things about myself, I can construct a purpose. The best purpose will be one that combines all of these three areas. In other words, if I am fortunate, I might find a purpose that combines something I am good at with what I like, and also what I believe to be important.

It is not necessary, however, for a purpose to combine all three of these. There are many examples of purpose that involve only one of the three areas. Many people can sing well. Many other people not only cannot sing but probably should not be allowed to sing. I belong in the latter category, along with most *American Idol* contestants. Those who can sing well have talent, the ability to construct pleasing melodies in space and time. They can do, almost without thought, things I will never be able to accomplish. I have known people who did not find singing particularly enjoyable. That is, they professed no special fondness or pleasure when singing. They did not sing when alone, just for the joy of it. Nevertheless, they possessed an "ear" for music and a voice that others found pleasant. The pleasure derived from the activity was from the attention they received. Being asked to sing and receiving accolades for the performance made the activity meaningful to them. This provides these people with a ready-made purpose.

Singing can become a way to connect with others. In choirs and concerts it can become a spiritual experience. It can even become a career. The purpose in this case is simply to make use of a natural talent. The sense of purpose derives from the use of the ability as well as the results obtained: the attention, money, and other benefits. For those fortunate enough to have a talent far above average, in any area, finding purpose can be straightforward. In the absence of active core issues serving to deprecate the significance of the talent, purpose becomes the exploitation of basic talent. Whether the talent is with music, numbers, mechanics, or paint, doing something I am good at can provide a sense of purpose. I have heard people describe this as fulfilling their destiny because they are "supposed to" or they "have to" practice the talents they have been given. That observation is a little too metaphysical for me. What I have observed is that folks who have an above average ability, of any kind, can find meaning in the exercise of that talent. This is purpose built on something I am good at (the first three questions in Table 14). In contrast, we can also gain a sense of purpose from some activities regardless of whether or not we are good at them at all or whether we derive any benefit.

I like to water. I will water anything, but grass is my favorite. Given the opportunity to water, I will stand all day long with a hose in my hand, watering. This is not necessarily a productive activity. I don't do it to accomplish anything or to please anyone. Indeed, it is probably inefficient considering that a sprinkler system on a timer would be less wasteful and require less attention. Many times, in point of fact, I hand water lawns that have automatic sprinkler systems installed. It also does not matter to me that the lawn is greener or covers better as a result of my watering. Strictly speaking, I do not do this in order to grow grass. I do it for the sheer joy of the activity.

While watering, I lose track of time. On occasion, I have become disoriented when interrupted, having been unaware of my surroundings while engrossed in watering. I do not think I am particularly good at watering. I don't even know what would constitute "good" watering. I also don't care. I don't care if someone else waters better than I do. I don't care if someone else thinks it is stupid or a waste of time. I don't care if the activity serves any larger purpose whatsoever. I just like to water. I never question the activity or attempt to justify it to myself. When walking along a particular sidewalk where I used to work, I would notice a bare patch of dirt at the edge of the lawn. The urge to water became almost instantly irresistible. If there was a hose available, I would have watered. This is only marginally under my control. I do not know where this impulse comes from. It may be genetic. It feels primal. It is not my fault. (If I have not been insistent enough by now, you should probably put the book down and go water something.)

This is an example of a purpose based on something that I just like to do (the second set of questions in Table 14). If one is lucky enough to notice such an affinity for a particular activity, passing time becomes easy. I can always water and not worry about anything, not even whether or not I feel good. I am beyond emotion. I am, in a sense, beyond purpose. When watering, I am fulfilled. Watering, for me, is a meditative state. This is somewhat different from a purpose based on values or service.

My father bequeathed to me a belief, a value actually, that we are all "part of the solution or part of the problem." I can remember him saying, along with my grandfather, that we all have an obligation to leave the world a little better than we found it. This is the founding principle for a purpose built on service or things we care about. If I believe in the reduction of suffering, or the preservation of the earth, or the need for more bees, or the importance of liberty, I can choose to put that belief into action. When I put my beliefs into action, I have purpose. When we consider the state of the world, and the inevitability of suffering by man and animal, the opportunities for this kind of purpose are boundless.

There are individuals who dedicate their lives to rescuing one breed of dog, for example. There are those who spend endless hours, and years, in pursuit of knowledge that will cure a disease.

Many people risk life, limb, and a lot of money to stop the harvesting of whales. Some people determine to become an expert in the propagation of certain types of plants. In all of these cases, the scope of the interest does not matter. Whether the result affects millions of people for thousands of years or simply makes one creature's life a little more pleasant, it is a contribution. It makes the world a better place because of my presence. That constitutes a value-based purpose. It does not have to matter to the entire world, or even a large part of the world. This kind of purpose does not have to be actually doing or accomplishing anything. It can be just putting up with something or someone.

Suffering in the place of or for the welfare of others can be a purpose. It has been said that "…suffering ceases to be suffering at the moment it finds a meaning."[51] If I choose to go without something so that another person's quality of life improves, this can give meaning. We can, in fact, make meaning, or purpose, out of almost anything. One important thing to keep in mind is that no single purpose is completely defining. We do not have to get it right, forever. We will be constantly redefining our purpose throughout life. There will be many purposes at different points in life. Coming up with purposes is an ongoing process. It is also a multifaceted process. By multifaceted I mean that it is possible, and desirable, to have more than one purpose at a time.

Our lives are complicated enterprises. Circumstances often dictate our activities. Having more than one motivating activity, more than one purpose, helps to insure that interruption of one activity does not result in a complete descent into depression. If a drenching rainstorm forestalls my watering, and I have nothing else about which I have passion, I am at a loss. If, on the other

---

[51] Frankl, 2006

hand, there are alternative activities in which I find purpose, I am stronger (if my alternate activity is singing, however, I might end up singing in the rain, and that would just be silly). Having more than a single purpose and being able to change purpose when necessary are both important skills. Remember, do not try to do this all at once, or once and for all.

Purposes change. Plus, the process of knowing me is ongoing because I change throughout my life. I need to make a habit of always being aware of myself and these areas of interest. There are other exercises available to help develop a sense of purpose. Just go online and search around. The important thing to remember is that my purpose does not have to be some earthshaking, monumental, or lofty goal. At a very basic level I am just looking for a reason to get up and put on my shoes in the morning. Secondly, my purpose is not something I am going to find lying around in a forgotten corner of the house. It is something I make up. The larger purposes are up to God or Nature or whatever. My purposes arise out of the context of my life, and the context of my life is restricted to my personal reality. Finally, making up a purpose is not a lifetime commitment like getting married. It is something I am going to be doing on and off for the rest of my life. It is whatever I am going to look forward to for now. I can, and often will, change it as I see fit. Creating purpose is best considered something like breathing. If I learn how to do it, and make it a habit, then I don't have to make a big project of it whenever it comes up. Just like breathing, if I don't do it regularly, I will suffocate. Constructing my purpose becomes an ongoing part of my life. The same caveats are true for making a place for ourselves.

In addition to having a purpose, I also believe human beings need to belong; we need to have a place. We are social creatures.

Most of us function better if we believe we are part of something larger than ourselves. It does not matter if that larger thing is a noble undertaking or a football team. When depressed, many people "feel" as if they do not belong. Thinking I am fundamentally different than other people sets me apart and leaves me without a sense of belonging. In this case I have lost touch with Fact #1: all people are people and I am one of them. On the other hand, perceiving me as part of a larger whole will result in a sense of completion and meaning—even if I see myself as just one pixel in the enormous mosaic of humanity. Being connected to that mosaic provides me a place. I belong. The fact is that all of us always belong; it is just that we cannot see it when we are lost.

Fact of Life #1 indicates that we are all people and, as people, we are all pretty much the same. What is often not obvious to many people is that we are connected. I have said it before and I will say it again: We are connected to other people, other species, all life, and at the end of the day, to everything. Assuming an optimal childhood, we retain an awareness of this connection into adulthood. Certain traumas of growing up, large and small, can serve to cloud our awareness and leave us out of touch with various facts of life. This results in one or more core issues. These distorted cognitive schemas all have one effect in common: They distort the perception of the context, the reality, of our existence. Most devastating of all, the distorted perception of our context can lead us to believe that we are alone and not connected to anyone or anything else by virtue of our difference.

Since all core issues are the result of trauma, and trauma veils our perception of the actual, immutable connection we all share, it is no surprise that some level of depression is associated with all of the core issues. Or, more succinctly stated, "Being abused is depressing."[52] One of the more important things we can do to overcome depression, or any core issues, is to verify the facts about our connection to others.

There was a friend of mine who became very depressed. He had lost a third significant relationship to divorce. He lived alone, had no pets or hobbies or activities. He came to sit on my porch and talk about his situation. As he talked, I listened carefully and heard his unstated belief that there was something wrong or different about him since nobody would stay in a relationship with him. One of his boyfriends had told him, on departing, "You are just too weird." As usual for me, I did not really know what to say. So, I listened and we talked for an hour or two. Several days later, I asked him to join me when I went to volunteer at a local soup kitchen, thinking it would do him good to simply get out of the house.

We arrived at the facility and began rather fevered work, as there were not many volunteers on hand. The activity alone had to be good for my friend, I thought. We finally had a lull and sat out back of the kitchen for a minute. I asked how he was doing and got the reply, "The same, maybe a little worse." My heart sank. My theory of "get off your butt and get active" was apparently not working. We went back to work. A second wave of customers rolled in, and we were so busy, I lost track. About an hour later, as things were starting to wind down, I noticed my friend sitting at a table talking with a man about the same age. Besides experiencing a little personal irritation that he was not in the kitchen helping, I did not think much about it.

Later still, I was through and ready to go. I found my friend still talking with the stranger. I let him know I was ready. After

---

[52] Ross (2000)

another few minutes, he shook the man's hand and came across the room. I could tell something was different just in the way he walked. Later in the car, he seemed to be much more engaged than he had been for a month. I asked what was up and he said:

"I started talking to that guy because he asked me a question about the kitchen. Then he started telling me about his situation. Man, that guy is *really* depressed."

"He's worse off than you, huh?" I was thinking the comparison had made a difference with my friend's perception.

"No, he is exactly like me!"

My friend had lost sight of the fact that we are all human and we are all in this together (Fact #1, page 4, All people are people). The sense of being apart and different was where he was lost. The chance conversation with someone going through a similar experience, and having the same thoughts and feelings, brought back the sense of connection and with that a renewed interest in life. Life might suck, but at least we are all in it together. Shortly after that, he got into a support group and began a rather quick recovery from his depression. My friend had become convinced that he was different and apart from the rest of the species. Meeting the other depressed person reminded him that we all face sadness and depression. It does not mean we are different; it means we are the same. Sadness and grieving are just part of the human experience. Even in the throes of severe pain, we are still human; we still belong. This sense of belonging gives meaning to our lives, sometimes even when we have created no purpose.

It is as if humanity represents a huge tapestry of billions of threads. Each thread is different in color and texture. Our particular life is a tiny collection of threads. From our vantage point we cannot see the overall pattern of the tapestry, if there is one. But we can see our place in it. So long as we are aware of how things fit together in our part of the tapestry, we have a sense of the context in which we live. We have a place. If we lose sight of this context and our place in it, we are lost. This kind of loss produces depression, and the only real cure is reconnection. We can try to numb the pain of being lost with medications, addictions, or distractions, but we will remain lost until we again see our place.

Grief

Grief is normal. Most people can grieve successfully without professional help. There are, however, those in my profession who act as if anytime someone is grieving, they need a counselor. This is ridiculous. Life is loss. Overall we get to keep nothing, and everything changes. If most human beings were not capable of coping with loss and trauma, we would not have survived as a species. Most people grieve successfully because it is a natural process, and the assistance of a professional does not make the process any easier or faster. Let me repeat and emphasize that no therapist, life coach, shaman, priest, doctor, friend, or relative can make the grieving process easier or faster for any of us. It is a natural process and a personal process that will run its course in due time if we do not interfere with it. "It is fortunate that, in the end, most people can cope with traumatic experiences if left to their own devices."[53]

First, let me point out some of the things that can be included as part of normal grief experiences: sadness, anger, guilt, anxiety, fear, loneliness, fatigue, helplessness, shock, yearnings, emancipation, relief, numbness, sense of unreality, various physical sensations (tightness in the chest or throat, breathlessness), confusion, preoccupation, hallucinations, sleep problems, appetite problems,

---

[53] Harvard Medical School (March 2006), page 1

MOOD DISORDERS AND GRIEF

dreams and flashbacks, restlessness, and crying.[54] This list is not exhaustive but it gives us an idea of the range of experiences associated with death and other significant losses. Some of these experiences can be quite frightening if we do not realize they are normal manifestations of grief. They are, however, completely normal.

About four months after my mother died, my father called me one night. Calling me was something he had never done much of, as it had been my mother's job, I suppose. So, I figured something was up. After some stalling around, he finally got to the point. He had a photo of my mother on the table next to his chair. At some point he looked at the photo, and my mother waved to him. He freaked out. His call to me was to find out if a) this was a paranormal experience, b) he was going crazy, or c) this ever happened to anyone else. I assured him it was a normal part of the grief process. He was somewhat reassured but called me several times over the following months to report repetitions of the experience and to inquire how long it was going to last.

Complicated grief occurs anytime the normal grief process is interrupted or incomplete. In these situations the grieving process either takes too long or is incapacitating. Grief itself is a process of putting the pieces back together. Remember that we constantly tell ourselves a story about life and our place in the world. Grief occurs when the story of our lives is disrupted. Abruptly my world does not make sense. The place I thought I belonged now looks different. Suppose again that my wife dies (I know, this is becoming tediously abusive). For my whole life my place was with her. Now she is gone and I have no place. For my whole life my purpose was to take care of her and share with her. Now I have lost

---

[54] Worden (2002), Neimeyer (2006)

that purpose. It becomes necessary to redefine my place and reconstruct my story. The story I had constructed before took many years and consisted of many details. All of this has to be redone. I have to have a new story in which she is no longer here, but is still a part of the story of my life. I have to develop new purpose and find a new place in life for me and a new place for her. This is not an easy process. It takes time.

There are at least five tasks or challenges that must be faced as part of the grief process:

1. Accept the reality of the loss.
2. Experience the pain of the loss.
3. Adjust to the new environment.
4. Redefine the relationship with the person or resource that is lost.
5. Reinvent yourself.

These are difficult and time-consuming tasks. Even when all are completed, the memory of the person lost will still remain, as will the fact of the loss. Things can never be the way they were. These tasks are not completed in any particular order, or in any particular time frame. The actual sequence is different for everyone. There are many variables that affect the length of time and the order in which the tasks are addressed.

The nature of the relationship is a very important variable. The closer, more intimate, and the longer a relationship has lasted will all impact the process. Relationships with unresolved issues can also take longer. The circumstances of the death are also significant. Sudden death early in life or very violent deaths will usually impact the process. Suicide often results in many more lingering questions than other types of death. Uncertain situations, such as someone lost and presumed dead, can also confuse the issue. Still, while it is possible to notice some of the factors affecting the grief process, it is not possible to predict how it will proceed for any individual person. The variables are too many and the interactions too complicated. Fortunately there are some things we can do to improve the odds that the process proceeds efficiently. Over my career I have found five actions that can be taken to move things along.

Believe in and remind myself of Fact #6 (things happen the way they happen).

Talk to myself and out loud to another person.

Do not isolate.

Don't start too soon.

Expect starts and stops, forever. It is not done all at once, or once and for all.

One of the most important things we can do to insure the grief process proceeds smoothly is to remember, and actually believe, Fact #6, "Things always happen the way they happen." Specifically, it is important to remember that death, or loss of any kind, is to be expected. In everyone's life, everything is ultimately lost. If a person lives a long time, it is reasonable to expect that many of those close to him will die. Discovering that someone has died should not really be a big surprise. It is to be expected. The same is true for loss of a job or property or anything. This is true whether we think the event was fair or not. Remember, life is uncertain. Bad things happen to good people, and good things happen to bad people—all the time. If I go around expecting that the way things are is the way they will be, I am going to spend a huge amount of time trapped in complicated grief. A true grasp of Fact #6 is critical. If we have this fact firmly embedded in our belief system, our overall approach to many things will change.

I find that I do best when I follow one simple sounding rule. Live every moment expecting only whatever happens next. The way things are is not the way they will be. Any given second could be the last. It is an excellent idea to remember this every day and pay attention to what is as though we will not have another chance to notice and appreciate. Thus, whatever comes next, loss or bonanza, would never be a total surprise. Approached with this belief, major losses are much more efficiently dealt with. This is something that benefits from advance preparation. In other words, if I have not believed that things happen the way they happen up until a loss occurs, I probably won't be able to suddenly view the loss in that context. Thus, thinking about death and loss—and coming to terms with Fact #6—is something we need to be working on at all times. After all, it is true at all times. It is no less true during a dramatic event than it was before or will be later. To be accurate, people who do not have this belief don't get stuck in complicated grief so much as they never truly start the grieving process.

As mentioned above, the process of grief is one of reconstructing the meaning, or story line, of our lives. The primary way we make up stories is by telling them. Storytelling is as integral to the development of the individual psyche as it is to the society. Educator Jim Trelease is reputed to have stated, "Story is the vehicle we use to make sense of our lives in a world that often defies logic." Thus, the primary activity of grief work: We must tell the story. There are lots of euphemisms for this activity. Counselors especially like to refer to "processing" our grief. "Grief work" itself is another bit of professional jargon. Redefine, reinvent, and reconceptualize—all of these words and phrases boil down to one thing: Talk about it. Talk about it to myself. Talk about it out loud. Talk about it to another person. Talk about it over and over. Reconstructing our story requires active storytelling. There is no substitute. The same is actually true for all types of trauma. The more we talk about any trauma-producing incident, the more normal it seems. Basically, if we tell the same story enough, it becomes boring. The problem with major losses is that we, and others, want to avoid the pain. Because the topic is uncomfortable, conversations about it become awkward. Also because of the pain, we may ourselves sidestep thinking about it. Attempting to elude the pain of the loss has deadly consequences. In order to avoid the pain, we avoid talking about what happened. Because we avoid talking about what happened, we can never move forward.

In the movie *The Everlasting Story*, there is a magical world called Fantasia, which is being destroyed because humans in the regular world no longer believe. This destruction is represented by an enormous, ever-growing dark cloud called "The Nothing." As human beings lose faith, The Nothing grows and is very close to consummating total destruction of Fantasia. The Nothing is a very good representation of what happens when we try to avoid thinking about and talking about the pain of loss. The grief just grows larger. Like The Nothing, it can, if ignored long enough, take over our inner world. The only tools we have in defense are self-examination and storytelling.

In the beginning, immediately following a loss, the talk will be, and should be, about what happened. The details of what happened are sometimes the very thing we want to avoid. Systematically recalling and retelling the events leading up to the loss, and the immediate impact, is a good place to start talking because it is a natural starting point. We can encourage this in one another by asking questions about what happened. "Were you there?" "What was that like?" "How did you hear about it?" Often asking what might be considered awkward questions gives others the permission they need to begin the process of storytelling.

There must be hundreds of workbooks dealing with grief. They offer countless exercises and activities to help "process" grief. Examined closely, the vast majority of these are simply structured ways of getting us to talk about, or write about, or think about what happened and how it fits into the story of our lives. The more active we are in talking about what happened and what we lost, the smoother will be our path. As implied, talking about the loss or the person lost should not be done in isolation.

Some writers view grieving as a social process that applies to families as well as individuals.[55] Thus, whenever possible, the primary talking and storytelling is best done with family members who most closely share the loss. In any case, it is vitally important to talk to someone, to stay connected to others. For some of us there is a tendency when injured to want to crawl into a hole and be left alone until it is better. This may work well when we are physically ill. I know when I have a cold, I prefer to stay in the bathtub and not have to deal with anyone or anything till it is over. For loss, however, this does not work so well. "…we are social beings who literally construct our identities in relation to the significant people in our lives"[56] Thus, in order to reinvent the story of our life, we need to reconstruct our relationship not only with the one who is lost, but with everyone else involved in the loss, especially family.

It is important not to isolate. The fact that bereavement leave in many places of employment is two weeks or less is actually helpful. While I suspect there are other considerations, possibly

---

[55] Walsh and McGoldrick (1991)
[56] Neimeyer (2006), page 46

financial, the fact is this arrangement forces us to reengage in our daily lives rather quickly. This is exactly what must be done to move the grief process along. We must be involved with others and go about our usual routines as quickly as possible. To sit and focus on the loss, outside of the social context of our lives, is to invite problems in grief. We need to be involved with others. Plus having to quickly reengage in our lives keeps us from attempting to resolve grief too soon.

Anytime we are in pain, there is motivation to get it over with as rapidly as possible. Unfortunately, with grief, this is just not feasible. On the contrary, attempting to process the grief quickly, immediately after the loss, can actually make things worse. For years a technique called Critical Incident Stress Debriefing was employed by professionals all over the country when major tragedies occurred. This consisted mostly of deploying professional counselors into the immediate aftermath of a disaster in order to get folks to begin the grief process as quickly as possible. The thinking was that the sooner one began to process grief, the less likely it would be to turn into complicated grief or PTSD. It turns out that Critical Incident Stress Debriefing was found to be "not only…ineffective for preventing PTSD, in some instances it appeared to increase the incidence of psychological distress."[57] Grief is a long-term process. It cannot be accelerated. In the initial days following a loss, we are struggling just to comprehend the reality of what has happened. To attempt to begin reconstruction of our assumptive world before the reality has sunk in will just complicate things. Things take time. Grief takes a lot of time. Attempting to hurry up the process does not help. Indications are that grieving the loss of a significant other will take anywhere

---

[57] Miller (2009)

from six months to four years. To attempt to resolve our grief in the first months, and especially the first few weeks, after a loss is just asking for trouble. The process is not quick and it is not predictable.

Not only is the course of the process not predictable, it is not constant. That is, we do not grieve continuously. Following a loss, there will be periods of intense pain and longing. Clearly during these times we are grieving. Then there will also be times when the pain is not so present. It is tempting to think we are done with grief at this point, but that is not the case. What we are actually doing is integrating the new meanings, the new story line, with what is going on in our life. We are learning to apply the new story. So the intensity of the process ebbs and then renews. Many people, on experiencing a renewed surge of pain and longing after a period of pretty normal adjustment, believe they have "relapsed" into grief and run in a panic to a counselor. This is not necessary. It is part of the process. If grieving is a process of reconstructing meaning, then it follows that the process will be similar to that for constructing meaning in the first place. Recall that constructing meaning is a skill to be applied as needed over a lifetime. It is not done once, nor once and for all. So it is with grief.

CHAPTER 8
Addictions

In my life I have seen a woman stop a ten-year heroin habit in one day. I have known men to suddenly walk away from years of meth use, without a backward glance. I have seen serious, long-term alcoholics abruptly quit drinking. In my own case I stopped a thirty-five-year heavy smoking habit in a minute flat. I have also, of course, seen hundreds of folks struggle for years, entire lifetimes in point of fact, with addictions they never quite conquer. From my perspective, the difference has always been in our belief system. Oftentimes there is also a genetic or physiological component to many addictions. In fact, studies suggest "…heredity accounts for about half of the risk that a person will develop an addiction."[58] I do not want to deny the fact that in these cases the task of quitting is harder. It is only harder though, not impossible. Genetics may spark but it does not fuel addiction. Even with this additional burden, the critical factor still appears to be the belief system and the extent to which the individual is in touch with the facts of life. First let me clarify my use of a couple of terms.

Addiction — by this I mean an obsession or compulsion to engage in certain behaviors (such as the use of substances, gambling, sex, work, or just about anything else). The defining characteristic is the involvement in the behavior despite serious and usually long-term negative consequences and despite repeated attempts to quit. I am not going to distinguish between dependence

---

[58] Miller (2006), page 8

and abuse as defined by some classifications. I am also not going to distinguish between chemical addictions (substance abuse only) and process addictions (behavior only).

<u>Addictive process</u> —The sequence of beliefs, thoughts, and emotions leading to or reinforcing addictive behaviors.

<u>Physical dependence</u>—A physiological condition in which there are physical symptoms produced in the body when a drug or medication is discontinued. This is a medical phenomenon that may or may not be associated with addiction. It is also the component of addictions that appears to be most associated with genetics.

<u>Tolerance</u> — Another physiological phenomenon wherein the dose of a medication needs to be continually increased in order to maintain its desired effects.

For me, there are two generally different addictive processes. These different processes involve core issues and therefore disregard the facts of life in slightly different ways. In my thinking, these are classified as 1) behavioral habits and 2) psychological dependence. Either of these may also be associated with physical dependence. These may furthermore be present together in the same person. First, let's look at the behavioral habits and use my smoking addiction as an example.

Behavioral Habits

We will start by going back to the basic A-B-C diagram. In Figure 1, we see an individual, myself in this case, who has stated, or been told, that he has to quit smoking. In actuality I told myself for a number of years that I should quit, and made many attempts without success. Eventually I wound up with diabetes, and my

ADDICTIONS

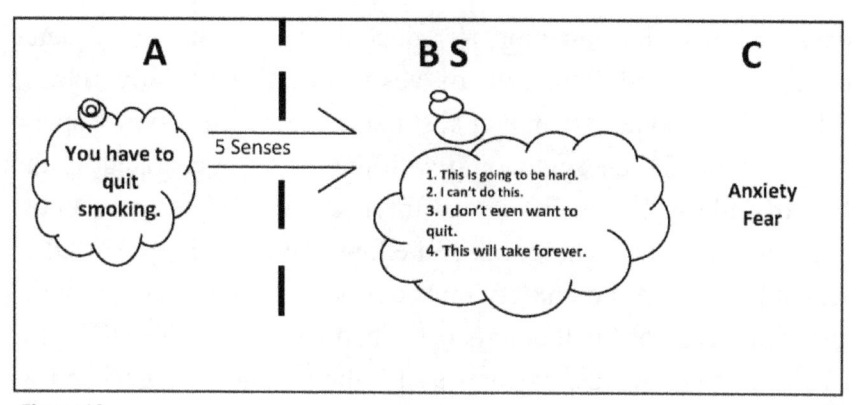

Figure 12.

doctor very convincingly showed me the data and explained how fast I was going to die if I didn't quit. None of this mattered to me, not in the least, and I kept on puffing. The reason I did not quit lies in my belief system. When the activating event of "having to quit" or "deciding to quit" occurs, several automatic thoughts immediately follow. Most readers will be able to imagine what they were. "This is going to be hard," "I can't do this," "I don't even want to quit," and "This is going to take a long time." (These are all shown under the BS in Figure 1.) Here, I am only addressing the automatic thoughts, not the underlying core issues. If you have paid attention to the previous chapters you know I have a core issue of competence, so it is logical that this generates and supports some of my automatic thinking. Especially the part about whether I can quit or not.

The result of this kind of automatic thinking, and the beliefs involved in the core issues, is the emotion of fear, or anxiety. I am going to use the word "anxiety" here because we are not talking about a specific object and because that is the way most of us would probably describe the experience. This set of automatic thoughts and the resulting anxiety drove my behaviors, which consisted of various attempts to reduce the anxiety (patches, plans, therapy, etc.) and the cycle of abstinence followed by relapse followed by another attempt at abstinence, etc. Typically, we spend a lot of time and energy coping with the anxiety generated by the fear of failure. If you have read the previous chapter, you know that anxiety is not a thing, but something we do. What we need to remember is that the anxiety only exists because of our thinking, and in the case of the thoughts described above, THEY ARE ALL LIES. In other words, as long as I believed the thoughts and as long as I kept lying to myself, it was going to be damned near impossible to quit unless I had almost superhuman willpower. In fact, very little willpower is required. Let's look at each of these thoughts individually.

"It is going to be hard." Really? I don't think so. Not doing something is hard? By the time I actually quit smoking, I had been alive for over fifty years. In that time I learned that some things are hard and some are not. Some things are harder for some people than other people. In general, I have found that digging a ditch is hard. Loading hay is also hard. Loading any kind of large truck is hard. Learning calculus was hard, for me anyway. Herding cattle, for my grandfather, was hard. In all my time, however, I found that doing anything is usually harder than not doing the same thing. Plus, I have never heard anyone else refer to doing nothing as a particularly difficult activity. So the idea that not having to look for my cigarettes, or other drug of choice, get my lighter, or other gear, and find a place where nobody will complain is altogether harder than having to do none of that stuff. When I tell myself that not smoking is hard, I am lying. If I quit lying, I quit creating the anxiety I will have to deal with. I will describe in a moment when and how this happened for me. Bottom line is that you have to learn to listen to yourself. Right now let's look at the second lie.

"I don't think I can do this." Here we have the direct effect of my competence core issues. In general, I never believed I could be successful at anything. Thus, I had all kinds of beliefs, self-talk, and intermediate beliefs telling me that I cannot do something. Often, as in this case, something I have already done. The truth is I had quit many times before. Remember, one of the things about the cognitive process is the way it filters information in order to confirm our beliefs. The assumptions I make to filter the incoming data are totally automatic and difficult to catch. "A person may not be aware of these assumptions any more than he is aware of the rules of grammar when he is speaking."[59] In this case I fail to notice all of the times when I had already quit smoking. Every day I sat through meetings, went to movies, quit smoking for a day or even two because of a respiratory infection, and engaged in all kinds of activities where I could not smoke. Unless the meeting or movie was very boring, I often didn't even think about smoking. The fact is that I quit all the time. However, this vital bit of data was excluded from my perception. Instead, if asked about quitting, for most of my life, I would reply, and firmly believe, "I can't. I have tried and I just don't have the willpower." Once again, I am not following the basic admonition: Listen to your self. Living in truth means I notice my self-talk, catch, and then stop the lies. If I quit lying, I quit the anxiety and a huge barrier is eliminated.

For many years when the subject of quitting came up, in addition to all my other objections, I would aver that the only reason to quit would be because someone else wanted me to (friends, doctors, etc.). I believed that I enjoyed it so much that no other factors could overcome the sheer pleasure. On the other hand, the habit did keep getting more expensive every year. Plus

---

[59] Beck (1985), page 63

keeping up with cigarettes and lighters, at all times, was always a pain, especially for someone with my attention issues. While true that I enjoyed it, I also enjoy living, and apparently I could not have both. So, if I really added things up, the conclusion is probably that I did want to quit. On any T-chart or other decision-making scheme, it is clear what the outcome would be. Once again, because of my beliefs that I couldn't and the fact that I was not listening to myself, I stayed in the fantasy that I enjoyed smoking, even more than life itself.

There are also the lies about how long it will take and the idea that I "need" the nicotine or whatever. Under logical analysis, these also fall apart. It takes no time to not do something; and, again, I had actually quit many times and gone for periods without smoking and without dropping dead. I might have been uncomfortable, but I got by. As with all of these lies, the real trick is to catch ourselves telling the lies to ourselves. We have to listen to the conversation in our head and actually pay attention to it. This is not easy because it is just like following the rules of grammar. With practice, however, and development of skills in meditation and critical thinking, we can learn to listen. The woman I mentioned at the top of this chapter, when asked if it wasn't hard to quit her heroin habit replied, "Nope, not once I really decided." What she was referring to was the moment when she heard herself telling the lies that lead to powerlessness. As soon as we actually hear that, we become powerful. For me it happened at a conference.

I was attending some sort of training in Phoenix, in a hotel off I-17. The morning session had been a long one, but we finally were told we could have a thirty-minute break. Great. I strolled out to the lobby to have a smoke and look around. When I reached into my shirt pocket, however, panic set in. I was out of cigarettes! I

ADDICTIONS

had run out driving over to the training and, running a little late, did not stop to stock up. I began to look around frantically to see if there was a gift shop in the hotel. I was also trying to remember if I had seen a convenience store nearby when I arrived. I began to engage in a very serious anxiety reaction. I remember thinking, *We only have thirty minutes, and I have got to have a cigarette.* That was when I heard the lie. That was the end of my addiction.

I noticed the thought "I have got to have..." and realized two things. This thought was the source of my fear and panic, and secondly, it was a lie. I clearly did not NEED a cigarette. I was not going to die without one. I did not "got" to have a cigarette. If I didn't bother to think about smoking, I would not even have any particular cravings. I had just gone about two and a half hours in the meeting without a cigarette and without even thinking about smoking. Clearly if I could do it for those two hours, I could do it for another two hours. I relaxed. I decided I would just wait and go to the store after the workshop. There was no hurry. Later, when the workshop was over and I was in the car, I decided that it was a lot of trouble to stop at the store right now because what I really wanted to do was get home. So I figured I would wait till later that evening.

I never have gotten to the store, never had another cigarette, and never had much of a craving that I remember. It did not seem to take much in the way of willpower. Like the woman who quit heroin, once I made the decision, it was not a huge problem. The key to the whole process, just as it was when I started going to the gym, was that I was listening to myself. I heard the lie. Once the lie was exposed, things could change.

I also did some other things once I realized the addiction was mostly in my head and based on lies. I did not set myself up by declaring that I was quitting. I thought of it as "I have not quit; I just haven't gotten around to going to the store." Thus I eliminated a lot of unnecessary anxiety. Eventually my wife noticed that I hadn't smoked in a while and asked if I was quitting. I replied that no, I just hadn't gotten to the store, and that was over fifteen years ago as I write this. Don't rush me.

Smoking is an example of a rather straightforward addictive process in that it is primarily a behavioral habit. Behavioral habits include not only the actual problem behavior such as smoking, but usually an associated set of behaviors. These associated behaviors result in construction of an environment in which the habit is supported. We tend to hang out with people who share the habit. Or go to places that facilitate the practice of the habit. There is a saying in the recovery community that in order to change an addiction, you have to change your playground and your playmates. This reflects the impact of associated behaviors. If I attempt to quit smoking but continue to be around people who are smoking, go to restaurants where smoking is allowed, and work in a smoke-filled environment, then my task is going to be more difficult.

If we examine the thinking involved in these associated behaviors, we will find cognitive distortions very similar to those shown in Figure 1. "I need to be with my friends." "I am more productive when I can smoke." "It would be too hard to change my friends." "I cannot do this without the support of my friends." All of these are lies or cognitive distortions and must also be deconstructed in order to eliminate the behavior which is the identified problem. I think no small part of my ability to quit was that the environment changed with the public restrictions on smoking. The playground had become smaller and less convenient. The combination of problem behaviors, together with the thinking producing it, along with associated behaviors and the thinking producing them makes behavioral habits seem very imposing. They can be difficult to change, but not impossible. Once the thinking or beliefs are changed, changing the behavior is relatively easy. This is much more difficult with psychological addictions.

Psychological Dependence

The second addictive process, psychological addiction, is more complicated and involves our core issues at a more significant level. Frequently, it involves the fear of self (described in the previous chapter). Remember that the fear of self involves the belief that there is something so different about me, something so defective, that I am not like anyone else and I am alone. Therefore, I am afraid of too much self-examination because I might then have to face the monster that I think I am. As I stated in the last chapter, if am afraid of myself, and I believe I am different from others, I have nowhere to turn.

In the case of addictions, however, we come to believe we have found a place to turn. We can turn to sex, drugs, and intensity-producing behaviors (still not willing to blame rock & roll), or many other behaviors that serve to numb the pain or distract us from the problem. A person suffering a psychological addiction is disregarding the fact that all people are pretty much the same (Fact #1, page 4), and has come to believe one or more lies about him or herself. An active core issue, of any variety, is a painful experience. When we believe ourselves to be inadequate in some way, or fundamentally different or broken or damaged goods, we experience shame. The fear of self is about the avoidance of the pain. When we discover even temporary relief with inebriation or intense, high-risk activities, it is easy to develop an addictive process around that substance or that activity.

We saw in Chapter 6 how the response to anxiety is often to turn off the alarm system. Rather than accept the pain and work through it, we seek to shut it down. Thus, again, we find relief. This relief is somewhat attenuated by the fact that no matter how intense the activity, no matter how much "fun" we are having, we still know, in the back of our mind, that we are not happy, and that there is something wrong. Nevertheless the partial relief granted by blunting the pain is very attractive and habit-forming. Believing that we cannot stand the pain and that we are powerless to change it, we seek to avoid it. At this point we have lost track of the fact that beliefs are ideas and all ideas can be changed (Facts 6, 7, and 8). In addition, the psychological addictive process will soon be joined by a behavioral addiction, as the ritual of the addiction becomes a strong habit. The addictive behavior itself has consequences of course, which further complicate the person's life and solidify the core belief of incompetence or lack of value. We can see how all of these forces come into play in the case of Sam.

Sam was forty-one years old when the bottom fell out of his life. The owner of a thriving healthcare business, with a net of over four million per year, Sam enjoyed all the benefits of a flourishing life. Sam's wife of seventeen years was successful in her own right, and their two children were the picture of a childhood in heart of the American dream. Then, just shy of his forty-first birthday, Sam was arrested in the parking lot of the ambulance service run by his company. Though he did not threaten anyone, Sam was carrying a loaded AK-47 and was thoroughly intoxicated, high on meth. The police took Sam to the local jail, and as a result of bizarre behavior, he was later transferred to the psychiatric wing of the county jail. Up to this point Sam had never received so much as a parking ticket in his life. He was raised by a devout Catholic family and attended the expected prep schools, eventually completing college with a business degree. There had been no physical or sexual abuse in Sam's childhood, and no overt abandonment. Sam also married his high school girlfriend, as expected. Also as expected, Sam took over a fledgling nursing home business from his father. In a little under ten years, Sam added the ambulance service and a medical laboratory to the business and became well established in his community.

On the night of his arrest, Sam's family and friends were astounded. They could not fathom any explanation for Sam's behavior and found it to be totally out of character. Many assumed it was a fluke, a one-time aberration in Sam's life that would soon be explained and forgotten.

Unfortunately, two months later, while Sam was attending his court-ordered group therapy sessions, he was arrested again for DUI. At this point, Sam spent a few days in jail and was ordered to extended treatment. Sam did attend the treatment groups as expected, but continued to act out in a disintegrating series of behaviors. His business began to suffer. Sam became irritable and verbally abusive at home and at work. His wife asked Sam to move out and eventually filed divorce papers. At work, Sam discovered his controller had been stealing from him, and the business, while still salvageable, was in serious trouble. However, Sam's continued use of meth and alcohol prevented him from coping with the business issues. Customers began using other labs and Sam finally lost the permits for his ambulance service.

During this time, Sam continued to live as though money would never be a problem. He spent lavishly on drugs and parties. Often, he would abandon the office to go ride his dirt bike through the desert, high as a kite, for hours at a time. Finally, Sam was arrested again when a woman accused him of kidnapping and extortion. These charges were dropped when it became clear the woman was herself on drugs and mostly angry that Sam did not seem to be romantically interested in her. This last arrest did, however, result in Sam entering a rehab and sobering up. At the point that Sam began his long road to recovery, his business had collapsed, and he was divorced and not allowed to see his children. Sam was living on friends' couches and driving around in an ambulance left over from his failed business. The IRS and creditors together claimed over two million dollars in outstanding debt. Suddenly it seemed he had nothing and nowhere to turn. Sam was now forty-three years old.

The question on everyone's mind, especially Sam's, was "What happened?" On the surface, there seemed to be no explanation. Just below the surface, however, the patterns were clear. Sam's father, while caring, was largely absent from Sam's early childhood. His older brother was rebellious and a problem until he ran away at seventeen and eventually moved to South America permanently. This left Sam at home with his mother. Sam and his mother became too close. With her husband emotionally distant, Sam's mother came to rely on Sam, emotionally and as the one to take care of things around the house. The impact on Sam was devastating. This almost incestuous enmeshment resulted in Sam being unable to experience true intimacy with women as anything but suffocating.

The abandonment by his father and the enmeshment by his mother (which also constitutes emotional abandonment) left Sam believing he was not good enough. Further, Sam came to believe that any value and worth he did have arose as a result of his taking care of others. In other words, Sam came to believe that, while he was valueless, he could compensate if he made himself important to others. Sam believed he needed to justify his very existence by taking care of others. It was clear that he did not matter to anyone else, but perhaps through his behavior, in the form of loyal problem solver and all-around nice guy, he could somehow come to matter.

Sam set out on a life course to make up for what he believed he lacked. He always did as expected. The effort could be seen early on. When his high school prom came around, and Sam was deathly sick with the flu and had a temperature of 104, his girlfriend stated, "Look, I bought this dress and it is not going to waste. Get up and get dressed." At his girlfriend and his mother's insistence, Sam went to the prom. When his parents wanted him to attend an exclusive prep school instead of the high school all his friends were attending, Sam complied even though he was not academically inclined. In fact, Sam always did what was expected of him. For forty years he kept putting off his own needs in order to live his life for others. Sam's assumption was, of course, that this would pay off somehow and that someday he would be rewarded by coming to believe that he was finally okay and deserving of life. Instead, he found that while he lived his life for others, the others went around living their own lives and Sam still did not feel complete or happy. Eventually Sam began to develop considerable anger and resentment. After all, he was doing everything he was supposed to do. "When do I get to do what I want?" "When does it start to pay off?"

Living his life for others also resulted in a total lack of knowledge about himself. In the absence of someone else's expectations of him, Sam did not exist. Sam did not have any ability to see himself except through the eyes of others. Sam defined himself by knowing that "I can be counted on." "I always do what is expected of me."

When Sam first encountered drugs, he was introduced to the first experience in his life in which there were no expectations.

When high, in addition to the pleasurable physical sensations, Sam found the first peace he had ever known. It was false, and it was temporary, but it let him be. Getting high and riding his bike full speed through the desert added another level of intensity that distracted him from the shame of not being good enough no matter how hard he tired. Sam could feel alive in a way he never could in his real life. The high let him forget about external and internal expectations. There was no "supposed to"; there was only Sam, the desert, and the wind. Since Sam had never learned to question the expectations placed on him, and self-awareness was never taught to him, the freedom of the high was irresistible.

Sam's story demonstrates a psychological addictive process. To understand it better, look at Figure 12. Here we have adapted the A-B-C illustration to include our behavior and to depict the ongoing evaluation that occurs when we are operating in a functional manner. There is a constant stream of sensations coming into us from activating events. There is also a continuous evaluation process in which the results of our emotions and behaviors are analyzed, and that analysis is used to evaluate the utility of our beliefs. Thus, all through life, we are constantly redefining ourselves. Our beliefs, values, and memories are up for consideration at all times.

When we pay close attention to ourselves, we have the ability to notice where our feelings are coming from, and we have the ability to make changes when necessary. This is why all people have the ability to be happy. The self-examination and the resulting self-awareness, the constant appraisal and reappraisal of the situation and our behavior allow us to adapt to changing circumstances. This is vital because we know that life is all about change. If we cannot adapt to constant and pervasive change, we will never realize what it means to be fully human—to remain

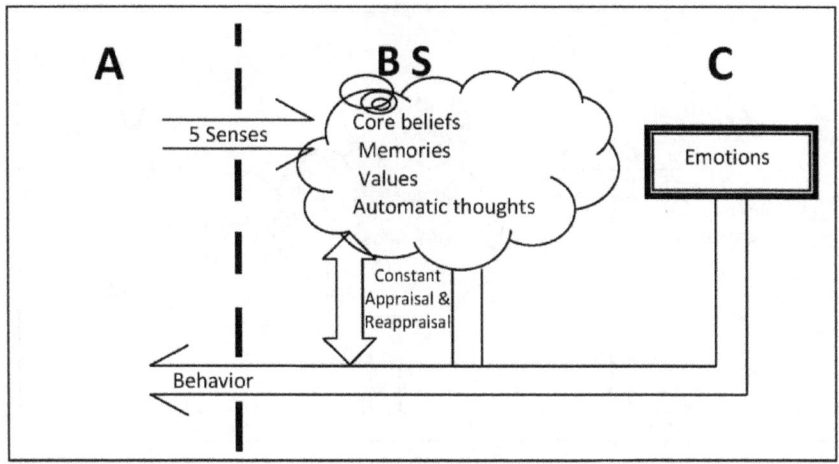

Figure 13.

connected and cognizant of the changing landscape no matter how drastic the changes might be. This provides stability to our sense of self. We no longer see the self as an immutable object but as a dynamic, adaptable process. This is the critical piece that is missing when we are engaged in dysfunctional behavior such as a psychological addictive process.

In Figure 14, we can see that the same general process operates. However, because of the fear of self and the numbing effect of the addictive behavior, we no longer are engaged in the evaluation of our behavior or of ourselves. Thus, nothing ever changes. The irrational cognitive distortions that pollute our thinking are never subjected to examination and modification. The complication can be exacerbated when the addiction involves the use of substances because many of the substances we use result in cognitive impairment, and we become unable to think clearly at all. This is why in co-occurring disorders (that is, in situations where core issues like depression result in the creation of psychological addictions, like alcoholism, so that both things are going on at once), it is necessary for the individual to become sober before

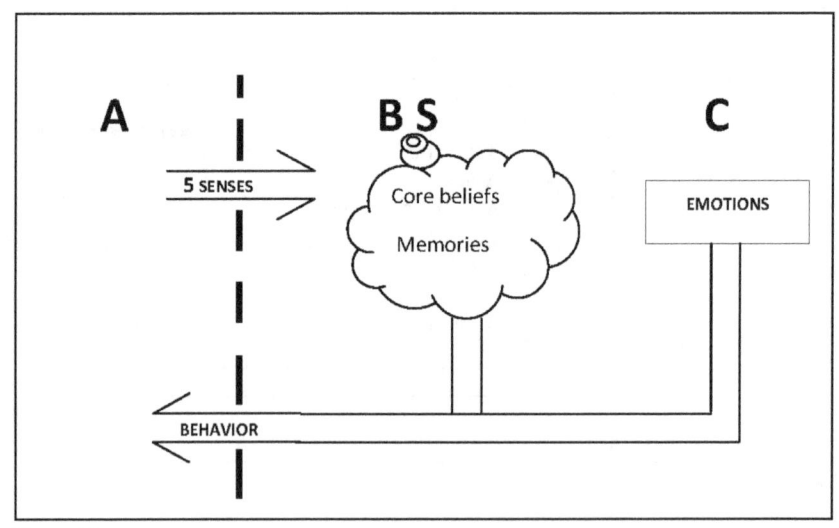

Figure 14.

attempting to modify the belief system. In other words, until we can think clearly, there is not much point in attempting an analysis of our belief system. Treatment in this situation often involves completion of two different approaches: one to deal with the addiction and the second to help resolve underlying core issues. This inability to think clearly is the situation in which Sam found himself.

With no real sense of self to begin with, except for the conviction that he was somehow "not enough," Sam entered into the use of drugs set up to become a full-blown addict. The meth prevented him from feeling, so he avoided the pain, but it also kept him from paying attention to himself. The numbing effect of the drug shut the door to experiences based in reality, and precluded Sam from being able to make the changes that would lead to true happiness. You can also see why, once Sam became sober, he was in great danger of a relapse. This is, in fact, what happened.

Sam got into recovery and was sober for several years. Unfortunately, the struggle to restore his place in the world with the added burden of a felony record and millions of dollars of debt proved overwhelming. In addition, Sam returned almost immediately to his previous pattern of needless, wantless behavior that led to his first crash and would eventually lead to another. He moved back in with his parents. He spent most evenings in the home of his ex-wife, taking care of the kids and helping around the house. He even loaned a friend several thousand dollars, which could have been used for attorney's fees to clear his record, or maybe a dirt bike so he could begin to enjoy his one healthy activity. Sam believed he had to earn his humanity so everyone else came first.

Furthermore, he thought, and still believes, he owed something for his very existence. Thus he continued to do things for others in the belief that his own needs would be met in return—without his having to worry about them himself. Sam had forgotten that our first duty to one another is to take care of ourselves so others don't have to. At no point in his recovery was Sam in good enough shape to be caring for others. Nevertheless, that is what he did. This is a very tangled set of beliefs that leads to a mostly painful existence. Ultimately the relief provided by the drugs is unmanageable and relapse occurs.

Eventually a business opportunity arose to partner with a previous competitor. Sam took a position making six figures, to establish and manage the operation. However, in order to meet regulatory requirements, a background check had to be conducted. Sam had neglected to take care of his legal situation and could not qualify. After only a few months, he found himself once more unemployed. The resulting emotions were more than Sam could manage and he relapsed. Still, Sam could not accept his humanity. As he struggled to recover once more, he still clung to the belief that he had to justify his existence by taking care of others. This led to disconnection because he did not believe he was like everyone else. It also led to anger and resentment because the world did not reward him for being such a nice guy, as he expected it should. His relationships remained primarily codependent, manipulative, and unsatisfying. Because of the underlying resentment generated by not being "rewarded" for doing the right thing, Sam could be testy, argumentative, and explosive in his relationships.

The frustration arises out of trying so hard and still feeling "less than" or unhappy. Ultimately the relief provided by the drugs is too seductive and relapse occurs. This type of psychological addiction is extremely difficult to end and often results in death. In Sam's case the final result is not clear as of this writing.

Psychological addiction can be complicated by the addition of behavioral habits, such as my smoking, and by the presence of genetic predispositions as well as tolerance and withdrawal issues. In cases where all of these factors are present, the outcome is bleak. Successful recovery in these situations can require inpatient treatment followed by extended residential care. The psychological addiction process plays a role in most process addictions (those addictions not involving the use of chemicals). We can, in fact, become addicted to almost any activity. The leading behaviors involve sex, food, and money, as these are pleasurable in their own right and normally legal. All such addictive processes share in common the disconnection from self and thus a loss of meaning and the ability to be truly relational with others. Even therapy can become an addiction.

Many times I have observed patients arrive in a treatment center or hospital with literally years of therapy behind them. I believe this results primarily from a fear of self and an avoidance of the lack of meaning that can face all of us. Five, ten, or twenty years of therapy are not uncommon. There was one woman who stayed to talk with me following a lecture. She had been in therapy for about seven years. Over the course of the conversation I heard her use the phrase "...work on my trauma..." a number of times. There was no doubt that her childhood had included horrific sexual and emotional abuse. Still, it seemed that she had made substantial progress, and was functioning quite well in her life. At some point I asked her, "What would happen if you no longer had to work on your trauma?" She became silent for a moment. I noticed a sudden change in her expression and she finally reported, "Sorry, but when you asked me that, I saw a big white blank and it scared me." It turns out that this woman's purpose in life had become "working on her trauma." The second she was confronted with the possibility that she might not be able to engage in that activity, she was confronted with the need to face the pain of having no other purpose or place. This constitutes a psychological addiction to therapy. In this case the therapist would do well to be shifting the focus from the trauma to helping the patient find some other meaning for the rest of her life.

Trauma work should not take up a lifetime, regardless of how severe it may be initially. Many times people become focused on the trauma to the point they are unable to function in the here and now. To be present with ourselves in the moment is necessary for true contentment. The "trauma excuse" we often use to avoid the pain of the present is a dead end.

Triggers

Triggers are a major topic in many discussions related to addictions. If you have read all of the preceding chapters in order, you will not be surprised to find me stating that triggers do not exist. At least they do not exist out in the world. Triggers are in the mind of the person being triggered. Often, following some type of relapse, I will hear someone say, "I was triggered" or "She triggered me." Frequently, I have observed those struggling with sex addiction inform someone else, "You are triggering me." It is amazing how often people accept this statement and accept responsibility for another person's behavior, especially when that behavior includes a relapse.

If I tell someone they are triggering me, what I am actually saying is that I am engaged in a boundary failure and I expect the other person to do something about it. While many people with their own boundary issues will accommodate such a request, it is not a functional approach for either person. It is no way relational and it is the very definition of codependence. This is the basis of much of the political correctness activity in our society, and it is a losing battle. Basically to be politically correct in all situations, I have to figure out, in advance, what everyone else is going to decide is offensive. This is impossible unless I am a mind reader because *offensiveness is in the mind of the offended*. Of course, reducing my exposure to unnecessary temptations to engage in an addiction is prudent. Ultimately, this approach is always going to be insufficient by itself.

Trying to avoid triggers, sometimes referred to as stimulus management, is an attempt to control what cannot be controlled: namely, the world. It's like trying to hide from the wind. You might be able to accomplish it, but only at the expense of your freedom. Remembering that things always happen the way they happen (Fact #6, page 37), we have to recognize that there are limits to our degree of control over the universe. Despite all of my best efforts, at some time, somewhere, I am going to have to face the stimulus I most dread. I cannot manage all of the things and all of the people, all of the time. If my approach to dealing with an addiction is based only on managing triggers, it will ultimately fail. I can, however, as stated by the woman in Chapter 2, manage my perceptions. While I cannot control the whole world, I can control my whole self. What I need to do is explore my faulty beliefs and thinking, by which activating events result in my cravings, and produce the repetitive decisions about my addictive behavior. Making myself into a ginormous victim by blaming the beer, or the affair partner, or the casino does not result in more manageability for me.

Triggers are excuses. Blaming does not alter present circumstances. Excuses do not alter consequences. A college student may have all kinds of excuses for not completing a course, or a degree: "I was sick a lot," "I have a learning disability," "It was an accident," or "I had to take care of my brother." All of these may be totally legitimate, but they do not alter the fact that this person will never get into medical school or whatever because, regardless of the excuse, he did not get a degree. Excuses do not change the outcome. All of the energy we put into development of excuses is energy devoted to a negative outcome. No justification is needed for failure. On top of that, nobody else really cares about my excuses. Very few people are interested in a conversation about why I am not a doctor or lawyer or rocket scientist.

My choice is clear in my approach to my addiction. I can attempt to manage all of my imagined triggers, or I can manage my perceptions. When perceptions actually change, the triggers disappear. I can try to manage the world, or I can manage myself.

To manage myself, I just have to increase my self-awareness, the key to it all.

Relapse Prevention

In my opinion, any conversation of addiction should always include a discussion of relapse prevention. It follows from the previous chapters that prevention of relapse is totally possible. In many treatment programs, relapse prevention is not given adequate attention. After years of working crisis lines, as well as responding to relapse calls from previous patients at treatment centers, I have seen firsthand how important it is. Over and over, when folks call in desperation because they have or are about to relapse, they report they did not follow, or never had, a relapse prevention plan. I consider it something of a moral responsibility to address the topic here.

First off, relapse is a process. It does not occur in an instant. The relapse process is distinct from the behavioral episode in which I take action. In other words, if I am an alcoholic, relapse starts when I begin thinking about drinking. Acting out is when I take the drink.[60] The relapse process that occurs prior to acting out is where we can take the most effective action because we already know, in advance, which activating events are going to be a problem.

If I have any type of addiction, especially if it has reached the level of interfering with my life and causing me to seek help, I know all I need to know about the activating events that are a problem for me. In other words, I know my "triggers." Now, remember that triggers only exist in the mind of the person being triggered. If I make myself aware of the things that "trigger" me,

---

[60] Gorski (1986)

what I have actually done is to make myself aware of the cognitive distortions and schema that result in the existence of the trigger. Eventually, this type of investigation will eliminate the trigger altogether. This takes time and while I am working on that, the world is still presenting me with problematic activating events. I need to have a plan for dealing with these activating events while I am working on the underlying core issues.

As stated above, I cannot control the world. I cannot plan to avoid all stimuli or activating events that might lead to acting out. I can, however, plan my responses to the activating events that may pose a danger. This is a relapse prevention plan. Essentially it is a list of the activating events that signal a relapse process is under way. The initial signs are usually internal, things such as difficulty thinking clearly, managing stress, or problems with memory. Later, signs begin to include more behavioral components such as sleep problems, loss of emotional control, return of impulsive behavior, and many others. There are at least thirty such signs outlined by recovery specialists.[61] The point is, since we can know in advance what the problem activating events are, we can do something about them.

I believe a good relapse prevention plan consists of the following:

Identification and anticipation of problem activating events, thoughts, and emotions
Becoming hypersensitive to the identified problems
Developing a preplanned response to each of the identified problems

---

[61] Gorski (1992)

Making a commitment to the follow-through response for each identified problem

Identification of the anticipated problems is best accomplished by first utilizing one of the available workbooks on the subject. Second, we must personalize these to accommodate our personal way of thinking and talking about them. This is the self-awareness process we have been describing throughout this book. It means simply identifying and then listing all of the persons, places, or things that we know will present some type of risk for relapse. The list needs to be as exhaustive and detailed as possible. In other words, do not use general statements like "Don't get overconfident." Instead, break it down into the actual thoughts that make up overconfidence. So, I might list things like "Notice when I start to think one drink is okay." Or "Be ready when the boss wants to go out after work."

Next we must make ourselves hypersensitive to the identified problems. One way to do this is to engage in the development of a *written* relapse prevention plan. The act of organizing these problems and committing them to writing heightens our awareness. For example, suppose one of my identified signals is addictive thinking such as "I've got this whipped. I don't have to worry about taking a drink now and then." This is the kind of thinking that we can engage in almost without awareness. These kinds of thoughts can be in the category of automatic thinking, which, as you recall, is unconscious. If, however, I have sensitized myself to the danger of such thinking, taken the effort to write it down as part of my relapse prevention plan, and devised a response, the odds are that I will become more conscious of such thinking. I will notice when I am engaging in that kind of thinking. This is the hypersensitivity we are looking for. Once I become sensitive enough to notice such thinking, or any of the other signs, I can plan for them.

Planning means coming up with a specific behavior I will engage in when I notice one of the identified problems. Thus, I might decide that the addictive thinking mentioned above is one of the problems. I might pick any number of behaviors to engage in. Generally the best ones have two characteristics: they are something I enjoy, and they require some level of concentration. I could decide that when I notice this kind of thinking, I will call my sponsor. I could also decide to call a friend who understands my situation and who I enjoy talking with. Perhaps I will decide to reread a particular book or section of a book that deals with this kind of thinking. At the very least I must select a behavior to engage in which will interrupt the relapse process and, hopefully, challenge the distorted thinking or beliefs involved. Once I have designed the behavior I will use as a response to the identified problem, I must commit to actually doing it.

One technique I have found useful is to make an agreement with myself that, if I am going to engage in a behavior, taking a drink in this case, it is okay so long as I have first completed the response I committed to in the relapse prevention plan. If I found myself in this situation, for example, in response to thinking about having a drink, I might have a commitment to go flying. I really enjoy flying and it definitely requires some concentration. Thus, if I actually follow through with a planned response of "go flying for two hours first," then the likelihood of acting on the impulse to drink is greatly reduced. Plus, as with my smoking, by making the response conditional, I have reduced the potential anxiety associated with following the plan.

Generally, I strongly recommend constructing an actual written relapse prevention plan, designed to assist in responding to every possible anticipated problem stimulus or activating event. This can be a little lengthy but, if constructed cleverly, can make the difference between a recovery lost and a recovery sustained.

CHAPTER 9
Things That Help

All that we have talked about so far is necessary to accomplish happiness. It is not, however, sufficient. The things that complete the task are generally straightforward in application, but they can be easily overlooked. This is especially true when we have become lost and confused about the ten facts of life. Just as we should not overlook these simple things in life, I did not want to close without including them here. So, here are a few things that can facilitate our work.

Therapy

I often have potential clients come to see me and ask for a particular type of therapy (EMDR, Therapeutic Touch, Somatic Experiencing, Inner Child Work, Shame Reduction, Hypnotherapy, Cognitive Therapy, DBT... The list is truly much larger than needs to be cataloged here). I almost always decline such clients. There are two reasons. First, such clients generally have some sort of magical thinking associated with the process of therapy, and this prevents them from dealing with core issues. It also is a set-up for me in that they will either be disappointed that I cannot produce the expected magic bullet, or they will become dependent on me and therapy to the point that they are blocking the self-awareness work they need to accomplish. Second, if these people already know the answers to their problems, why do they need me? The answer is, of course they don't.

It is as if a person has a problem with their car. They go to a mechanic and the first question is "Do you use Craftsman tools or Snap-on?" Clearly the choice of tools is better left to the mechanic. The focus on technique rather than the problem is counterproductive and seldom leads to a positive outcome. Of course people are a little more complicated than cars, and therapy is somewhat more complex than engine repair. Still, in my experience, this is not the most productive way to benefit from counseling. The approach that works best is one that keeps in mind a couple of the facts of life we have discussed.

First, when I go to a therapist, I need to keep in mind the fact that I already have everything I need to be happy (Fact #3). Belief in this fact can be difficult because it really means there is no easy way out of my misery. Second, therapy generally should be brief. Years of analysis are nice if you have the luxury of time and funds and nothing else to do, but it is not necessary. It is only necessary to come unstuck and begin the journey. Completing the journey is what is called life.

The ultimate goal of therapy is to come to know our true selves. In the glare of the facts of life, we discover that we are simply human. By walking along with us, a therapist can help us see past the fear of self and reconnect with the facts of our existence. Once I am in touch with the facts of life and the facts about my self, serenity is accomplished. It is difficult to surmount the fear of self and explore the depths of our experience. With someone walking along we can more quickly discover the truth that, if you look deep enough into your heart, you will find nothing wrong there. There is nothing to prove and nothing to fear. With this discovery is freedom. The details are myriad. They may take a long time to work out. Once I am no longer afraid of my self, however, I can usually proceed on my own. Selecting a therapist who can help with this process is the critical step.

A therapist is not the same as a physician. When I use the word "therapist," by the way, I mean *psychotherapist,* often in the form of a psychologist, counselor, social worker, etc. (If I have need of referring to other kinds of therapists, I will be specific.) This is a very arbitrary distinction that I just made up, but I think it is important.

A physician cures us. When I go to a physician, the presumption is that there is something wrong with me that I know very little about and cannot fix. The physician knows a lot about it and, if all goes well, can fix me. A physician may have advice for me and give me instructions to help with my recovery (take two of these and call me in the morning; eat your vegetables; don't eat bad stuff; quit smoking, etc.). A therapist, on the other hand, is in quite the opposite situation. A therapist cannot cure me. I know much more about me than she does. Not knowing much about me, she cannot automatically fix me. Further, even if she did know all about me, she could not fix me because I am the only one who has direct access to the parts that need fixing—my sensations, my beliefs, my mind, and my feelings. A good therapist will have few instructions and little advice for me. She may suggest I try certain things. These are only suggestions and experiments though, not prescriptions.

Because people are all human, there are certain principles that apply. A therapist will have been trained in and will have knowledge of these principles. Because all people are individuals, however, no one can say exactly how the principles will apply to me. A therapist cannot know about me in advance. On the other hand, a therapist can have experience in applying the principles. First, the therapist can have applied the principles to her self. This is invaluable experience. It comes under the heading of "practice what you preach." A therapist who espouses various procedures for clients, but does not apply them in her own life, will not be as effective a guide as one who follows their own precepts. She might have encyclopedic knowledge of techniques and principles, but having never used them herself, she will not have the experience. Secondly, a therapist will have experience guiding others to the goal. The more successful trips, the more likely she will be helpful in the future.

Imagine life as an immense swamp. At the center of the swamp is a clearing which contains happiness. All around are various tangles of growth and complications of terrain. As happiness radiates out from the center, the closer a person gets to the center, the happier they are. The complications of terrain present different problems to different people. There are tunnels which cannot accommodate very tall or large people. There are pathways in the trees that only work well for tall people. There are places where swimming is required. There are bugs and snakes and all manner of creatures. There are situations that require courage and other situations that demand curiosity or caution. There are all sorts of tricky situations involved. The only thing we know for sure is that, for every person, of whatever stature and temperament, there is at least one path to the center. We also know that every person starts from a slightly different point on the edge of the swamp, so even those with very similar abilities will need to find unique paths. The edge of the swamp allows room for many peoples of different abilities and cultures and languages.

Now suppose there are guides available to help me figure out how to get to the center. The best guide, of course, is one who has been to the center herself, from all possible starting points. This is not going to happen, because every starting point is unique. We would probably like to have a guide who possesses technical knowledge about the swamp and how to navigate in it. She should be able to recognize quicksand and use a compass and know things like the difference between an open and a closed crimp. In addition, she should know which bugs are dangerous and which bugs may be eaten (hey, I never said it was going to be a completely pleasant journey, or a short one). Also helpful would be someone who has at least found their own path to the center. Even better is someone who has found their own path and has been invited to walk along with many others. This person has seen a number of starting points. Some of the people she has traveled with have made it to the center. Some have made mistakes and become lost on the path. In either case, the guide will have learned from the experience. She knows in which general direction the center lies, because she has been there, and she has seen many mistakes and many successes. She knows things a person can try and things to avoid. She still will not have the answers for me, but she will have knowledge and experience that can make my journey a little less difficult. My odds of discovering my path will be improved by having her walking along, watching me and commenting. Once discovered, I still must walk the path on my own; this is true for all of us. With my guide at the start, however, the passage will be less frightening. I will not walk alone.

The guide must also have one more characteristic. I must feel a connection with the guide. At least we must be able to communicate, to use the same language, to share. This can be true because my therapist started out from a point close to me on the edge of the swamp and thus has similar values and a common culture and language. It can also result from the guide having extensive experience with many people, using many languages and using many different starting points. Regardless of how her connection skills were acquired, I must be able to communicate with my guide or her knowledge is lost to me. So, how does this metaphor translate into practice?

First, let's talk about knowledge. While I am generally opposed to bureaucracy, I must grudgingly admit that, in some situations, it can be useful. Most states have some sort of examining board or other licensing mechanism for therapists of various types. The designation Licensed Professional Counselor (LPC), or Licensed Mental Health Counselor (LMHC), is used in many states. There are a number of other designations also used for mental health counseling. These include designations for clinical social work or marriage and family therapy, psychologists, and psychiatrists. The thing all licensure has in common is a required course of postgraduate study. This provides a broad knowledge base in the field of human development and behavior. In addition, most licenses require several thousand hours of supervised practice.

In my opinion, using a therapist who does not hold a professional license issued by the state government is taking a huge chance. There certainly are many practitioners who have been to the center of the swamp without the formal training and education, but there is really no way for a person to know. Often such practitioners only know one path to the center and are not familiar with the larger knowledge base of professionally licensed counselors. This is a relatively straightforward issue. The issue of connection is not so clear cut.

To know if an otherwise knowledgeable therapist is right for me, I believe I have to try them out. I do not know of any other way to figure out if a particular therapist is able to speak my language than to try talking with them. I enjoy hearing a potential client tell me they are "looking for a therapist." In other words they are interviewing me to see if there is a fit. In my practice there is no fee for a first meeting, a consultation, the sole purpose of which is to see if there is a fit. Some professionals may not like this approach. As a client in search of a therapist, it is also expensive and time consuming, and it requires that I tell my story over and over until there is a good fit. However, when I find a person in this manner, it is clear, before the journey starts, that she speaks my language and will be a comfortable companion on my journey through the swamp.

For me personally, "swamp" is a very good description of what is going on here in my head. I would not want to be stuck in a boat in this particular bog with someone not of my ilk. So, my suggestion for selecting a therapist boils down to two items: 1) Select from the pool of licensed mental health professionals and 2) schedule single appointment "interviews" with several until you find a good fit.

So far I have not addressed the question of when to seek professional help. This is a very personal issue. My own first two experiences with therapists were totally unsatisfactory. I believe this was largely due to the fact that, at that time, I really did not need a therapist. I was premature in my efforts. Generally I believe therapists can only be helpful when the pain of our current approach to life outweighs all other considerations. If I am on the verge or close to becoming nonfunctional in work or relationships or recreation, then help is advisable. I do not want to wait until I am attempting suicide, have lost the ability to keep a job, losing a marriage, or not having any fun in life, though many people do. At the same time, I do not need a therapist for every little bump in the road. I have had many folks ask if I would become their life coach. This is not a role for a therapist. This is a role for someone to help with legal, financial, and career decisions. Therapy is, in my opinion, to be reserved for those situations in which I have become lost and disconnected from myself, when I am so anxiety ridden or so depressed that I can barely leave the house, and life has no passion—when I am on a course of behavior that is killing me, or when I am in grave danger of dying before I ever even approach the refuge in the center of the swamp.

Forgiveness

I am including a few words on forgiveness here because of all of the people I have known who refused to forgive and, therefore, cannot move on with their life. Many of these people I have loved dearly and thus share some considerable pain with them. There is the wife who, after discovering her husband was having an affair, cannot let go of the pain, shame, and anger. She clings, ten years later, to the dream that there is a way to make him pay and somehow return to the way things were before the betrayal. She cannot move on, is chronically depressed, constantly on the verge of killing herself. She poisons her relationships with the rest of her family and her life.

There are friends who experienced the death of a son as a result of someone's irresponsible drinking and driving. These people, years later, cannot forgive the person. Even the conviction for DUI and manslaughter and a fifteen-year prison sentence does not satisfy. They torture themselves with thoughts of "what if" and "if only" and most devastatingly "he shouldn't have." These are all thoughts and beliefs. These people have lost touch with the fact that things happen the way they happen, and it is neither fair nor unfair or anything else. It just is. (See Fact of Life #6, page 37.)

Our lot in life is not to change the way things happened, but to cope with what is (Fact #6 again, things happen the way they happen). It is also not a matter of forgetting what has happened to us, but acknowledging it as part of our human experience. Often the "shoulds" involved in this type of thinking include moral judgments—invocations of absolute right and wrong. This is an attempt to impose my moral values on others. It has never been done successfully. Despite all the propaganda and wars and crusades and terrorist activities over the millennia, people usually stick to their own beliefs when it comes to morality or any sense of right and wrong. This is because, ultimately, right and wrong are personal issues.

I can believe that people who do not believe as I do are damned. I can believe that people who do not accept the facts of life as I know them will never be truly happy. I can believe that those who do not accept Christ into their lives will be consigned to hell. I can believe that oranges are evil or, perhaps, the nectar of salvation. One thing I cannot do in this regard is to believe for someone else, or force someone else to believe as I do. I am not a religion or a priest or shaman with some sort of direct connection to God or whatever. Thus I cannot know what is right or wrong for someone else. I have enough trouble figuring out what is right for me.

So long as I make forgiveness conditional on other people's compliance with my personal values and morals and judgment, I am doomed to a life of frustration and desperation. Forgiveness does not require the other person's apology or contrition. It does not occur because the other person suffers. It is not at the discretion of the other person in any way. It does not depend on the fairness of things or the morality of another person's behavior. Forgiveness is not about the other person at all. Forgiveness is about me and my expectations of the world.

Forgiveness is about my accepting that, whatever happened, it does not change who I am. Forgiveness does not condone another person's behavior, but acknowledges their behavior as a fact of my life. Forgiveness is about knowing the difference between things I can control and those I cannot. Forgiveness is mostly about recognizing that whatever has been done to me, I am still able to seek my own measure of peace and happiness. And, forgiveness also confers the freedom to seek a life of serenity, no matter what has happened. Forgiving is actually the only way we can find peace of mind. Failure to forgive is to stubbornly continue to punish myself for the behavior of others. Forgiveness is about my claiming the rest of my life despite what someone has done to me. Once again I refer the reader to Fact #6 (things always happen exactly the way they happen).

The opposite of forgiveness is righteous resentment. Something happened in a way I did not expect or prefer. In response I decide to hold on to my expectation at all costs. I justify this response by pointing out that whatever happened was against the laws of God or man or nature. Thus, my stubborn refusal to accept what is becomes justified on moral and ethical grounds. Sadly, these justifications do not lessen the cost to me. The main cost of my resentment is my own serenity. In addition, I have afforded the other person tremendous power.

By refusing to give up my resentment and anger, I am providing the other person with the entertainment of watching me continue to suffer. This is over and above whatever damage may have been done to me originally, If, in the course of my misery, I seek and obtain some sort of revenge, nothing of significance has changed.

Suppose that someone commits a wrong to me. I become angry and resentful. I am, in fact, consumed with my righteousness. I file a legal action. The suit proceeds through the court system, and let's says two years elapse. Eventually a finding is rendered and I win! Perhaps I can now drop my resentment and move on, somewhat.

This is great. It is also beside the point here. Our concern here is that during the two years, I made myself miserable—and I did not have to. Furthermore, in my experience, while the court ruling might bring some relief, most people who have not been able to forgive while awaiting retribution will still harbor some resentment or outright hate toward the other person. This is just sad. It is also silly. Regardless of the rightness or wrongness of whatever happened, we all have the ability to retain our serenity in such situations. To give up our serenity in the process is quite simply stupid. If necessary I can retaliate and still maintain my serenity, but only if I first forgive.

Sleep

Sleep is important. You probably knew that at some level. What I really mean to say is that sleep is important to emotional and intellectual functioning. There are physical and psychological consequences if we tolerate chronic sleep problems. We are not going to go into the process in any great detail here because considerable literature exists on the Internet and in your local bookstore. There are only a couple of points I wish to make. First, in my experience, sleep disorders are associated with most diagnosable behavioral problems. At least 80 percent of the patients I have worked with in psychiatric facilities experience some sort of sleep disturbance. It is estimated that "two-thirds of Americans have sleep problems… They enjoy life less, are less productive, and endure more illnesses and accidents at home, on the job and on the road."[62] We could spend a lot of time here discussing the casual relationship between emotional upset and loss of sleep, but that is a cart-and-egg type of issue. The reality is

---

[62] The Harvard Medical School (2010)

that neglecting either will result in problems with the other. In practical terms, we know emotional stress can keep us awake. We also know that severe lack of sleep can keep us from thinking clearly or paying attention. So, sleep is not just a good thing in itself, but healthy sleep hygiene is one of the prerequisites for sustainable happiness. Sleep should not be neglected.

The second thing I would like to note is that most sleep problems can be ameliorated. The principles of sleep hygiene are well established. In addition, sleep centers can evaluate and treat many kinds of sleep disorders. If you are suffering from any kind of sleep disorder, the matter should be brought to the attention of your physician or therapist. Go online to the American Academy of Sleep Medicine (www.aasmnet.org) to locate a physician or sleep center near you. It is not necessary to tolerate sleep problems.

Finally, it is very important to be aware that sleep patterns are as varied as people. No one sleep pattern fits all. Genetic, cultural, and personal factors determine the amount, type, and pattern of sleep that is right for each individual. Not everyone should be sleeping eight hours a night in one stretch. Some people sleep in two sessions a night rather than sleep straight through. Determining the pattern that suits us can help to eliminate unnecessary struggle trying to force ourselves to sleep all night. For many years I strove to force myself to sleep all night. When I woke up at around 2:00 a.m., I would stubbornly stay in bed and try to sleep. It was pretty miserable. Then I learned that many people experience a first and second sleep. On learning this, I began to just get up at 2:00 and do something, take a shower, read, write. The result is that the sleep I did get was better, more restful. In addition, rather than fighting to sleep for two hours a night, I spent the time being productive. This book was in truth mostly written in the middle of the night, during my *night watch*.

So, like the other topics in this chapter, sleep should not be neglected. As with many behavioral problems, rather than simply medicating with drugs, it is important to establish good sleep hygiene and seek treatment if necessary to accomplish this. Research shows, in fact, that medication alone does not provide a long-term solution. It is changing our thinking that has the most lasting impact.[63] As we have seen throughout this book, our thinking can be under our control. It may seem at times as though my depression or anxiety or eating disorder needs to take precedence and that lack of sleep is just a side effect of my larger problems. In fact, sleep loss can be part of the solution for the other problems. Sometimes, taking care of the small things is all we need to do.

Exercise

(Those who exercise regularly and especially those who enjoy exercise are encouraged to skip this section.)

The body-mind connection is real. This book has been focused primarily on the mind and its contents. Beliefs, thoughts, purpose, and place are not physical entities. On the other hand, it is clear that mind arises out of the existence of the body. Like our system of TV production, there are necessary hardware components, such as actors, cameras and microphones, transmitters, satellites, internet connections, receivers, screens, speakers, smartphones and viewers. These correspond to the sense organs, brain, muscles, and bones of the body. Obviously, without these nothing much is going to happen. It is also true, however, that setting up all of this equipment and making sure it is working properly does not, by itself, produce a single minute of programming. There must also be

---

[63] The Harvard Medical School (2010)

content. Content is not physical. Content consists of ideas. (I know, a screenplay is physical because it is written on paper. I am hoping the reader will cut me a little slack here.) The quality of the content is arguably the most important aspect of the system to the people watching. I say "arguably" because, judging by the inferiority of what we put up with from the media, it is not at all clear we really care about quality of programming. On the other hand, if the equipment is not up to par, and the signal suffers, and the viewer is plagued with fuzzy pictures and scratchy sound or interruptions in the program (especially on fourth down and inches to the goal), then the overall experience is degraded. The better the equipment, the better the signal, and the better the fidelity in the transmission of the content. The quality of the content does not much matter to the equipment. The quality of the equipment does, however, impact the quality of the overall experience. Ultimately, I will not be able to have great viewing experience if I cannot transmit a signal effectively. How many times can a movie be interrupted with the notice "Loading" before we give up? The same is true for our bodies and minds.

If I do not take care of my body, there will be limitations on my brain's ability to collect and process data. If I do not eat properly, I will not have adequate energy. If the neurons of my brain do not facilitate pattern recognition, causal reasoning, and learning, my mind will be correspondingly limited. There is now plenty of evidence those neurons, the cellular foundation of the brain, are just like the other cells of the body. They are enhanced by physical activity. It appears that not only can we make ourselves physically sick with dysfunctional thinking; we can also make ourselves mentally ill by not keeping our bodies in shape. That may be a bit of an exaggeration. Nevertheless, there is mounting evidence that indicates that exercise can, in fact, make us smarter.[64]

As a student in physiological psychology, I was taught that once the brain is developed in adolescence, it quits growing. It was made quite clear that we only get so many brain cells, and once they die, they can never be replaced. Over the last decade or two, research has been demonstrating this is not the case. In fact, it turns out that new brain cells are created all the time. Scientists have now isolated proteins in the brain that stimulate new growth of brain cells. I will spare you the technical details of the brain chemistry (mostly because I apparently do not exercise enough to keep from being confused by those details). The main growth factor, BDNF (brain-derived neurotrophic factor), turns out to be generated by exercise, and especially aerobic exercise. In other words, besides the fact that exercise can make us feel better physically, it is also the case that exercise causes increased levels of BDNF, which contributes to improved learning, memory, and other cognitive abilities. A number of schools have begun to take advantage of this by instituting early morning exercise programs. The results show that an hour of aerobic exercise prior to the start of the school day can significantly improve student performance.

If exercise improves brain functioning, it follows that exercise will also improve our mind and therefore our ability to be happy. Problems with depression, anxiety, addictions, etc. are made worse by inactivity. It has been pointed out that only those organisms that can move have brains. In other words, we think because we move. It follows that if we want to improve our thinking, it helps to increase our movement through physical activity.

---

[64] Ratey (2008)

Even prior to the recent research showing that exercise can make you smarter, most people would acknowledge that exercise is good for you. In spite of this, studies show that most Americans do not get enough exercise. A CDC study found, in 2005, about 40 percent of Americans "...engaged in no leisure-time physical activity..."[65] The study also reported that only about 30 percent of adults engaged in regular leisure-time activity. This leaves about 30 percent who, it can be presumed, engage in occasional leisure-time activity, which is inadequate. Thus, about 70 percent of Americans do not get enough exercise. The reason for this is, of course, in our thinking. Most of us prevent ourselves from doing anything physical because we believe it is too much trouble or it is too hard or we are too out of shape. This is very similar to my struggle with smoking and to the struggles of Susan to take care of her apartment or anything else. Remember, there is no such thing as laziness. It is actually a set of beliefs and automatic thoughts. This automatic thinking leads us into emotions such as anxiety, and behaviors such as procrastination. There are no actual physical barriers for most of us. Even a prisoner can do pushups in the cell. It is possible for almost every person, even those with physical disabilities, to find a way to get some exercise. Being clever folks though, most of us can talk ourselves out of it.

Recall in Chapter 2 that I mentioned my introduction to the gym in preparation for a major surgery. Well, I eventually did have that surgery. I felt as prepared as I could be as a result of my almost daily workouts. What the surgeon failed to advise me about was something he called "deconditioning." Basically this means that following the surgery, I lost almost all of the benefit I had gained in my previous six months of workouts! In fact, I found

---

[65] Barnes (2007)

myself weak as a kitten. I was confined to bed for a number of weeks and had every excuse in the world to stay that way. Eventually, I had milked the situation to the point that my loving family members began to wilt in their devotion to providing for my every little whim. Things became boring. I had a decision to make. I knew that I needed to start getting some exercise. The problem was, when I observed my present condition, or "de-condition," I told myself that it would be too much work. It would take way too much time. I wasn't even sure I would live long enough to benefit. I was, after all, in much worse shape than I had been before my previous attempt to exercise. I was in the worst shape of my entire adult life. I had no shape at all. These thoughts and others are depicted in Figure 15. I have also indicated that both an emotion of anxiety and a behavior of procrastination were produced. The overall result was that I created an insurmountable obstacle with my thinking. I did, however, find a way out.

The way out was somewhat the same that I used to quit smoking. First, I did not set a goal of getting back into the shape I was prior to surgery. That did appear to be a huge task, one that I was not sure I was up to. Instead I set a goal that I knew I could accomplish. Believing that any exercise was better than no exercise, I decided first that I would attempt to do one pushup a day. I did not commit to actually doing a pushup, which was out of the question as far as I could tell. I just committed to getting down on the floor and attempting one. As I recall, the first day or so just getting out of bed and down on the floor pretty much wore me out. I believe my brother had to come get me back in bed. Eventually I managed one very shaky pushup. I did not change my goal; I just committed to keep doing the one pushup per day. I knew that eventually I would get a little stronger, and a second pushup would become not only possible, but also relatively easy. By scaling down my commitment and expectation to something I knew I could accomplish, I reduced the anxiety. I could mentally say, *yeah, but it's only one attempted pushup.* I did the same thing with aerobics. After a couple of weeks of one pushup a day, I decided to see how far I could walk. Turns out I could only make it to the end of the driveway before collapsing. However, I then made the commitment to attempt to walk to the end of the driveway every day. Again, I did not add a lot of pressure about actually making it to the end of the driveway. I just said I would try. With both the pushup and the walk, I had two rules. First, never feel that I have to increase the commitment for any reason. In other words, only commit to what I know I can do *easily.* Second, if I did once *happen* to increase the level, say up to two pushups, I could never go back. After all, the new level was now part of the definition of "easy."

So, basically I never made a commitment to increase the level of exercise unless I just felt like it. I did not set long-term goals. I stayed away from thoughts like *I will be able to bench press 300 pounds by December.* For me, goals equaled pressure, and pressure created anxiety, and that would result in all of my competence core issues coming up in the form of the thinking depicted in Figure 1.

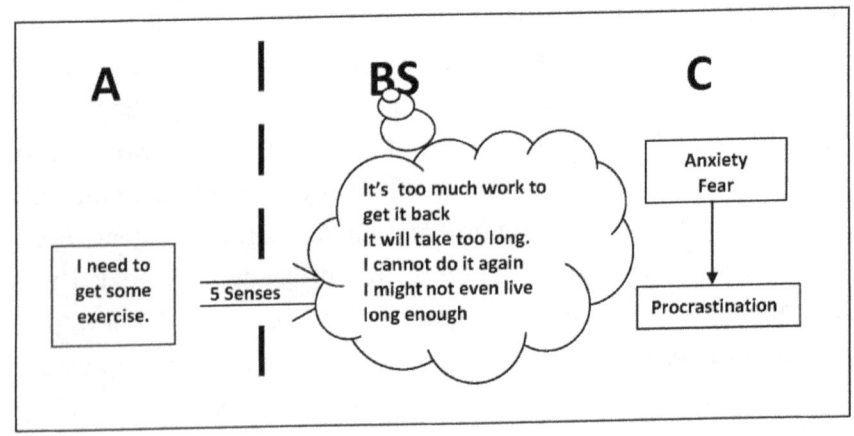

A: I need to get some exercise.

5 Senses

BS: It's too much work to get it back. It will take too long. I cannot do it again. I might not even live long enough.

C: Anxiety, Fear → Procrastination

Figure 15.

THINGS THAT HELP

The idea was that any exercise was better than nothing. Basically, always do only what I am comfortable doing. If I know that what I am committed to is easy, I am much more likely to actually try to do it. Changing my thinking about exercise resulted in my getting some exercise rather than none. The results were very satisfying.

Because I did not make a huge commitment, I could take a sense of satisfaction and accomplishment from the slightest effort, After all, I did get out of bed and attempt a pushup. Sure, my brother had to help me get back in bed, but at least I followed through on my commitment. Secondly, pretty soon, a few weeks I think, I found I could just as easily do two pushups. Within a couple of months I was doing five pushups and walking to the end of the block, all without really trying to do anything that was not easy. Granted, this may not seem like a huge accomplishment. Remember the principle though. Something is better than nothing. If the something is only what I can do easily, it still is better than nothing. I am pretty sure that fitness experts and the entire "no pain no gain" crowd will scoff and probably even decry my approach as inept and inadequate. All I can offer in rebuttal is my own self. I am a person who is constitutionally opposed to exercise. As mentioned in the previous chapter, the facts of exercise do not recommend it to those of us in touch with reality (that is, all of us with couch potato genes). It makes me sweat. If I am not careful it hurts. It is very inconvenient. It is boring. My approach may flaunt conventional wisdom, but it does get past these problems. Despite the rather lackadaisical approach, at my last annual evaluation, the doctors did comment that "You are actually very fit." Of course, I don't believe I should head out to a bodybuilders competition any time soon. While I am in no danger of becoming muscle bound, the actual benefits, for me, are very clear.

I feel better. I feel better physically. I think better. My attitude is better. I can pick up a bag of dog food without thought. There was a time when picking up that bag of dog food was a project. I began feeling better after three days. The approach I have used is designed with this simple goal in mind. Feel better. Remember, that is the purpose of this book. The other choice is to continue to feel bad. Now that we know exercise can have a positive impact on depression and anxiety, there is a clear choice. I can continue to feel bad or I can feel better. It is within my power. I believe, with the appropriately comfortable level of commitment and a studious avoidance of long-term fitness goals, everyone can make himself or herself feel better. At this point, four years after my first pushup, I have somehow arrived at a routine that actually meets the recommendations of one expert for thirty minutes of exercise two to three times a week. I have no idea how I got here. I did not set out to accomplish this. Most people would say that is a ridiculous amount of time to take several years to make it to this point. I say, who cares. I got here. That is the beauty of not worrying about long-term goals. All I needed to do was get off my butt and do *something*. If you do that, the rest will follow. In the meantime, you will feel better and think better starting with the first day.

Meditation

Not infrequently I have had people say to me, "I tried CBT (or DBT or whatever) but it didn't help much. Now I am into meditation." This is a little disturbing to me because the fact is, cognitive therapy of any variety is all about mindfulness. Mindfulness is a necessary requirement for contentment. It is, by itself, not sufficient but is absolutely essential. One topic we have discussed on and off throughout various sections of this book is self-awareness. We have to be aware of our selves, how we make

THINGS THAT HELP

meaning and emotions, if we want to have any control over our contentment. Meditation is a discipline of self-awareness. That makes it one of the most important endeavors we can undertake.

Almost any type of meditation will improve our self-awareness. According to Merriam-Webster, the definition of meditating is "to engage in mental exercise (as concentration on one's breathing or repetition of a mantra) for the purpose of reaching a heightened level of spiritual awareness."[66] Remember from Chapter 3 that awareness is a basic requirement for making any significant changes to our belief system. Typically, meditation is used in conjunction with other supportive practices like therapy and twelve-step groups. It is also becoming a growing trend in the medical and research communities.

Meditation is old in tradition, linked back to the ancients in every culture and widely researched to have health and wellness components. The University of New Mexico did a study with women, during the first four weeks postpartum, and found that less anxiety and depression were experienced at the end of the trial period following guided imagery.[67] Dr. Daniel G. Amen writes that meditation is a "behavioral intervention" that helps "anxious overeaters," "adrenaline overloaded anorexics," "menopause," "perimenopause," "heart health," "boost energy," "increase brain cells," "sleep," "calm stress," "PMS," "attention and planning," "depression," "anxiety," "weight loss," "muscle tension," "tightens skin," and "protects the brain from cognitive decline associated with normal aging."[68]

Meditation can be done in many ways, and there are many different styles or types of meditation that are executed with or

---

[66] Meditating
[67] Rees
[68] Amen

without guided imagery. For example, some people prefer to meditate in silence with their eyes closed in a dark room while sitting cross-legged on a matt. Others prefer to meditate in the morning, while watching the sunrise, sitting on a chair, reflecting on a daily reading. You can also take the time at work during your fifteen-minute break: Close your office door and turn up the imagery. And there are those who prefer to meditate with guided imagery and music in a closed room, at home, lying down on a soft surface.

It is important to note that diaphragmatic breathing is often incorporated into guided imagery or meditation. Diaphragmatic breathing is also referred to as belly breathing or yoga breathing. The basic principle of diaphragmatic breathing is to have your belly move in and out and have little to no movement in your chest while breathing. There are also mantra-based meditation practices such as Transcendental Meditation. In my experience all methods of meditation are effective and generally reach the person's desired goal. Those goals can include conditioning or training our minds and bodies to relax on cue. Research also indicates that while a person is actively meditating, their physical ailments begin to decrease and recovery time is shortened.

The mind to body connection is real; researchers to philosophers support this claim. As I looked into journal articles and books related to the mind-body connection, I continued to turn up references to the autonomic nervous system (ANS). The ANS is our body's automatic response to the function of our organs, such as intestines and stomach for digestion or lungs and diaphragm for breathing.[69] Generally speaking, the ANS functions with or without our conscious effort to control it. This system is further

---

[69] Mockus

THINGS THAT HELP

broken into two divisions: sympathetic and parasympathetic. The sympathetic division is associated with mobilizing our body under stress into the "fight or flight" response. The parasympathetic system is associated with "rest and digest." Oftentimes, we become familiar with chaos and constant motion; in other words, our sympathetic nervous system is on overload. Living life in chaos, as you would expect, lessens peace, and we are not able to know our selves. The byproduct of constant stimulation is that we become fearful in our own skin. Chaos keeps us from truly experiencing spirituality because we become connected to deadlines, money, status, drugs, sex, or other means that we have employed to avoid ourselves. The greatest means of attaining spirituality is connecting to our selves, then to those around us, not to things or status. Claudia Black writes, "By definition, spirituality is derived from the Latin word *spiritus*, which means 'the act of breathing.' Breathing allows you to be open within your own body, to go 'inside'. Once your physical body is relaxed, it is necessary to relax your mind and let go of thoughts and worries."[70]

The goal of attaining happiness is to focus on the self, and meditation can be used as that tool for distraction and bring us back to homeostasis. Of course, for many the idea of sitting still is ridiculous or too "New Age." They have employed business or avoidance as a defense mechanism far too long, and the idea of shifting defenses is frightening beyond all belief. Dr. Amen writes, "If you actively distract yourself from repetitive thoughts or block them, over time they will lose their control over you."[71] Through repetition, the messages received in guided imagery can be the

---

[70] Black
[71] Amen

distraction you need until you are more apt to automatically employ your parasympathetic system—"rest and digest."

Remember from Chapter 2, values determine what we pay attention to. If I am going to value my self, I need to pay attention to my self. Meditation is practice in controlling our attention and directing it toward our inner experience, toward our selves. One of the major themes of this book has been the importance of self-awareness. Not many of us are taught to be aware of the state of our physical, emotional, or existential being. Meditation can provide both a starting point for the connection to self and for advanced awareness.

We know ourselves most intimately when surrounded by silence in the here and now, the present. Researchers have found that meditation "tunes people in, not out." Meditation provides a sort of checks and balances from the stressors we have in our daily lives. We begin to learn how to calm a fearful mind and teach ourselves skills to shift our attention from negative thoughts to productive rational thinking. Of course, it is impossible to avoid all chaos in the world today, but we can limit the amount that enters our minds. "It is meditation that allows you to completely stop, to let go of thoughts about the immediate past or future, and simply focus on being in the here and now."[72] Marketing companies strategically use "relaxation" as the selling point for vacationing, but why not achieve self-enhancing relaxation daily? Through meditation, and following the facts of life, relaxation on a daily basis is absolutely attainable. All persons can benefit from meditation, and the benefits are endless.

---

[72] Black

Humor

Life should not be taken too seriously. Every analysis I have undertaken has come to one conclusion. Life is preposterous. There is no way to win and nobody gets out alive. We are not consulted regarding the circumstances of our birth or death or much of what happens in between. Life is a setup. Nevertheless, most of us cling to it desperately. In the face of the setup, we can give up, go through life wringing our hands in anxiety, or just appreciate the ridiculous coincidences and amazing twists of fate that continuously arise. I vote for the latter.

I have observed that it is possible to find humor in the grimmest of circumstance. The combat humor of soldiers, the gallows humor of men in prison, the comic relief of police and first responders in the face of appalling tragedy all attest to this. In fact, there is no arena in which I have not found some form of humor. Life is a giant soap opera and often the best response is to sit back and watch the show. There has to be a reason why humor exists in every human culture. It clearly must be adaptive. We have emphasized throughout this work the importance of patterns. There are some who claim that pattern recognition is an innate skill we all possess, and this ability helps to define what it means to be human and forms the basis of humor.[73] I have to agree that the ability to find some level of humor in stressful or gloomy situations is an earmark of the adaptive, mentally tough individual.

In all of the counseling sessions I have ever engaged in, formal and informal, there has almost always been a moment of humor. At some point in discussions of death and depression, suicide and panic, there has appeared a joke. Whether it is the dark humor associated with "failed" attempts at self-harm, or the lighthearted

---

[73] Clarke (2008)

assessment of abusive family dynamics, most people can see and appreciate alternative patterns of meaning. Sadly, when this is not the case, in my experience, the prognosis is grim indeed.

On the pattern recognition theory of humor, the ability to perceive various patterns in available phenomena is fundamental. It is also a survival tool. My experience is that it is definitely an indicator of success in therapy. After all, if a person is not capable of noticing alternative patterns, then they cannot appreciate alternative meanings. It will be very difficult to be able to see the patterns of thought and behavior in the inner self without this skill. If we cannot notice our current patterns of thought and behavior, it is almost impossible to imagine, affirm, or practice new patterns, patterns of functional thoughts, feelings, behavior, and meaning. Humor is practice in pattern recognition and develops proficiency of finding alternative meaning. The more we laugh the more capable we become of seeing our self and our beliefs in a different light. Given that the mechanisms of pattern recognition are physical, mostly in the brain, we find that, once again, the mind-body connection is real!

Practicing humor can have a positive impact on the maintenance and growth of those parts of the brain responsible for pattern recognition. This enhanced mechanism is more effective at discerning the current patterns of our thoughts, feelings, and behaviors and in imagining new patterns. When viewed from this perspective, one conclusion is obvious. Humor is serious business. For this reason, humor is one prescription I can make for everyone, problem or dilemma they face.

Writing this little book has been an adventure for me. It has clarified my thinking and forced some needed discipline. It has also been a journey of discovery as some of the twists and turns and insights have been completely unanticipated. I have, in fact, tickled myself as I discovered new and interesting patterns in my own life and in the work I do with others. In that vein, I find it delightful to discover that the last two words of this work, and some of its best advice, turns out to be…lighten up.

Bibliography

Adler, Mortimer J., editor (1952). The Great Books of the Western World, Volume 12, *The Discourses of Epictetus*. Chicago: Encyclopedia Britannica, Inc.

Allen, James (2006) *As a Man Thinketh*. New York: Jeremy P. Tarcher/Penguin, a member of the Penguin Group (USA) Inc.

Amen, Daniel G., M.D. (1999). Change Your Brain, Change Your Life: The Breakthrough Program for Conquering Anxiety, Depression, Obsessiveness, Anger, and Impulsiveness. New York: Three Rivers Press.

Amen, Daniel G., M.D. (2010). Change Your Brain, Change Your Body: Use Your Brain to Get and Keep the Body You Have Always Wanted. New York: Harmony Books.

American Psychiatric Association (2013). Diagnostic and Statistical Manual of Mental Disorders, Fifth Edition. Washington D.C.: American Psychiatric Association.

Argyle, Michael, Veronica Salter, Hilary Nicholson, Marylin Williams & Philip Burgess (1970): The communication of inferior and superior attitudes by verbal and non-verbal signals. *British Journal of Social and Clinical Psychology* 9: 222-231.

Barnes, Patricia (2007). Physical activity among adults: United States, 2000 and 2005. Center for Disease Control online article at cdc.gov/nchs/data/hestat/physicalactivity/physicalactivity.htm

Bateson, Gregory (1972). *Steps to an Ecology of Mind.* New York: Ballantine Books.

Bateson, Gregory (2002). *Mind and Nature; A Necessary Unity.* Cresskill, NJ: Hampton Press, Inc. and the Institute for Intercultural Studies.

Beck, A.T. (1964). Thinking and depression: II. Theory and Therapy. *Archives of General Psychiatry,* 10, 561-571.

Beck, Aaron T. and Emery, Gary with Greenburg, Ruth L. (1985) *Anxiety Disorders and Phobias: A Cognitive Perspective.* Basic Books, a Member of the Perseus Books Group.

Beck, Judith S. (1995). *Cognitive Therapy: Basics and Beyond.* New York: The Guilford Press.

Beck, Judith S (2005). *Cognitive Therapy for Challenging Problems.* New York: The Guilford Press.

Begley, Sharon (2008). Train Your Mind, Change Your Brain: How a New Science Reveals Our Extraordinary Potential to Transform Ourselves. New York: Ballantine Books.

Black, Claudia (1999). *Changing Course: Healing from Loss, Abandonment and Fear.* Bainbridge Island, WA: MAC Publishing.

Bradley, Brent and Furrow, James (2013). *Emotionally Focused Couple Therapy for Dummies.* Mississauga, ON: John Wiley & Sons Canada, Ltd.

Bradshaw, John (2005). *Healing the Shame that Binds You.* Deerfield Beach, FL: Health Communications, Inc.

Brown, Brene (2007). I Thought It Was Just Me (But It Isn't): Making the Journey from "What Will People Think?" to "I Am Enough." New York: Gotham Books.

Burns, David D. (1999). *Feeling Good: The New Mood Therapy.* Revised and Updated. New York: Avon Books.

Chodron, Pema (2003). *When Things Fall Apart: Heart Advice for Difficult Times.* Boston: Shambhala Library.

Clarke, Alastair (2008). *The Pattern Recognition Theory of Humour.* Pyrrhic House.

Clancy, Susan A. (2011). The Trauma Myth: The Truth About the Sexual Abuse of Children—and Its Aftermath. Basic Books.

Downs, Alan (2012). *The Velvet Rage.* Boston: Da Capo Press.

Dutton, D. G. and Aron, A. P. (1974). Some evidence for heightened sexual attraction under conditions of high anxiety. *Journal of Personality and Social Psychology,* 30, pp. 510-517.

Ellis, Albert and Harper, Robert (1961). *New Guide to Rational Living*. North Hollywood, CA; Melvin Powers Wilshire Book Company.

Ellis, Albert, McInerney, John F., DiGiuseppe, Raymond, and Yeager, Raymond J. (1988). *Rational-Emotive Therapy with Alcoholics and Substance Abusers.* Boston: Allyn and Bacon.

Frankl, Viktor E. (2006). *Man's Search for Meaning*. Beacon Press.

Gardner, Daniel (2008). *The Science of Fear.* New York: Dutton, Penguin Group (USA), Inc.

Gorski, Terence T., and Miller, Merlene (1986). *Staying Sober, A Guide for Relapse Prevention.* Independence, MO: Independence Press.

Gorski, Terence T. (1992). The Staying Sober Workbook: A Serious Solution for the Problem of Relapse (Revised Edition). Herald Publishing House.

Harvard Medical School (March 2006). First Aid for Emotional Trauma: When and how must we act to prevent lasting damage. *Harvard Mental Health Letter*, Volume 22, number 9: Harvard Health Publications.

Harvard Medical School (2009). *Coping with Anxiety and Phobias: Special Health Report.* Boston: Harvard Health Publications.

Harvard Medical School (2010). *Improving Sleep: A Guide to a Good Night's Rest.* Boston: Harvard Health Publications.

Harvard Medical School (2008). Measuring empathy in psychotherapy. *Harvard Mental Health Letter*, Volume 24, Number 8: Harvard Health Publications.

Hsee, Christopher K., Elaine Hatfield & Claude Chemtob (1992). Assessments of the emotional states of others: Conscious judgments versus emotional contagion. *Journal of Social and Clinical Psychology* 14 (2): 119-128.

Kaviratna, Harischandra (1980). *Dhammapada: Wisdom of the Buddha.* Pasadena, CA: Theosophical University Press.

Keller, Helen (1957). *The Open Door.*

Kennedy, Eugene C. (1974). *Believing.* Garden City, NY: Doubleday & Company, Inc.

Kinney, Jean (2000). *Loosening the Grip: A Handbook of Alcohol Information* – 6th edition. New York: McGraw-Hill Higher Education.

Koontz, Dean (2001). *One Door Away From Heaven.* New York: Bantam Books.

Kopp, Sheldon B. *If You Meet the Buddha on the Road, Kill Him! The Pilgrimage of Psychotherapy Patients.* Palo Alto, CA: Science and Behavior Books, Inc.

Meditating. (2010). In *Merriam-Webster Online Dictionary*. Retrieved April 15, 2010, from http://www.merriam-webster.com/dictionary/meditating

Mellody, Pia (1989*). Facing Codependence: What It Is, Where It Comes From, How It Sabotages Our Lives*. New York: Harper One.

Mellody, Pia; Miller, Andrea; Miller, J. Keith (2003). *Facing Love Addiction: Giving Yourself the Power to Change the Way You Love*. New York: HarperCollins Publishers, Inc.

Miller, Michael Craig (February 2006) editorial. Is addiction hereditary? *Harvard Mental Health Letter*, Volume 22, Number 8: Harvard Health Publication.

Miller, Michael Craig (October 2009) editorial on psychotherapy for those exposed to trauma. *Harvard Mental Health Letter*, Volume 26, Number 4: Harvard Health Publications.

Mockus, Susan M., Ph.D. (2002). The Gale Group Inc., Gale, Detroit, Gale Encyclopedia of Nursing and Allied Health. Retrieved April 15, 2010 from
http://www.healthline.com/galecontent/nervous-system-autonomic?utm_term=ans&utm_medium=mw&utm_campaign=article

Neimeyer, Robert A. (2006). *Lessons of Loss: A Guide to Coping*. Memphis, TN: Center for the Study of Loss and Transition.

Peck, M. Scott (2003). The Road Less Traveled, 25th Anniversary Edition: A New Psychology of Love, Traditional Values and Spiritual Growth. New York: Simon and Schuster.

Rando, Theresa (1993). *Treatment of Complicated Mourning.* Champaign, IL: Research Press.

Ratey, John J. MD (2008). Spark: The Revolutionary New Science of Exercise and the Brain. New York: Little, Brown and Company.

Rees, Barbara L., Ph.D., R.N. (1995). Effects of relaxation with guided imagery on anxiety, depression, and self-esteem in primiparas. University of New Mexico. *Journal of Holistic Nursing.* Retrieved October 15, 2009, from http://highwire.Stanford.edu

Richardson, Sandy (2006). *Soul Hunger: A Personal Journey.* Ozark, AL: Remuda Ranch.

Ross, Colin A. (2000). *The Trauma Model: A Solution to the Problem of Comorbidity in Psychiatry.* Richardson, TX: Manitou Communication, Inc.

Ruiz, Don Miguel (2004). *The Voice of Knowledge.* San Rafael, CA: Amber-Allen Publishing, Inc.

Satir, Virginia (1988). *The New Peoplemaking.* Mountain View, CA: Science and Behavior Books, Inc.

Schachter, S., & Singer, J. (1962). Cognitive, social, and physiological determinants of emotional state. *Psychological Review*, 69, pp. 379-399.

Tzu, Lao, Tzu Chuang and Tzu Lieh (2007). *Tao—The Way: The Sayings of Lao Tzu, Chunag Tzu and Lieh Tzu*. Translated by Lionel Giles and Herbert A. Giles. El Paso: El Paso Norte Press.

Walsh, Froma and McGoldrick, Monica (1991). *Living Beyond Loss*. New York: Norton.

Watzlawick, Paul; Beavin, Janet Helmick; Jackson, Don D. (1967). *Pragmatics of Human Communication: A Study of Interactional Patterns, Pathologies, and Paradoxes*. New York: W.W. Norton & Company.

Wilson, R. Reid. (1996). *Don't Panic*. Revised edition. New York: HarperCollins Publishers, Inc.

Worden, J. William (2002). Grief Counseling and Grief Therapy: A Handbook for the Mental Health Practitioner. New York: Springer Publishing Company, Inc.

Yontef, Gary M. (1993). *Awareness Dialogue & Process: Essays on Gestalt Therapy*. Goldsboro: The Gestalt Journal Press.

Young, Jeffery E., and Klosko, Janet S. (2006). *Schema Therapy: A Practitioner's Guide*. New York: The Guilford Press.

Index

Abandonment, 186
A-B-C model, 15
Active Listening
  Clarifying, 134
  Minimal Verbal
    Responses, 132
  Nonverbal Management, 127
  Paraphrasing, 132
  Reflecting, 133
  Summarizing, 135
Addictions, 233
  Addiction definition, 233
  Addictive process, 234
  Behavioral Habits, 234
  Physical dependence, 234
  Psychological Dependence, 241
  Tolerance, 234
Alarm system, 82, 192, 193, 194, 195, 196, 197, 198, 204, 242
Anxiety, 194
Automatic Thoughts. *See* Belief System
Behavioral Habits. *See* Addictions
Belief System
  Automatic thoughts, 27
  Core Beliefs, 20
  Memories, 23
  Values, 25

Believing
  I am different, 1, 202, 241
  In object permanence. *See* Object permanence
  In other persons, 10
  That others have the answers, 39
Bibliography, 286
Body-Mind Connection. *See* Mind-body connection
Boundaries, 102, 155, 156, 157, 158, 159, 160, 161, 162, 163, 164, 165, 170, 179, 180, 181, 185, 190
  and limits, 161
  Functions, 159
  None, 158
  Types, 157
  Walls, 158
Codependence
  Definition, 167
Cognitive distortions, 39, 42, 51, 52, 53, 56, 68, 84, 90, 189, 240, 247, 255
  Cognitive distortion, 51
Connection, 4, 5, 6, 48, 100, 109, 110, 111, 113, 120, 124, 126, 131, 137, 154, 155, 157, 158, 160, 187, 202, 207, 211, 221, 222, 223, 263, 264, 267, 280, 282, 284

Definition, 111
Contentment, 4, 6, 7, 8, 13, 31, 40, 58, 65, 66, 70, 79, 80, 82, 86, 93, 108, 121, 137, 192, 251, 278, 279, *See* Happiness
Definition, 8
Core Issues. *See* Model of Dsyfuntional Developmennt
Critical Incident Stress Debriefing, 231
Depression, 208
Dissociation, 28, 29, 34, *See* Automatic thoughts
Emotions, 4, 12, 36, 37, 38, 42, 45, 46, 47, 48, 51, 54, 62, 67, 68, 69, 70, 84, 87, 89, 91, 97, 99, 115, 117, 121, 122, 136, 138, 139, 158, 161, 166, 167, 176, 178, 179, 185, 198, 199, 206, 208, 209, 234, 246, 249, 255, 274
Are Indicators, 61
Benefits of, 62
Continuum of intensity, 63
Definition, 61
Dysfunctional emotions, 67
Functional emotions, 62
Instrumental, 65
No independent existence, 64
Not good or bad, 62
Physical component, 62
Primary, 64
Secondary, 64
Three levels of, 64
Will not kill you, 65
Enmeshment, 187
Excuses, 178, 191, 253
do not alter consequences, 253
Trauma excuse, 251
Exercise, 271
Facts of Life, 191
1 People are people, 4
2 Happiness is not something that happents to us, 7
3 We all have everything we need to be happy, 12
4 Everyones reality is different and valid, 18
5 My feelings always come from my belief system, my thoughts, 36
6 Everything always happens exactly the way it happens, 37
7 The belief system consists of ideas, not facts, 38
8 All ideas can be changed, 38
9 Everyone's behavior is mostly about them, not me, 120
10 Meaning depends on context, 184

Fear, 6, 47, 90, 97, 118, 119, 130, 133, 138, 166, 167, 186, 187, 198, 199, 200, 201, 204, 206, 208, 224, 235, 236, 239, 241, 247, 250, 260
   of self, 201
Feelings. *See* Emotions
Forgiveness, 266
Functional families, 185
Grief, 224
Happiness
   Definition, 8
Humor, 283
   Is serious business, 284
   Life is preposterous, 283
Intimacy
   Definition, 126
Limits. *See* Boundaries
Meaning, 212
   Place, 220
   Purpose, 213
Memories. *See* Belief System
Mind-body connection, 10, 11, 16, 41, 58, 61, 62, 68, 84, 88, 90, 91, 93, 98, 103, 113, 119, 121, 122, 123, 141, 156, 165, 179, 184, 193, 194, 196, 202, 207, 209, 210, 211, 219, 242, 244, 252, 254, 260, 268, 271, 272, 273, 278, 280, 281, 282, 284, 287
Model of Dysfunctional Development
   Core issues, 84

Safety, 93
Spirituality, 108
Value, 98
Nonverbal, 115, 116, 127, 132, 140, 141, 142, 149, 150, 152, 153, 162, 170
Object permanence
   Definition, 20
Panic Attacks, 203
Parasympathetic nervous system, 194, 196
People are people, 4
Personal Boundaries. *See* Boundaries
Phobias, 206
Psychological Dependence. *See* Addictions
Purpose, 213, *See* Meaning
Reality, 17
   Everyones is different and valid, 17
Roles, 99, 155, 156, 172, 177, 184, 185, 188, 189, 190
   Family roles, 184
Safety. *See* Model of Dysfunctional Development
Schemas, 84
Sleep, 269
Speaking For Myself, 136
   I statements, 137
Stories
   Chuy, 95
   Helen, 30
   How I quit smoking, 234

Jim, 149
Karen, 99
Mandy, 144
Mikes Core Issue, 105
Rebecca, 9
Sam, 242
Singing, 216
Soup kitchen, 222
Squad leader, 151
Susan, 172
Swamp of life, 262
Tennis elbow, 197
Tumbleweed, 89
Watering, 217
Wayne and Jill, 116
Sympathetic nervous system, 194
Ten Facts of Life, 191
Therapy, 259
Trauma, 89, 90, 221, 251, 289, 292
Underlying Messages, 140
Values. *See* Belief System

CPSIA information can be obtained
at www.ICGtesting.com
Printed in the USA
BVHW070052260719
554329BV00001B/80/P

9 781478 722595